LEGENDARY LOCALS

OF

ST. CHARLES

MISSOURI

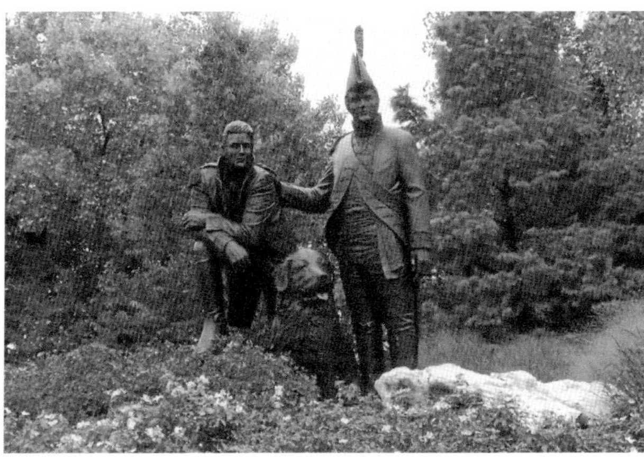

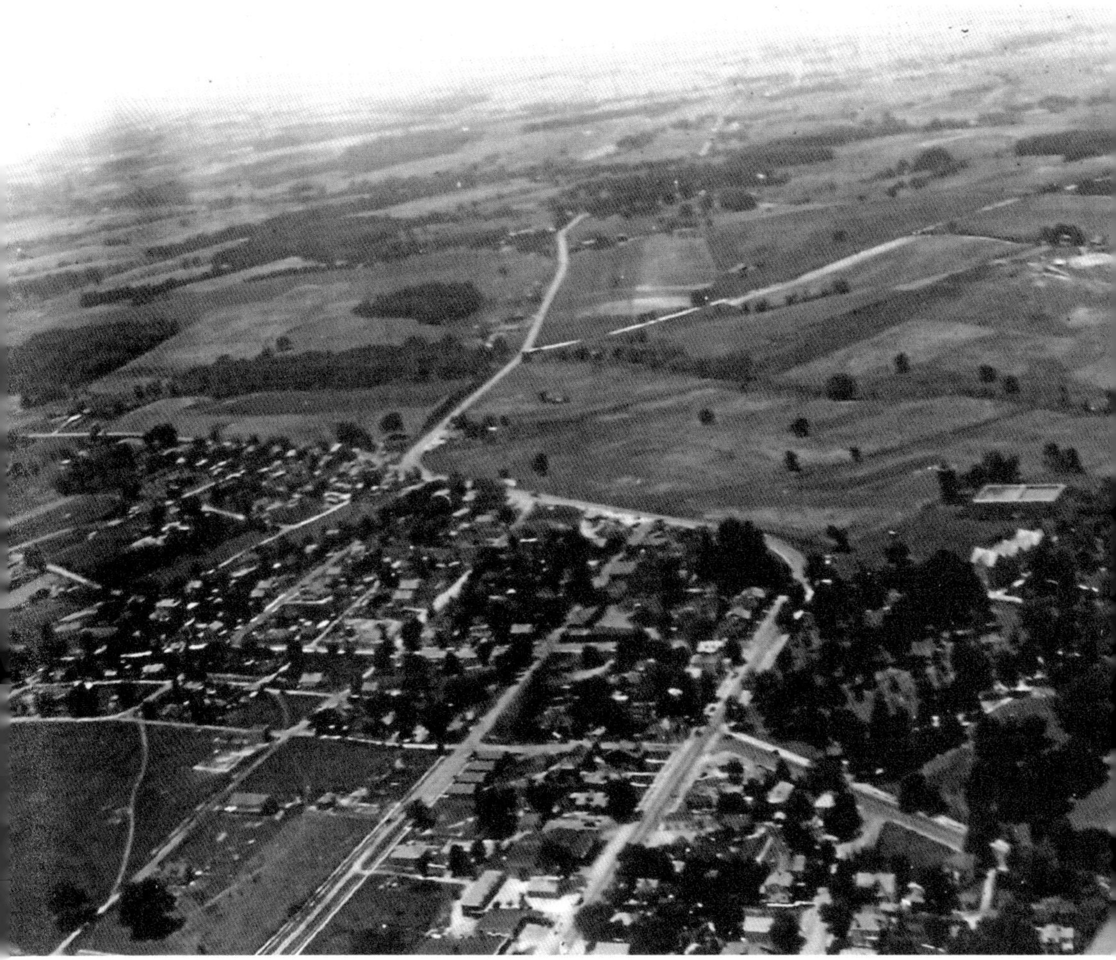

Aerial View of St. Charles
Taken about 1932, this photograph captures west St. Charles, including what was then Clay Street and Lindenwood College. Clay Street was renamed First Capitol Drive in 1970. Today, Lindenwood University is a sprawling four-year liberal-arts institution. (Courtesy of St. Charles County Historical Society.)

Page 1: Meriwether Lewis and William Clark
St. Charles is proud of its connection to Lewis and Clark and the Corps of Discovery expedition. In 2003, a 15-foot-tall statue, designed by artist Pat Kennedy, was dedicated to the explorers in Frontier Park, near the site from which the expedition to the Louisiana Purchase territory departed in 1804. (Photograph by author.)

LEGENDARY LOCALS

OF

ST. CHARLES

MISSOURI

DON AND DIANNA GRAVEMAN

FOREWORD BY GRACE NICHOLS

LEGENDARY LOCALS

ISBN 978-1-4671-0231-5

Legendary Locals is an imprint of Arcadia Publishing
Charleston, South Carolina

Printed in the United States of America

Library of Congress Control Number: 2015910879

For all general information, please contact Arcadia Publishing:
Telephone 843-853-2070
Fax 843-853-0044
E-mail sales@arcadiapublishing.com
For customer service and orders:
Toll-Free 1-888-313-2665

Visit us on the Internet at www.arcadiapublishing.com

Dedication

For the special people in our children's lives, David Cattani, Maxwell Knocke, and Melissa Graveman. You three are legendary in our minds.

On the Front Cover: Clockwise from top left:
Sr. Anna Mae Marheineke, educator (Courtesy of Academy of the Sacred Heart; see page 39), Marvin Hohman, musician, music educator, and director of the St. Charles Municipal Band (Courtesy of St. Charles County Historical Society, photograph by Michael Schlueter; see page 107), Melvin Washington, civic leader and educator (Courtesy of St. Charles County Historical Society, photograph by Michael Schlueter; see page 40), Bobbi Smith, bestselling author (Courtesy of Bobbi Smith; see page 114), Norbert Wapelhorst, founder of St. Charles Park and Recreation Foundation (Courtesy of St. Charles County Historical Society; see page 82), Patt Holt Singers, world-renowned show group (Courtesy of Todd Luerding; see page 108), Rudolph Goebel, photographer (Courtesy of St. Charles County Historical Society; see page 27), Grace Nichols, first female mayor of St. Charles (Courtesy of St. Charles County Historical Society, photograph by Michael Schlueter; see page 101), Edward Pundmann Jr., civic leader (Courtesy of St. Charles County Historical Society, photograph by Michael Schlueter; see page 76).

On the Back Cover: From left to right:
Archie Scott, founding member of the South Main Preservation Society (Courtesy of St. Charles County Historical Society, photograph by Michael Schlueter; see page 84), Dr. Henry W. Clever Jr., pediatrician and civic leader (Courtesy of St. Charles County Historical Society, photograph by Michael Schlueter; see page 87).

CONTENTS

FOREWORD

St. Charles has been an exciting place to live and work since the arrival of Louis Blanchette and the visit of Meriwether Lewis and William Clark prior to their travels to the West Coast. The people of St. Charles have been both cautious and welcoming to those who followed the early explorers, surviving many challenges throughout history, including Civil War divisions that separated family members. The impact of Rose Philippine Duchesne, founder of the Academy of the Sacred Heart, and of George and Mary Sibley, founders of Lindenwood University, has been significant in the worlds of education and religion. Nothing has stood still in this fast-moving community, from the transition of the Katy Depot to Frontier Park to the development of the Katy Trail; from the opening of the Lewis and Clark Boathouse Museum to the advent of riverfront gaming; from the building of the St. Charles Convention Center to the opening of the Family Arena; and from the renovation of the Foundry Art Centre to the booming growth of Lindenwood University. Countless people have devoted their lives to the betterment of St. Charles. Through it all, citizens, merchants, and leaders have stood fast, celebrating the past and welcoming the future.

—Grace Nichols, 2015

ACKNOWLEDGMENTS

Many thanks to all of the folks who gave us permission to use their photographs, sent us information, or suggested people for inclusion in this book. Special thanks to Amy Haake, archivist at St. Charles County Historical Society, for lending her time, knowledge, and expertise to this project; the board of directors at St. Charles County Historical Society for supporting us in this effort; Scott Grimwood at SSM Health Archives for helping with research; and Grace Nichols for graciously agreeing to write the foreword. Special thanks to Elizabeth Knocke for lending her proofreading skills.

INTRODUCTION

The people of St. Charles, Missouri, past and present, are a varied lot—some history-minded, some focused on the future and town growth, some young and ambitious, others who reflect on their life's work and accomplishments. This book is a compilation of photographs and information about some of those people, including founders like Louis Blanchette, the first of three commandants appointed while this area was under Spanish rule in the late 1700s. But it is not all ancient history, as these pages include stories of contemporary citizens, too—athletes, journalists, performers, and business and civic leaders. While not all of them have lived long enough to achieve true legend status, each of them are notable for their contributions to the St. Charles community and to the other places where they have lived or worked.

The story starts in 1764, when Louis Blanchette met French trapper and hunter Bernard Guillet on the banks of the Missouri River. Guillet had landed near the river sometime around 1740 and lived in the area before being taken captive by the Dakotas. He later married into the tribe and became chief after his father-in-law's death. Guillet returned to the Missouri River many times, and it was during one of those visits that he came upon Blanchette, who asked him what he called this place. Guillet replied, "Les Petites Côtes," meaning "The Little Hills."

In 1769, Blanchette returned to the area with his Pawnee wife and his children to found a settlement, eventually becoming its commandant. He is also credited with founding the first church in the settlement. When the Spanish lieutenant governor of Upper Louisiana, Don Manuel Perez, visited Les Petites Côtes, he signed a petition granting permission for the church. Records show the meeting took place at Blanchette's home. When the church was dedicated in 1791, Perez named it San Carlos Borromeo, for the former cardinal of Milan. The name of the village was then changed to San Carlos de la Rio Misuri (St. Charles of the Missouri River).

St. Charles is the oldest city on the Missouri River, and its quiet claim to fame lies in its quaint historic district, which has become a jewel of the Missouri tourism industry. For five years, Missouri's state capitol was here, and St. Charles became a place for the comings and goings of politicians like Sen. Thomas Hart Benton. The town, once a thriving trading center, launched the Louisiana Purchase expedition, led by Meriwether Lewis and William Clark. Even Zebulon Pike came this way in 1806 on his trek west, during which he tried and failed to summit the mountain that bears his name. Though the image of St. Charles today is not one of a bustling, big city, but rather of a place from another time, residents are not timid when it comes to promoting town pride. French heritage shines through each time Les Petites Côtes is invoked during the Festival of the Little Hills. A larger-than-life statue of Lewis and Clark and their dog, Seaman, stands in Frontier Park. Daniel Boone, bronzed and life-size, sits down to welcome visitors near the site of what was the beginning of Boone's Lick Trail. The town boasts many firsts—the first interstate highway in the United States had its beginning in St. Charles; St. Rose Philippine Duchesne founded the first Society of the Sacred Heart School here—but, just as important, many citizens have gone out into the world and made their hometown proud. Others have stayed in St. Charles and dedicated their lives to the continued growth and development of the city and its people. Some left their homes in other parts of the state or country—or even the world—and came here for the benefit of all. Leona Erhard's family came here from Alsace, France, and Dr. Benjamin Geret was a native of Bavaria. Their contributions are a treasured part of the town's history.

Legendary Locals of St. Charles focuses, as much as possible, on notable visitors, workers, and residents of the city of St. Charles. Many truly legendary locals live and work in unincorporated St. Charles County and in St. Peters, Wentzville, O'Fallon, Cottleville, Augusta, Lake St. Louis, New Melle, Flint

Hill, Foristell, Portage de Sioux, St. Paul, Weldon Spring, and West Alton. It would be impossible to include everyone who deserves mention from the entire county in one book of this style and size. Therefore, after much discussion and forethought, it was decided that the people included here will have been born in the city of St. Charles, gone to school here, worked here, lived here, or made some of their greatest contributions in the city of St. Charles.

Even so, many more people than those profiled in this book deserve mention. The authors have tried to include the names of some of those folks in the introduction to each chapter. Also, some of the people profiled are talented in diverse areas and should be included in multiple chapters, but they had to be limited to one. Peter Carlos, for example, is a poet, scriptwriter, filmmaker, and educator (and probably something else we left out). This book is not complete—nor could it ever be. St. Charles is just too rich in talent, drive, creativity, brainpower, kindness, generosity, and down-to-earth energy for one book to include photographs of every notable citizen, past and present. The authors hope that, within these pages, the reader will learn something new about a St. Charles local who has used his or her gifts for the betterment of the community and beyond.

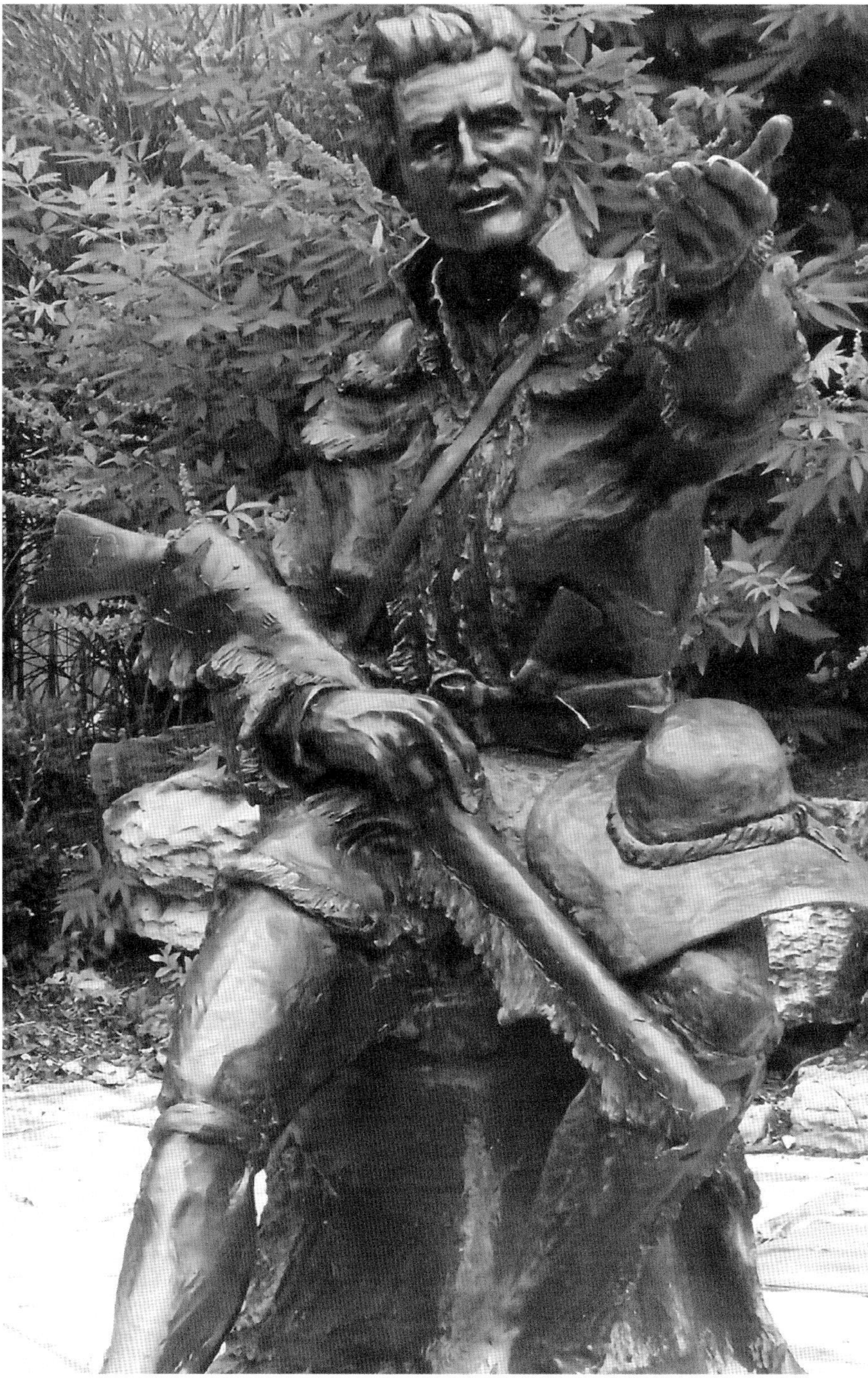

Daniel Boone's Welcome

Daniel Boone's statue, designed by Harry Weber, welcomes visitors to South Main Street, near what was the beginning in 1808 of the trail to Fort Osage, later called the Boone's Lick Trail. (Photograph by author.)

CHAPTER ONE

Settlers, Famous Visitors, and Early Residents

Don Carlos Tayon was the second of three commandants in the village of San Carlos while it was under Spanish rule. He was named to the post upon the death of the first commandant, Louis Blanchette, in 1793. The third and final commandant was Don Santiago "James" MacKay. Bernard Guillet, who played a role in the naming of Les Petites Côtes, is discussed in the introduction.

Other early notables who deserve mention are Francis Duquette, a French-Canadian who established a windmill, acquired land, and became a principal trader and merchant in the area in 1796, and Rev. Timothy Flint, who established a Presbyterian church in 1816. The first recorded marriage in the village involved John Baptiste Provost and Angelique Savanges. They were wed on September 25, 1792, firmly securing the couple's place in the history of St. Charles.

Robert McCloud produced the *Missourian*, the first newspaper published in St. Charles, which is said to have also been the first, outside of St. Louis, published west of the Mississippi. McCloud was its reporter, editor, business manager, publisher, and printer. The *Missourian*, published during the years that St. Charles was Missouri's capital, was succeeded by the *Clarion*.

All of these events and many more, some described briefly in the profiles that follow, make up a rich and vibrant past that is celebrated by St. Charles residents and visitors, who hope to catch a glimpse of yesterday as they stroll along the cobblestones of the historic district.

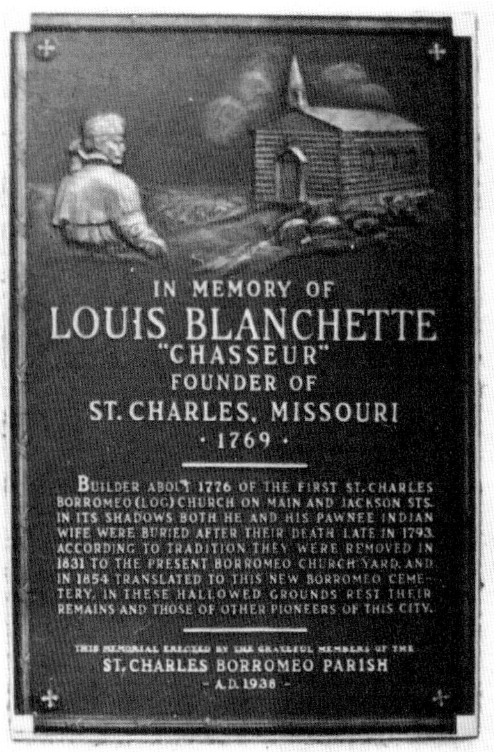

Louis Blanchette
In 1764, Louis Blanchette, a French hunter and trapper, came to the area now known as St. Charles. He returned to the area in 1769 with his Pawnee wife and their children to found the first permanent settlement in the Spanish territory. (Courtesy of St. Charles County Historical Society.)

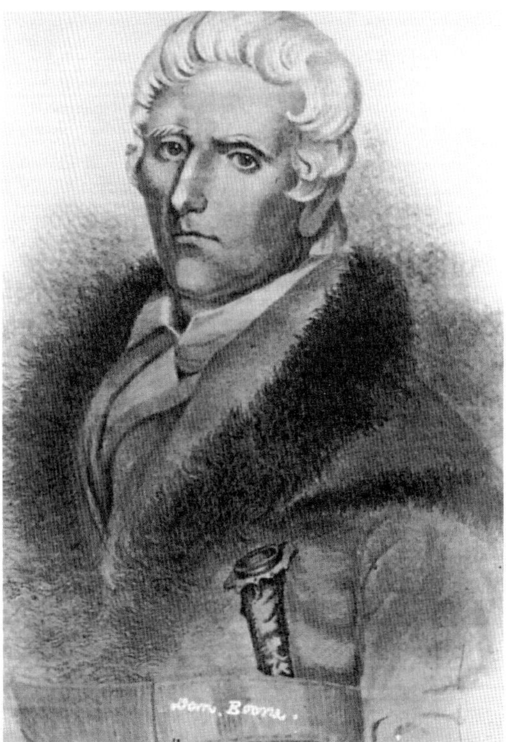

Daniel Boone
Explorer Daniel Boone was not the only member of the Boone family to come to the St. Charles area. In 1797, Daniel Morgan Boone came here at the request of his famous father. He and his brother Nathan forged the Boone's Lick Trail to connect St. Charles with a salt lick near present-day Boonville, Missouri. (Courtesy of St. Charles County Historical Society.)

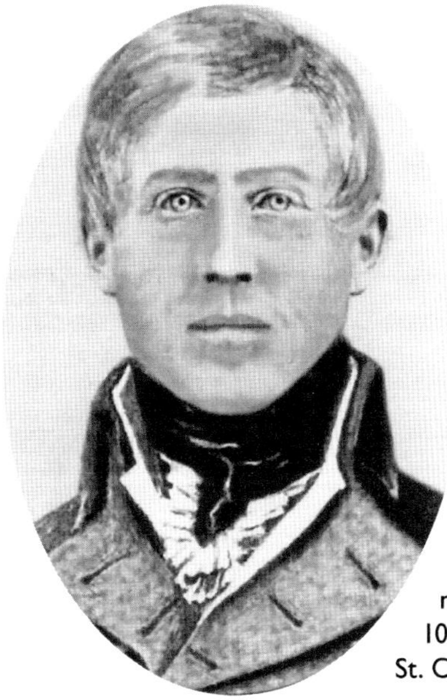

Don Santiago MacKay

Don Santiago "James" MacKay was the third and final commandant of the District of St. Charles, from 1801 to 1804. He succeeded Don Carlos Tayon and Louis Blanchette. MacKay, born in Scotland, is reported to have been the first English-speaking settler in Spanish service in this region. Known as Jacque MacKay by the French and as Don Santiago MacKay by the Spanish, he is believed to be the author of the first detailed map of the Missouri River, which was used by the Lewis and Clark expedition. The original is now in the Library of Congress. Pictured below is the home at 1017 South Main Street where he lived in 1797. (Both, courtesy of St. Charles County Historical Society.)

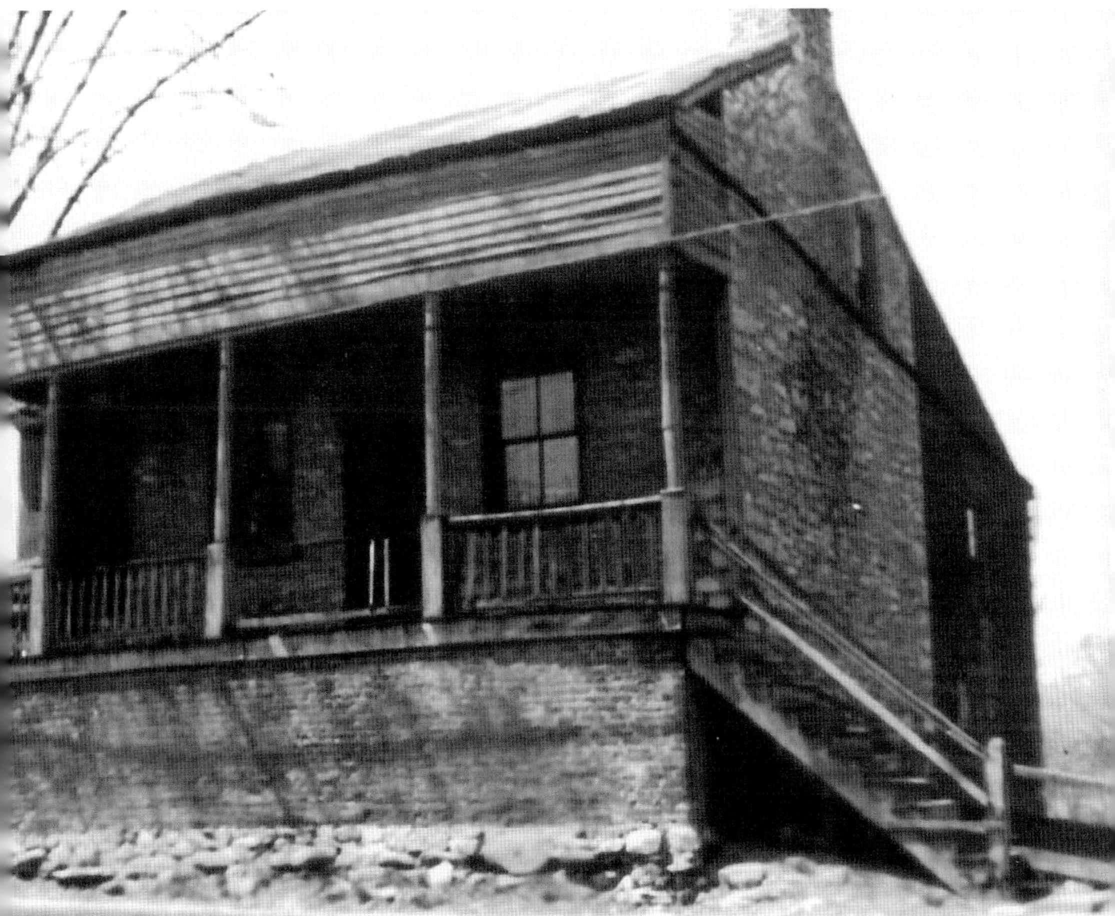

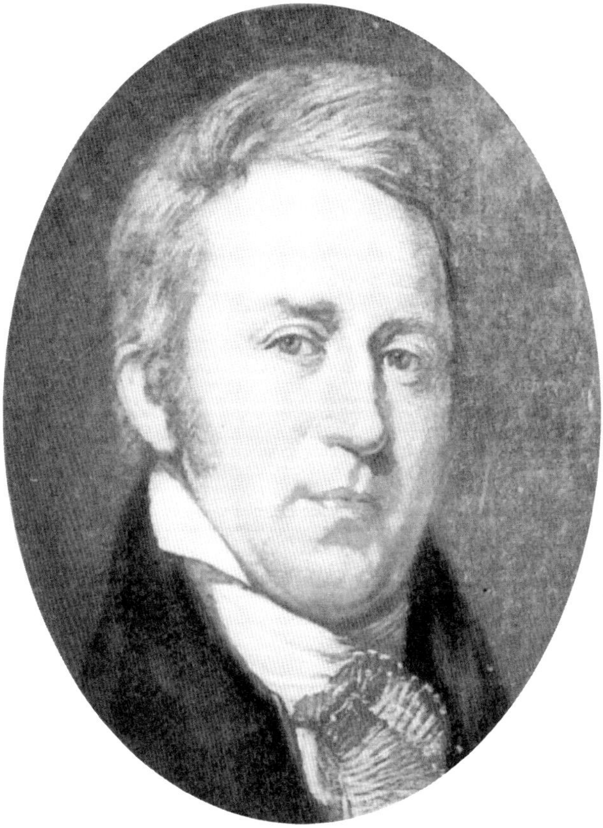

William Clark

On May 14, 1804, William Clark stepped out of his boat and onto the banks of the Missouri River in St. Charles. Clark was waiting for his friend, Capt. Meriwether Lewis, to arrive. On May 21, Lewis and Clark departed on their famous expedition to explore the recently acquired Louisiana Purchase territory. (Portrait by Charles Willson Peale; courtesy of Library of Congress, LC-USZ62-10609.)

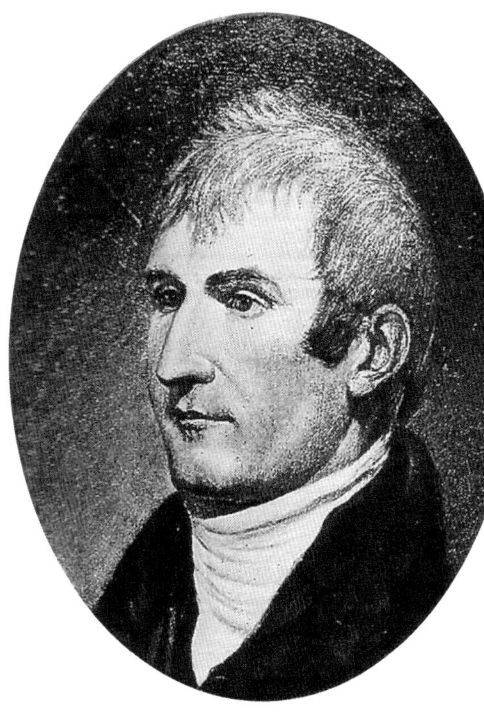

Meriwether Lewis

The other half of the famous exploring duo, Meriwether Lewis joined William Clark in St. Charles in May 1804 before the group, known as the Corps of Discovery, embarked on its journey to explore the Louisiana Purchase territory. (Portrait by Charles Willson Peale, c. 1807; courtesy of Library of Congress, LC-USZ62-20214.)

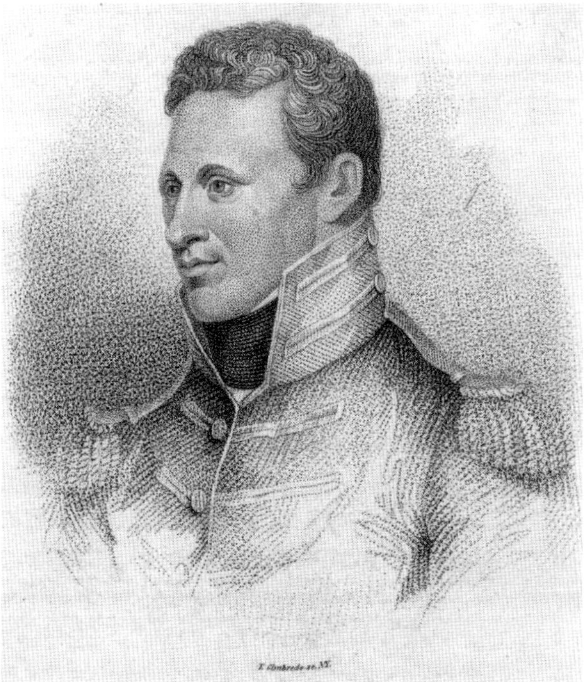

Zebulon Pike

While many will question the inclusion of Zebulon Pike in a book about St. Charles, Pike's visit here loosely belongs in the same category as that of Lewis and Clark. In 1806, Pike led 22 men up the Missouri River from Fort Bellefontaine, passing through St. Charles. During that expedition, Pike traveled to present-day Colorado, where he tried and failed to climb the mountain that would later be called Pike's Peak. (Courtesy of Library of Congress, LC-DIG-ppmsca-03211.)

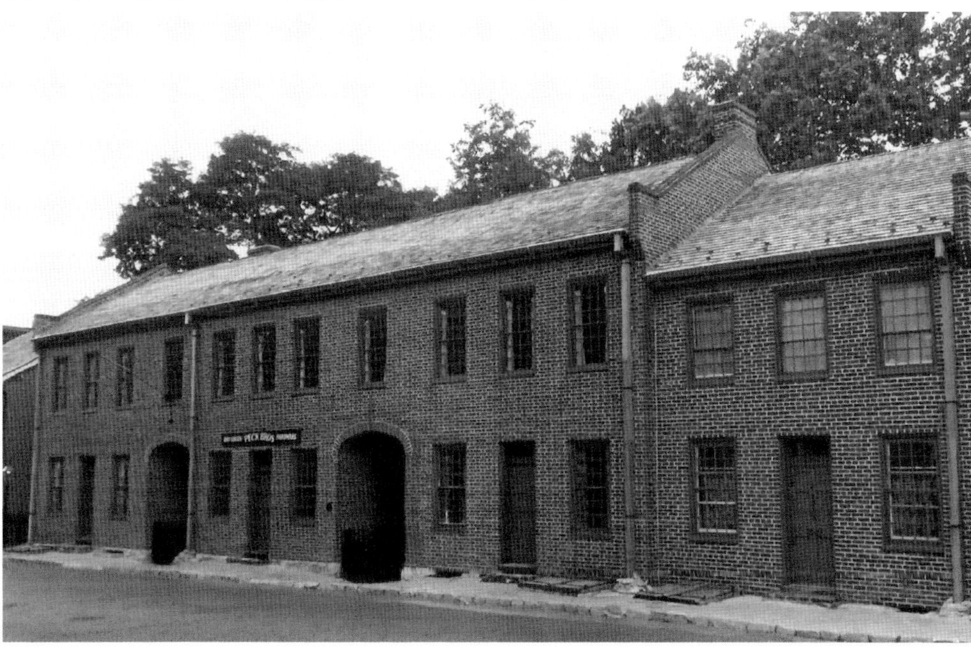

Charles and Ruluff Peck

Early prominent merchants Ruluff and Charles Peck erected these buildings at 206–214 South Main Street in the early 1800s, using part of the structure as their store and residence. After the Constitutional Convention in St. Louis in 1820, when St. Charles was selected to be the first state capital, the second floor of "Peck's Row" became the site of the capitol. The structure is pictured here in 2015. (Photograph by author.)

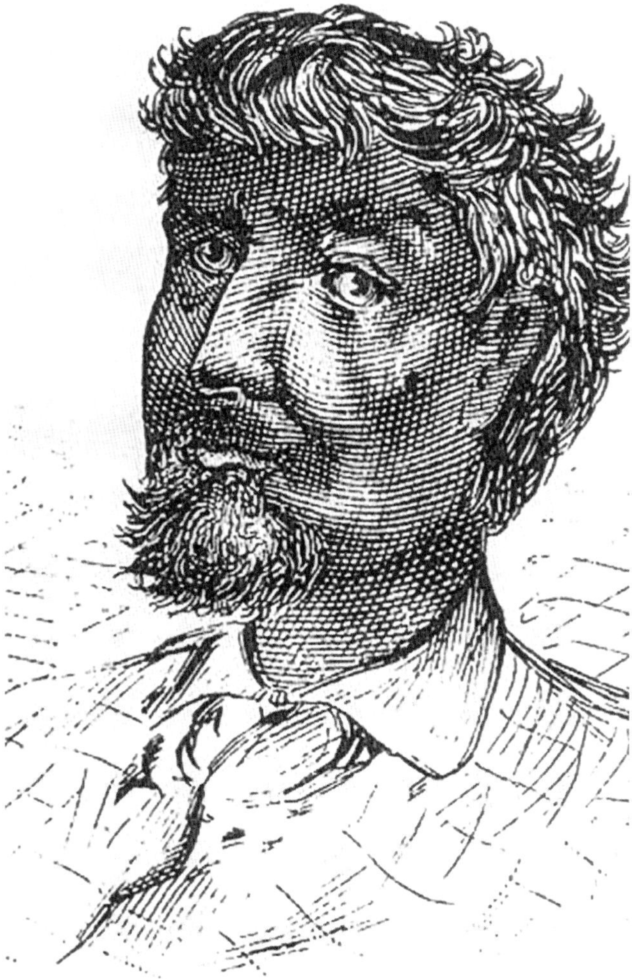

Jean Baptiste Point du Sable

Known as the "founder of Chicago," du Sable was the first permanent resident of an area that would later become that city. His birth date and place are not known, but he is believed to have been from Haiti. No known official portraits were made of du Sable during his lifetime. Accounts suggest that, from about 1768, du Sable was a fur trader with an official license from the British government, managing a successful trading post in Indiana. He established a farm in Chicago about 1788 with his wife, Catherine, and their children. The couple's farm prospered after the end of the Revolutionary War and was known as far away as the East Coast for producing fine crops.

Sometime between 1800 and 1809, after his wife died, du Sable sold his land in Chicago and moved to St. Charles, Missouri, where he was commissioned to operate a ferry across the Missouri River. He bought a house that would later be the home of Alexander McNair, Missouri's first governor. In 1814, du Sable declared bankruptcy. He died impoverished in 1818 and was buried in an unmarked grave in St. Charles Borromeo Cemetery. The parish burial register suggests his remains were moved twice, each time the cemetery was moved. A permanent marker was placed at what is believed to be du Sable's final resting place during a service at the third St. Charles Borromeo Cemetery.

Chicago's Du Sable Museum of African American History carries his name. (Image from *History of Chicago. From the Earliest Period to the Present Time*, published 1884 by A. T. Andreas, courtesy of Library of Congress, LC- rc-01001859..)

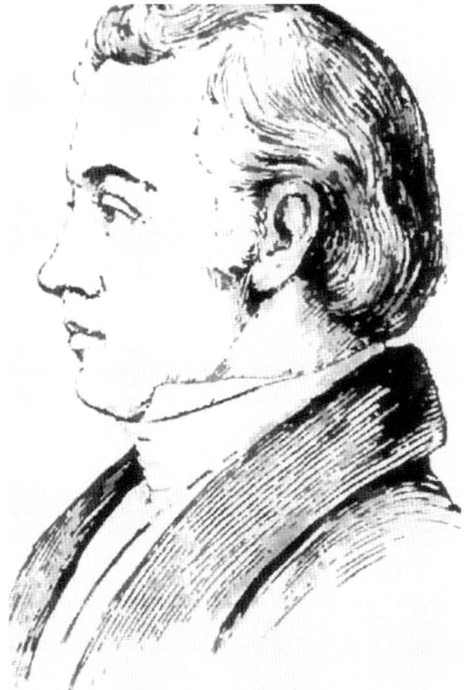

Elijah P. Lovejoy

Noted abolitionist Elijah Lovejoy was a Presbyterian minister and a publisher and printer of antislavery literature. Lovejoy lived in St. Charles, Missouri, at his wife's uncle's home at 301 South Main Street (below). On October 1, 1837, a mob attacked him and threw his printing press into the river. He escaped to Alton, Illinois. Several weeks later, he was killed in another mob attack, and his press was again thrown into the river. (Right, image from *Appletons' Cyclopædia of American Biography*, Volume IV, published 1888by D. Appleton and Company, courtesy of Library of Congress, LC-06043076; below, photograph by author.)

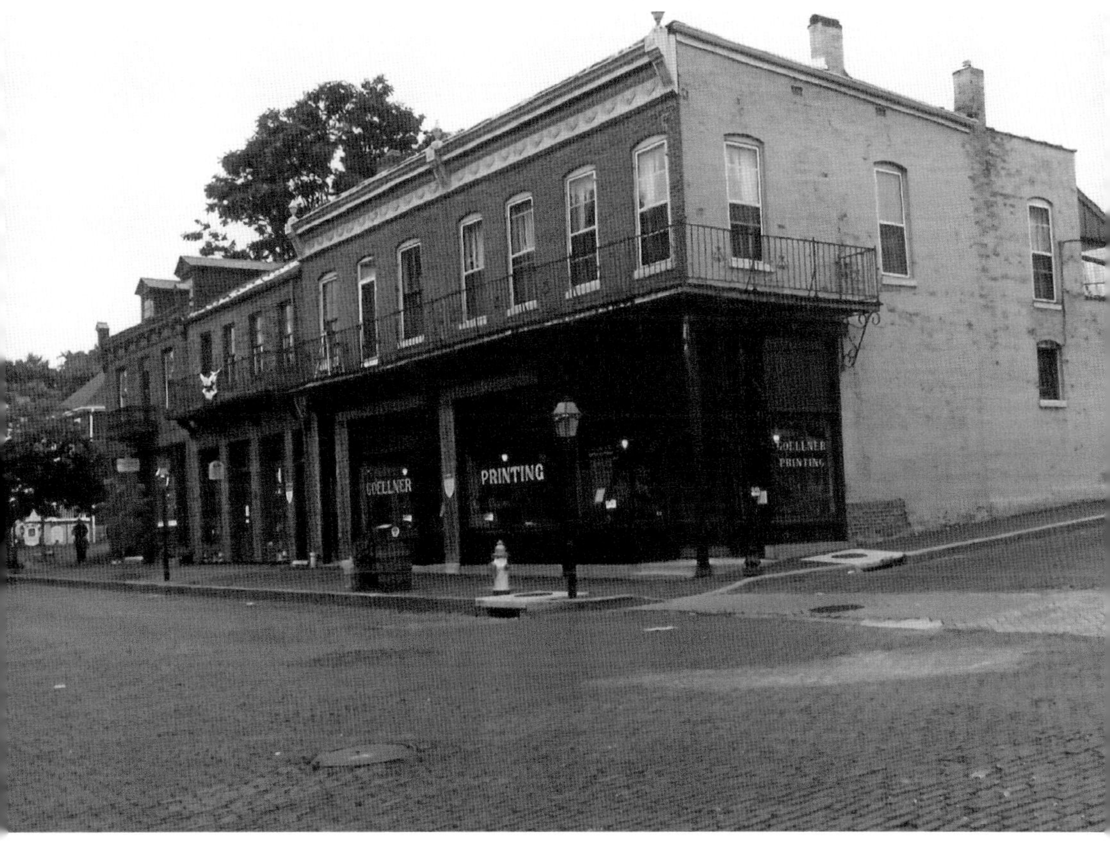

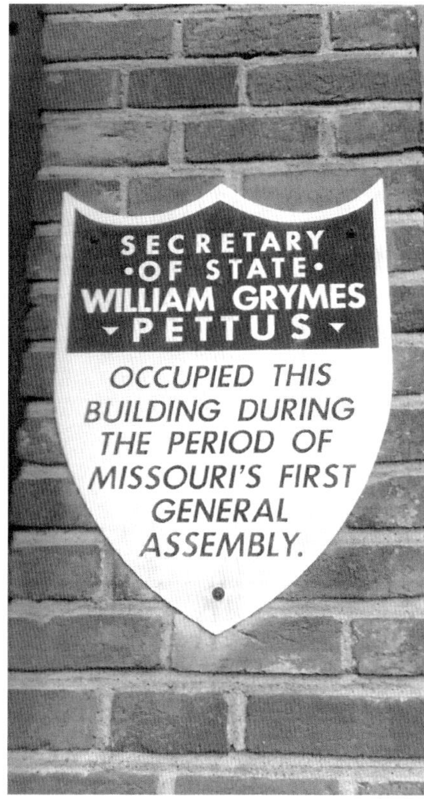

William G. Pettus

Pettus, a veteran of the War of 1812, was appointed secretary of state after Governor McNair was elected and St. Charles became the first state capital. The building at 307 South Main Street, built in 1821, was his home and office, as it was close to the capitol building but less crowded. The building is now the site of popular Main Street Books. (Photograph by author.)

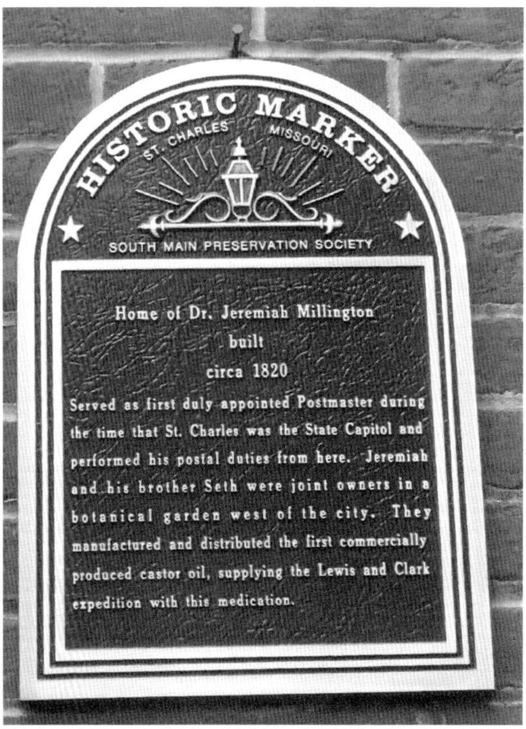

Dr. Jeremiah Millington

Jeremiah Millington and his brother Seth were two of the first doctors to settle in St. Charles. Originally from New York, the two are said to have been the first to commercially produce castor oil, giving some to the Lewis and Clark expedition for use during its journey. Dr. Millington also served as the first postmaster when St. Charles was the state capital, operating his medicine practice, his castor-oil business, and carrying out his postal duties, all from his house at 332 South Main Street. (Photograph by author.)

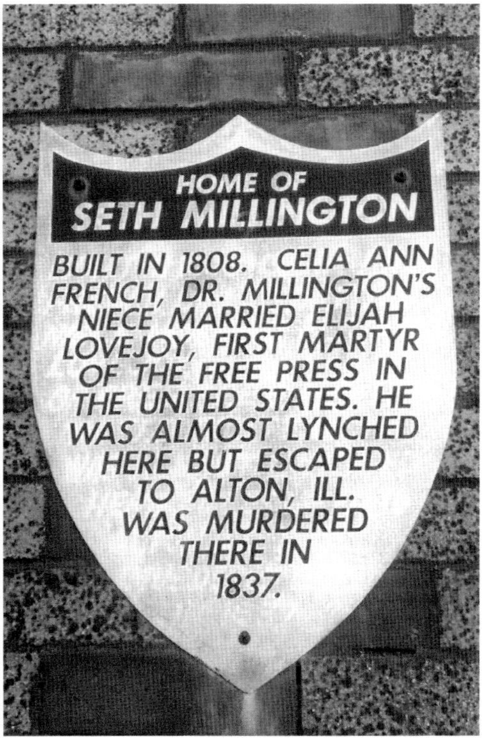

Dr. Seth Millington

Seth Millington's house at 301 South Main Street was built in 1808. He was the uncle of Elijah Lovejoy's wife and brother of Dr. Jeremiah Millington, with whom he owned a castor-oil-making business and later a coal mine, after the discovery of coal on his farm outside of town. The brothers were known for their botanical gardens west of St. Charles, where they grew several acres of castor beans. (Photograph by author.)

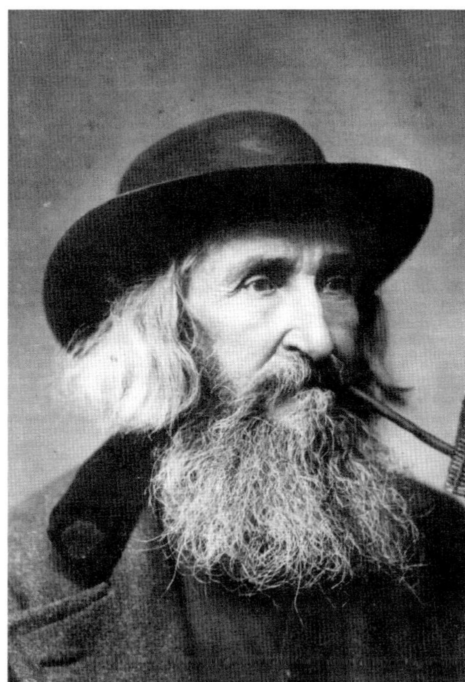

Doc Carr

St. Charles legend states that Doc Carr was the inventor of the corncob pipe. He whittled the first pipes by hand and sold them for 5¢ each. At various times, Carr also tried his hand as a hunter, newspaper editor, and baggage man. (Courtesy of St. Charles County Historical Society.)

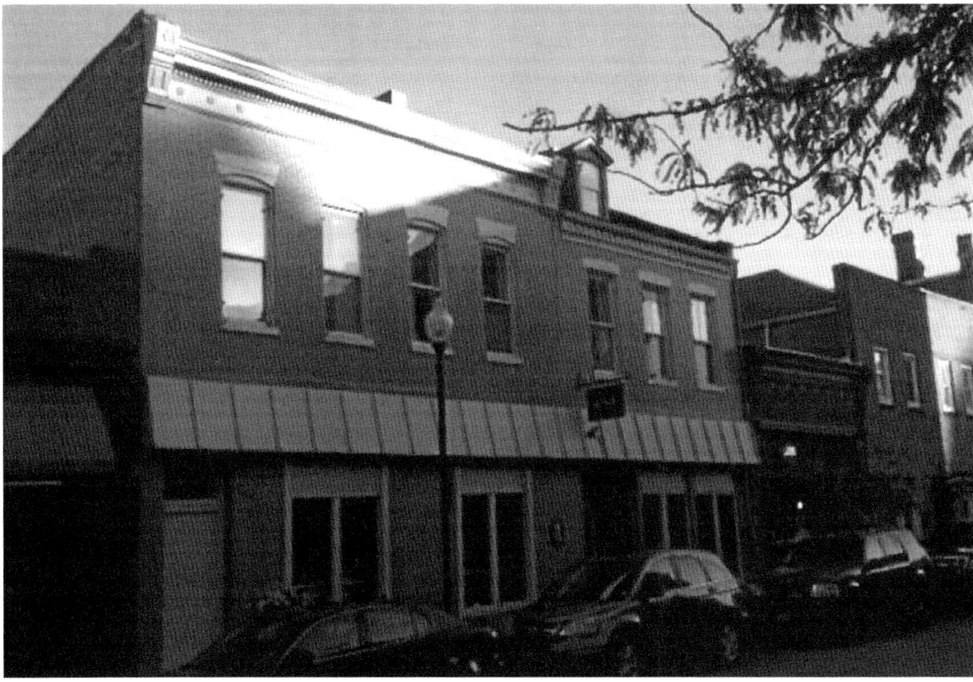

William Sublette

St. Charles's own mountain man was known as Bill Sublette. His family lived in a brick building on North Main Street (pictured). In 1822, Sublette became part of the trapping group known as Ashley's Hundred, named for William Henry Ashley of the Rocky Mountain Fur Company. The group included several other mountain men, including Jim Bridger and Jedediah Smith. According to legend, Sublette was the first to bring wagons back to the Rockies, helping to forge the Oregon Trail by way of a shortcut known as Sublette's Cut in Wyoming. (Photograph by author.)

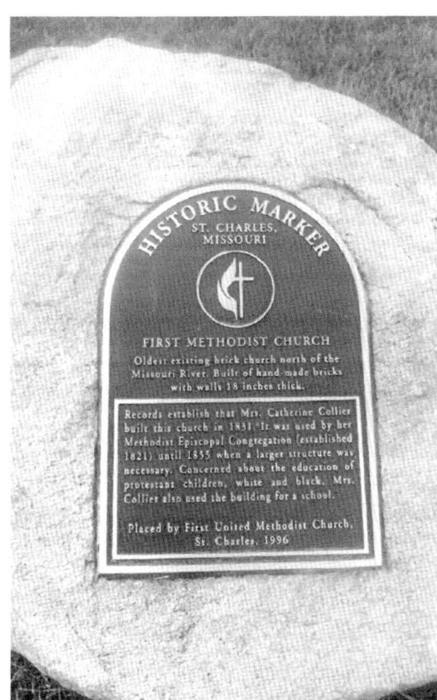

Catherine Collier

In 1830–1831, Catherine Collier erected the first Methodist church in St. Charles at 617 South Main Street. With her son George she also founded St. Charles College. George Collier established the mill in 1843 that would later become the famous Griffith Mill, said to have been the largest flour mill west of the Mississippi River. (Photograph by author.)

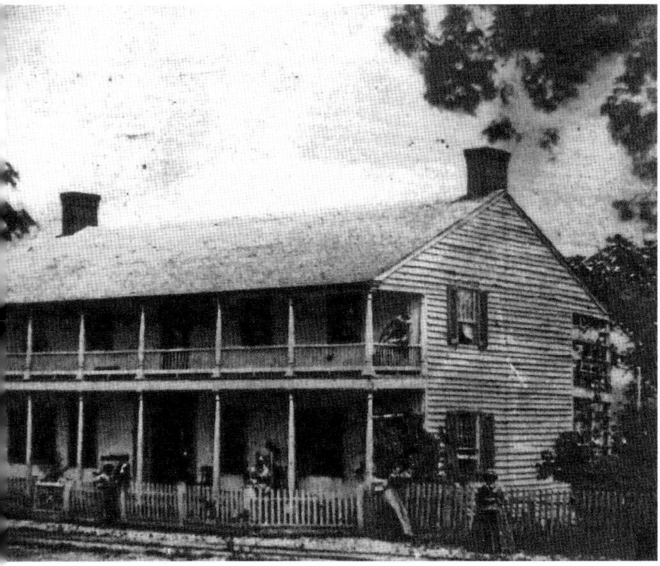

Dr. Henry Behrens
About 1830, Henry Behrens occupied the first doctor's office in St. Charles, along with Dr. J.R. Mudd, another early St. Charles physician, at 116 North Main Street. Pictured is the home of Dr. Behrens in 1850, which was located at Clark and Main Streets. It is said that Dr. Behrens took care of Mother Rose Philippine Duchesne during her last illness. (Courtesy of St. Charles County Historical Society.)

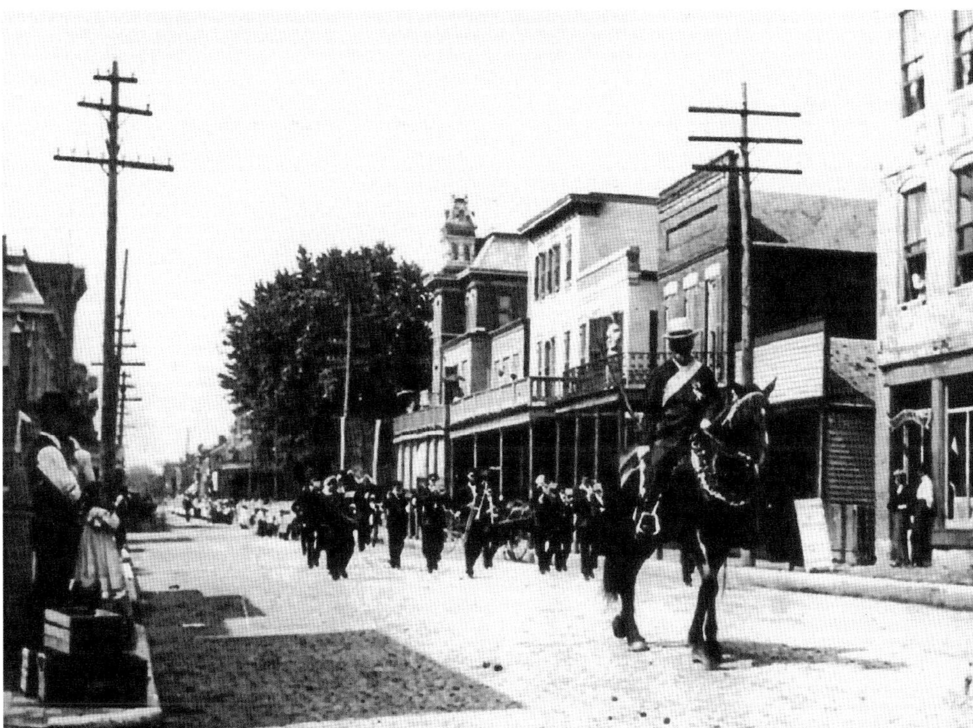

Dr. Charles Montgomery Johnson
A native of Virginia, Dr. Johnson sided with the Confederate army during the Civil War, eventually being captured and held prisoner by Union soldiers. Records show he had been sentenced to death but was subsequently paroled. After the war, Dr. Johnson moved into the city of St. Charles and returned to practicing medicine, partnering with Dr. John E. Bruere, a Union veteran. Here, Dr. Johnson leads a parade on horseback after returning from the Civil War. (Courtesy of St. Charles County Historical Society.)

Sr. Mary Elizabeth Becker

One of the founders of SSM Health St. Joseph Hospital–St. Charles, Sr. Mary Elizabeth Becker was one of five sisters, including Mother Odilia Berger, who came to St. Louis from Germany in 1872 to establish a religious community, the Franciscan Sisters of Mary, the founding order of SSM Health. The sisters began caring for patients in their homes shortly after arriving in town. Near the end of 1873, at the insistence of Rev. Charles Edward Koch at St. Peter Church in St. Charles, the sisters established a house here from which they provided private nursing for families. Sr. Mary Elizabeth was in charge, and she had two sisters to assist her. Unfortunately, during the sisters' stay in St. Charles, Father Koch became ill, and Sr. Mary Elizabeth nursed him until his death. In 1884, Rev. Francis X. Willmes, pastor of St. Peter Church, requested that the sisters return to St. Charles to treat patients. Franz Schulte of St. Charles provided his house at 305 Chauncey Street for use as a hospital, and the sisters took charge of the hospital in November 1885. Sr. Mary Elizabeth Becker was the first superior. The house was small and could accommodate only a few patients, so the sisters devoted most of their time to nursing people in their homes. Becker died at age 57 from complications related to tuberculosis. (Courtesy of Franciscan Sisters of Mary.)

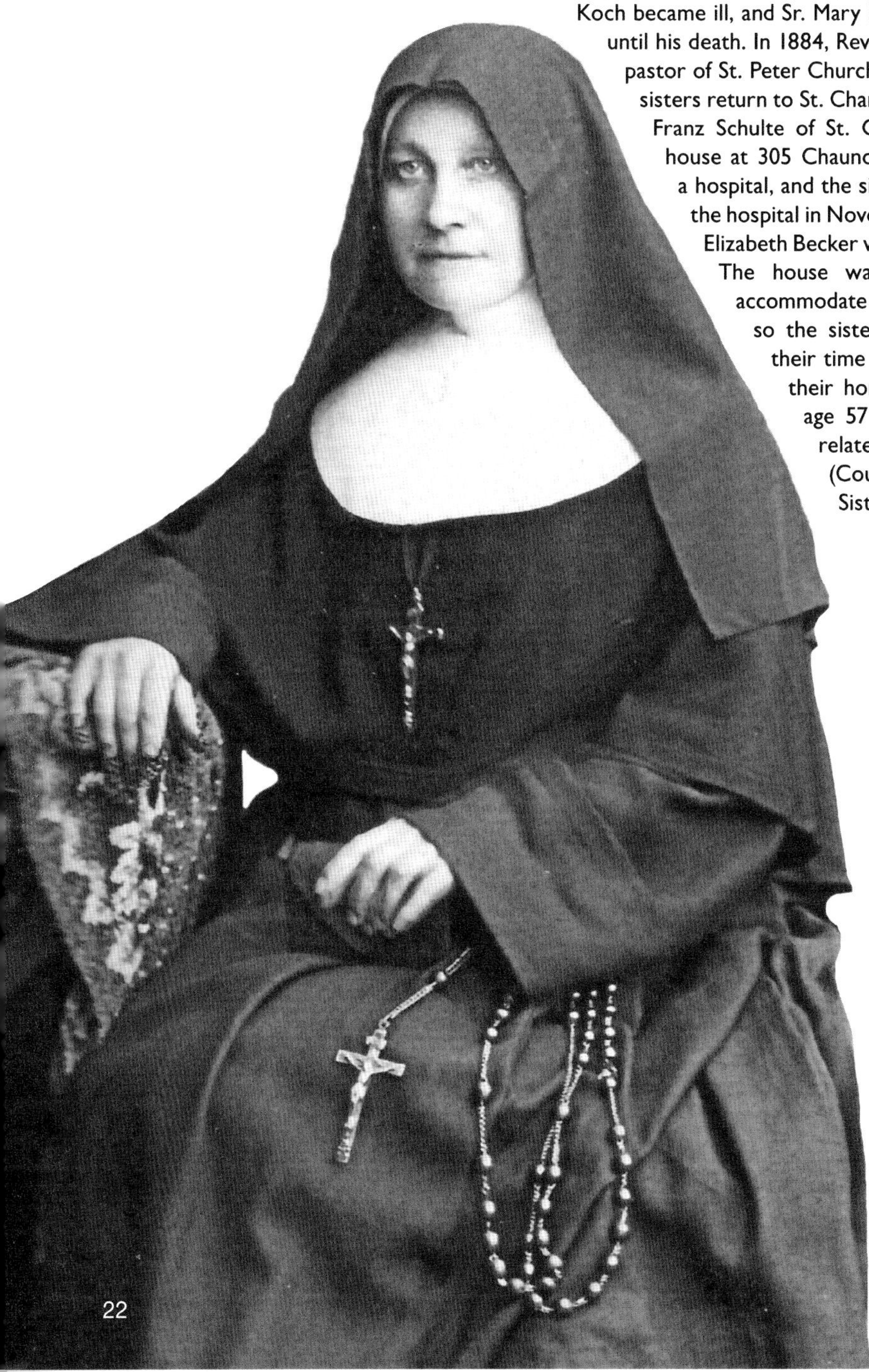

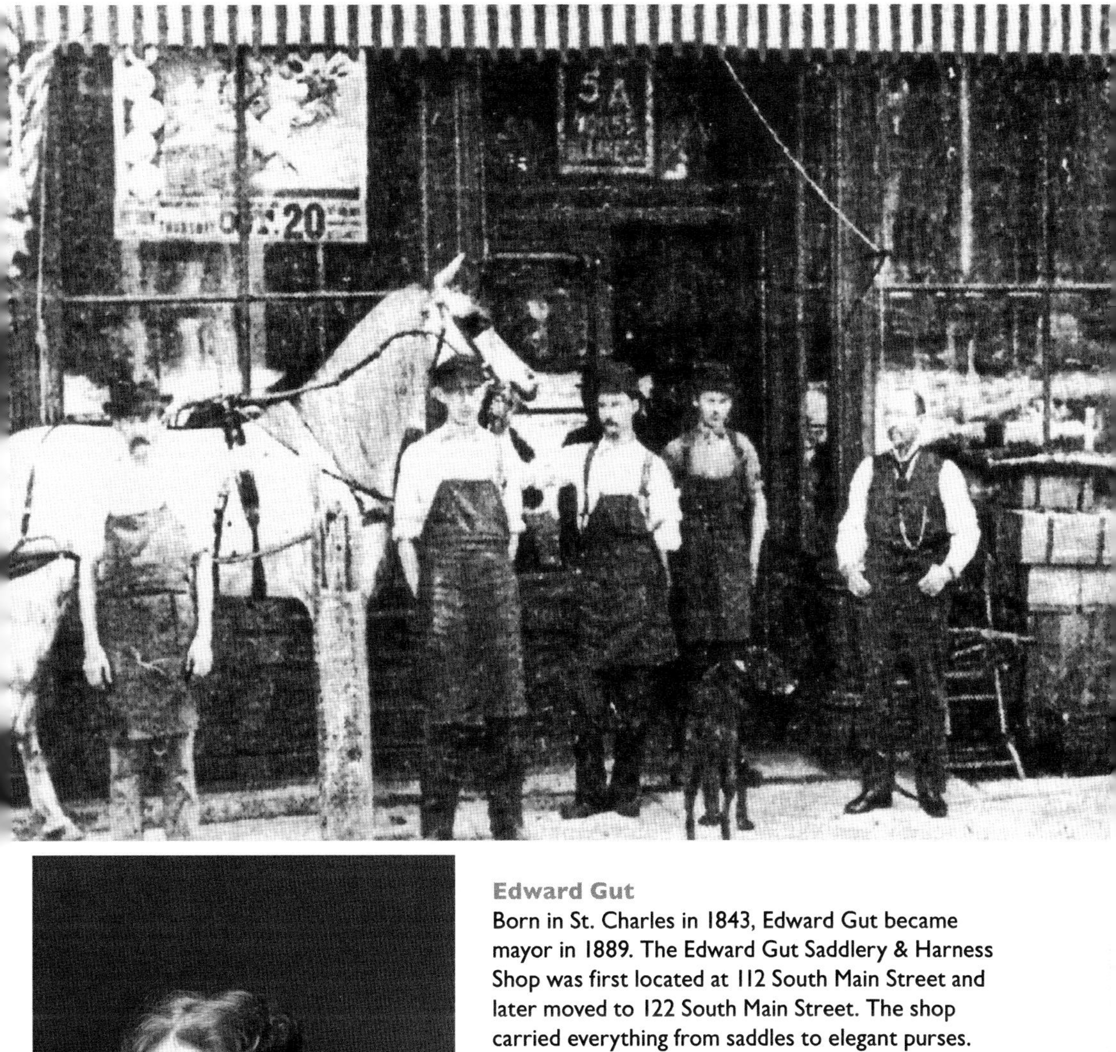

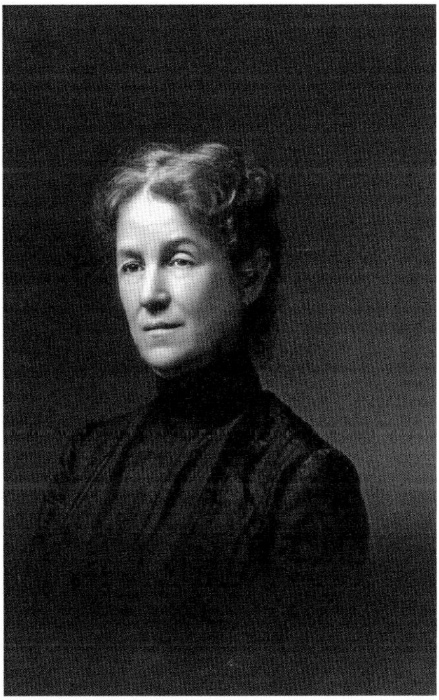

Edward Gut

Born in St. Charles in 1843, Edward Gut became mayor in 1889. The Edward Gut Saddlery & Harness Shop was first located at 112 South Main Street and later moved to 122 South Main Street. The shop carried everything from saddles to elegant purses. Gut was also president of First National Bank. Gut's shop is seen here about 1880. He is believed to be the man on the far right, shown here with his employees. (Courtesy of St. Charles County Historical Society.)

Mary Louise Bailey Gatzweiler

Mary Louis Gatzweiler was born at Pond Fort and came to St. Charles to teach school. In the late 1890s, she opened Gatzweiler's Elegant Millinery at 102 South Main Street. Her shop remained open for 34 years. (Courtesy of St. Charles County Historical Society.)

Henry B. Denker

Born in Hanover, Germany, in 1839, Henry Denker came to the United States in 1859, where he eventually became a resident of St. Charles. Originally, he opened a grocery and meat-packing business. After the car-repair shop of the North Missouri Railroad closed in 1867, causing a loss of employment in St. Charles, Denker, with the help of other citizens, provided the funds to reopen the company as St. Charles Car Manufacturing Company in 1872 or 1873. Originally, the company considered producing farm machinery, but it eventually became a railway-car manufacturer. Denker served as vice president of the company until 1895 and then became president. In later years, the company built horse streetcars, trolleys, and freight cars for steam railroads. The company's name was shortened to St. Charles Car Company about 1880, and it began building passenger cars for steam railroads in 1886. The company was one of 13 that merged in 1899 to form American Car & Foundry, now known as ACF Industries, a national manufacturer of railcars and railcar components. Henry Denker was mayor of St. Charles from 1902 to 1910. (Courtesy of St. Charles County Historical Society.)

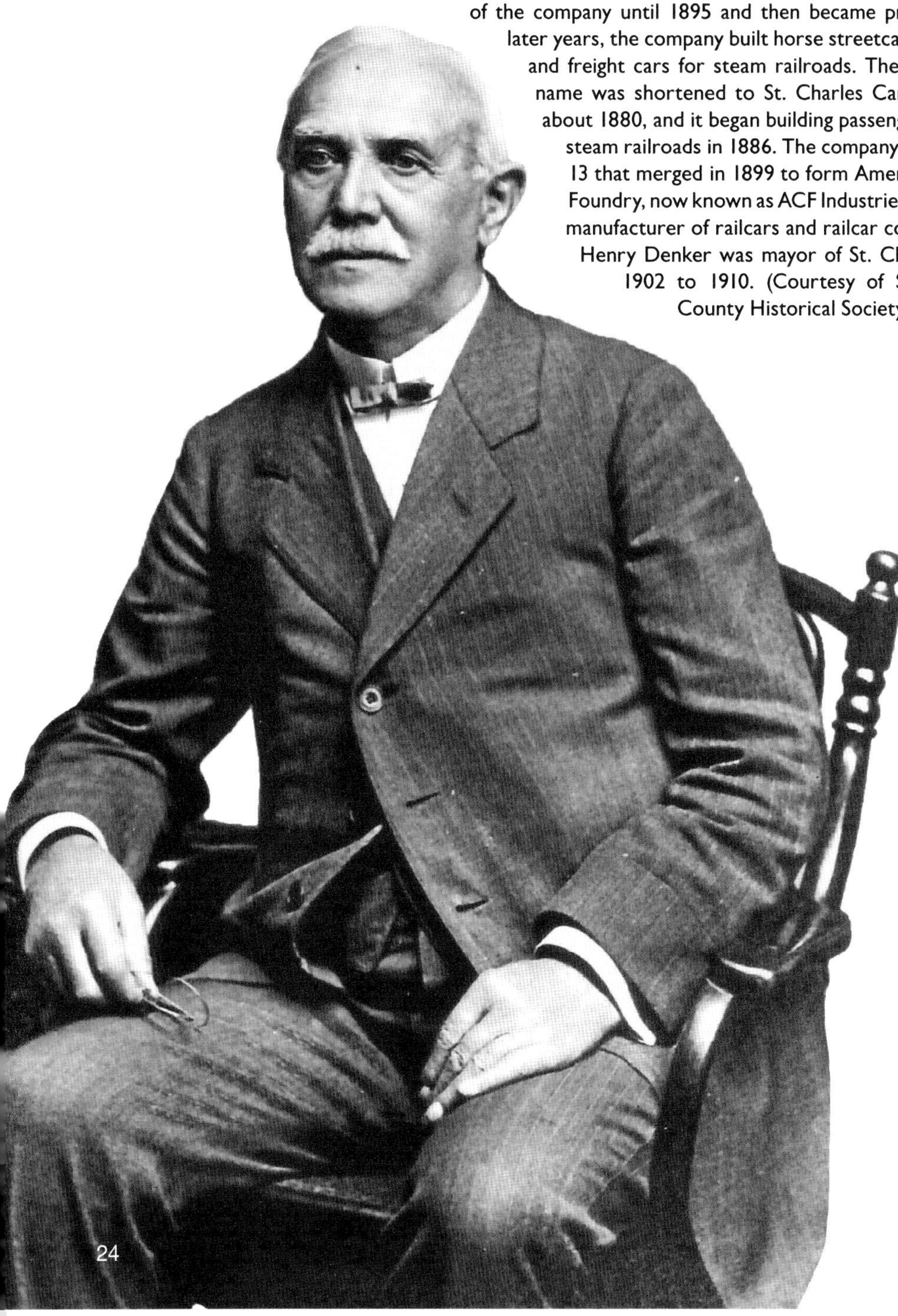

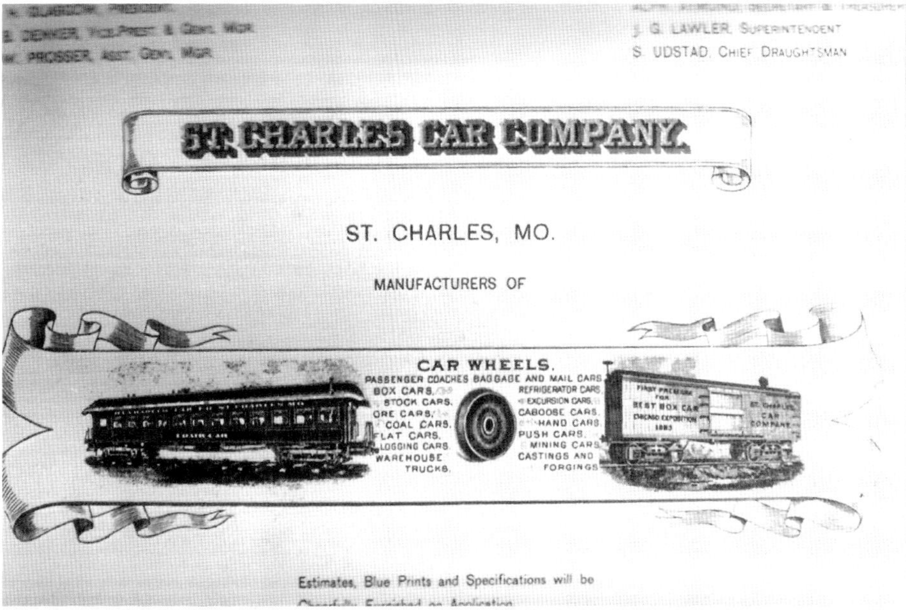

James Lawler

James Lawler came to St. Charles from Indiana in 1879 and became a blacksmith with the St. Charles Car Company (later American Car & Foundry). Known for leadership, he became district manager 20 years later and held that position until his death. It is said that his funeral was the largest in the history of the town up to that time. In the below photograph, Lawler (back row, fourth from left) poses with other men from the St. Charles Car Company. In no particular order, they are: George F. Hoehn, J.C. Prosser, Frank Timpken, Adolph Aymond, John Pfeiffer, F.C. Becker, W.H. Glasgow, William Patterson, J.R. Mudd, John Gruenberg, H.B. Denker, Sigwald Udstadt, and ? Beason. William Buckner is at the window. (Both, courtesy of St. Charles County Historical Society.)

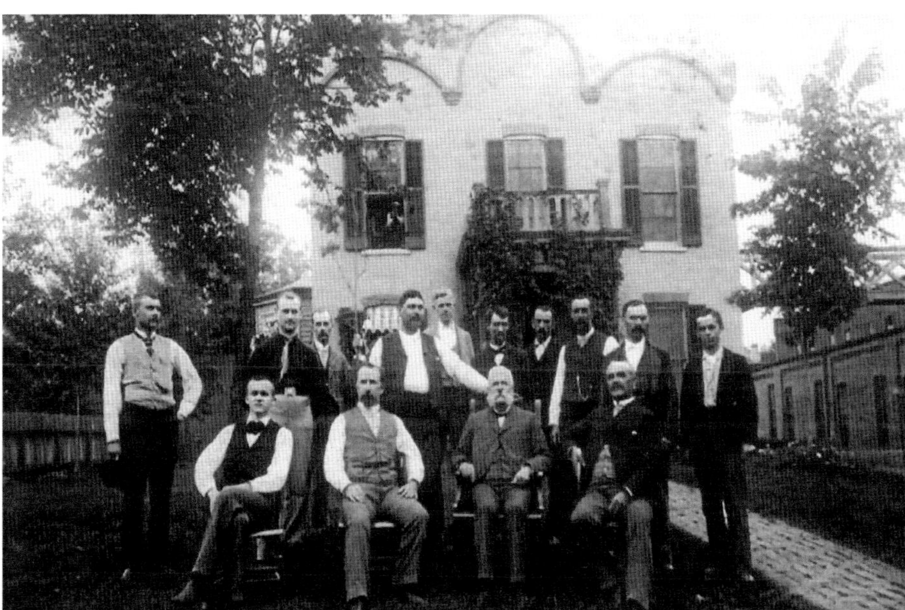

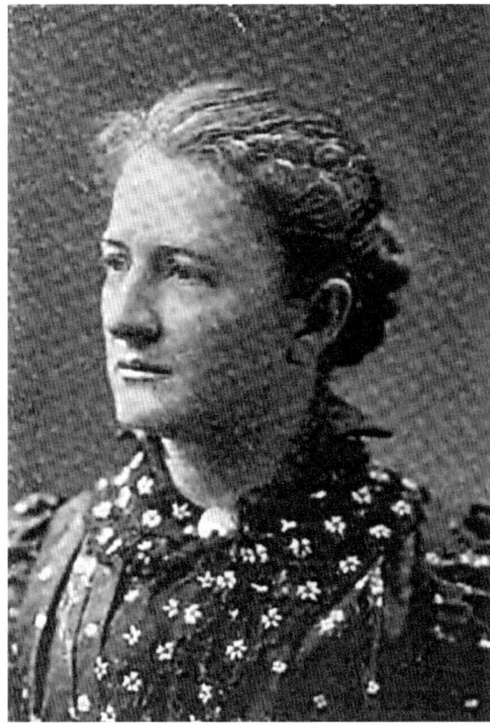

Ellene Alice Bailey

E.A. Bailey, an inventor from Pond Fort in St. Charles County, lived for a time with her sister Mary Gatzweiler at 310 Jefferson Street in St. Charles. Her first invention was the Pond Fort Boot, for which she obtained American and Canadian patents in 1880. Her second invention was the Pond Lily powder puff (below), patented in 1882. Her inventions led her to move to New York, where she continued to invent other commercially useful products. (Both images from *American Women: Fifteen Hundred Biographies*, Revised Ed., by Mary Ashton Rice Livermore and Francis Elizabeth Willard, published 1897, courtesy of Library of Congress, LC-06045834.)

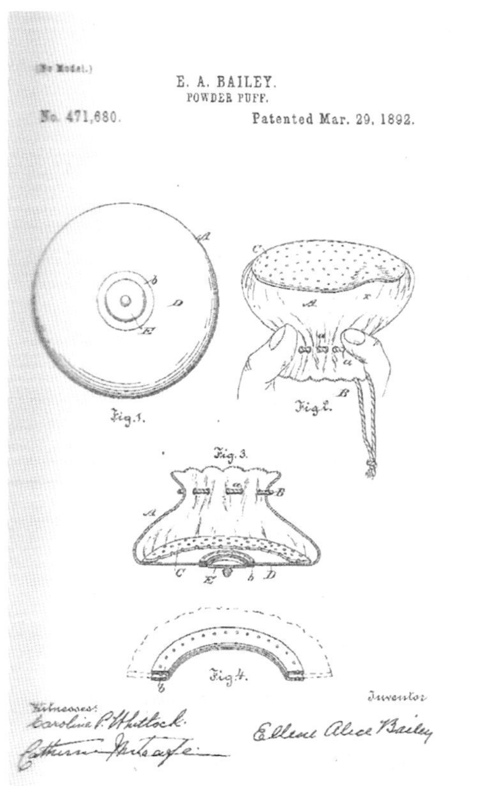

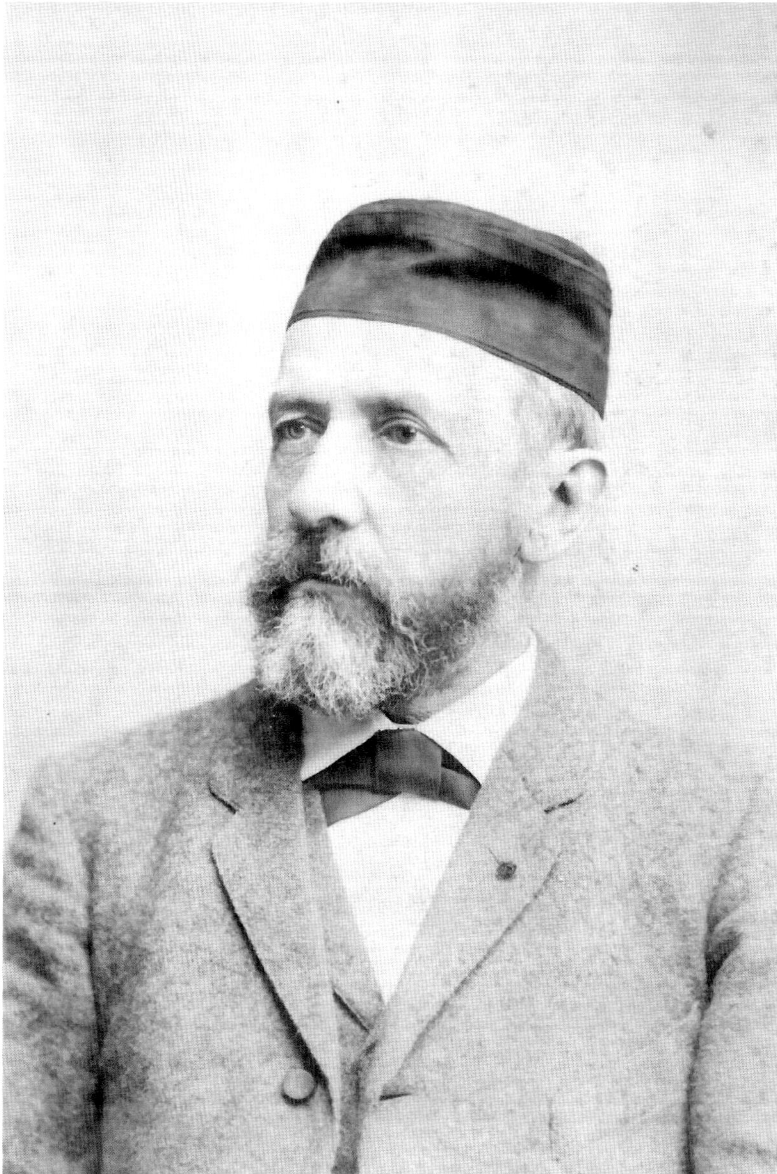

Rudolph H. Goebel

Rudolph Goebel chronicled St. Charles history in photographs for more than half a century. He was born on January 20, 1835, in Buer, Germany. His wife, Amelia, was a native of Hamburg, Germany. Records indicate that Goebel paid $15 to become a licensed photographer in St. Charles, Missouri, in November 1862. According to markings on his photographs, his studio was located opposite the St. Charles Courthouse during the Civil War. His subjects included the St. Charles Bridge and views of the city after an 1876 tornado. From about 1877 to 1880, Goebel toured the countryside around St. Charles, often traveling by horse-drawn wagon, taking photographs and producing dozens of photographic negatives. Accounts differ, but it is believed he may have continued to take photographs in St. Charles from 1880 until about 1916. Rudolph Goebel died in St. Charles on May 8, 1923. (Courtesy of St. Charles County Historical Society.)

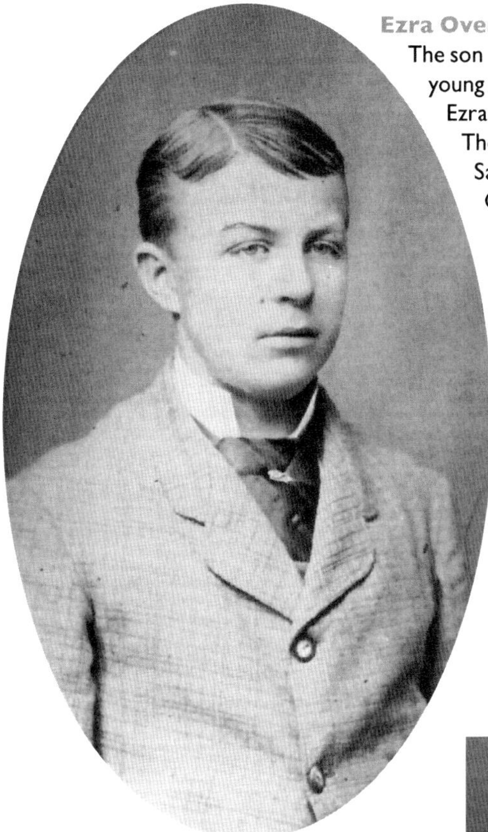

Ezra Overall

The son of Asa N. Overall, mayor of St. Charles (1861–1862), young Ezra Overall was also the nephew of Asa's brother Ezra, an early St. Charles attorney and land speculator. The elder Ezra Overall, first president of the Union Savings Bank in 1870, later became a benefactor of St. Charles College. (Courtesy of St. Charles County Historical Society.)

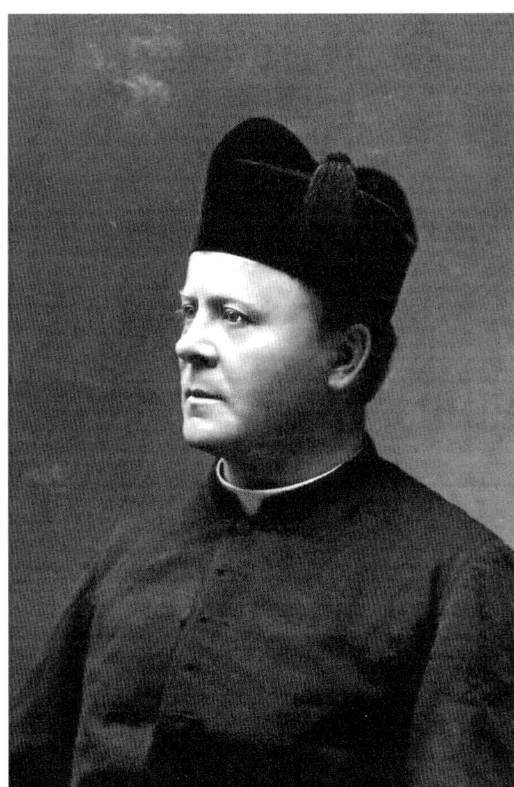

Rev. F.X. Willmes

Fr. Francis Willmes became pastor of St. Peter Church on January 1, 1882, and remained the pastor for 50 years. Under his careful leadership, the church grew in size and added new buildings, including a new parish school. Father Willmes was also active in the community, along with the priests of St. Charles Borromeo Church. (Courtesy of St. Charles County Historical Society.)

CHAPTER TWO

Educational Leaders

Education is a large part of the heritage of St. Charles, Missouri. Many early citizens were involved in one way or another in the founding, building, or supporting of schools. St. Rose Philippine Duchesne helped found the first Society of the Sacred Heart school in America in St. Charles, and Mary Easton Sibley and George Sibley founded Lindenwood College, now Lindenwood University.

Today's citizens of St. Charles are committed to education, too. The brief biographies of contemporary or recent St. Charles residents show that Lindenwood University figures heavily in the list of organizations where locals perform civic duties.

Among the many beloved educators in St. Charles's past are Melvin Washington, Sr. Anna Mae Marheineke, and Terry Gravemann, all of whom are featured in this chapter. However, today's educators are challenged even more than those in the past to meet the needs of diverse groups of students, and most of them perform an exemplary job—leading youth into the future or supporting adults in the furthering of their education. These professionals demonstrate a dedication to education that makes the town proud. Special mention goes to Kathleen Hopper, former principal at Academy of the Sacred Heart, who left a legacy of devotion and caring when she retired after four decades at the school. Teaching can be an exhausting job, but thankfully, plenty of talented St. Charles locals find it to be a rewarding job, too.

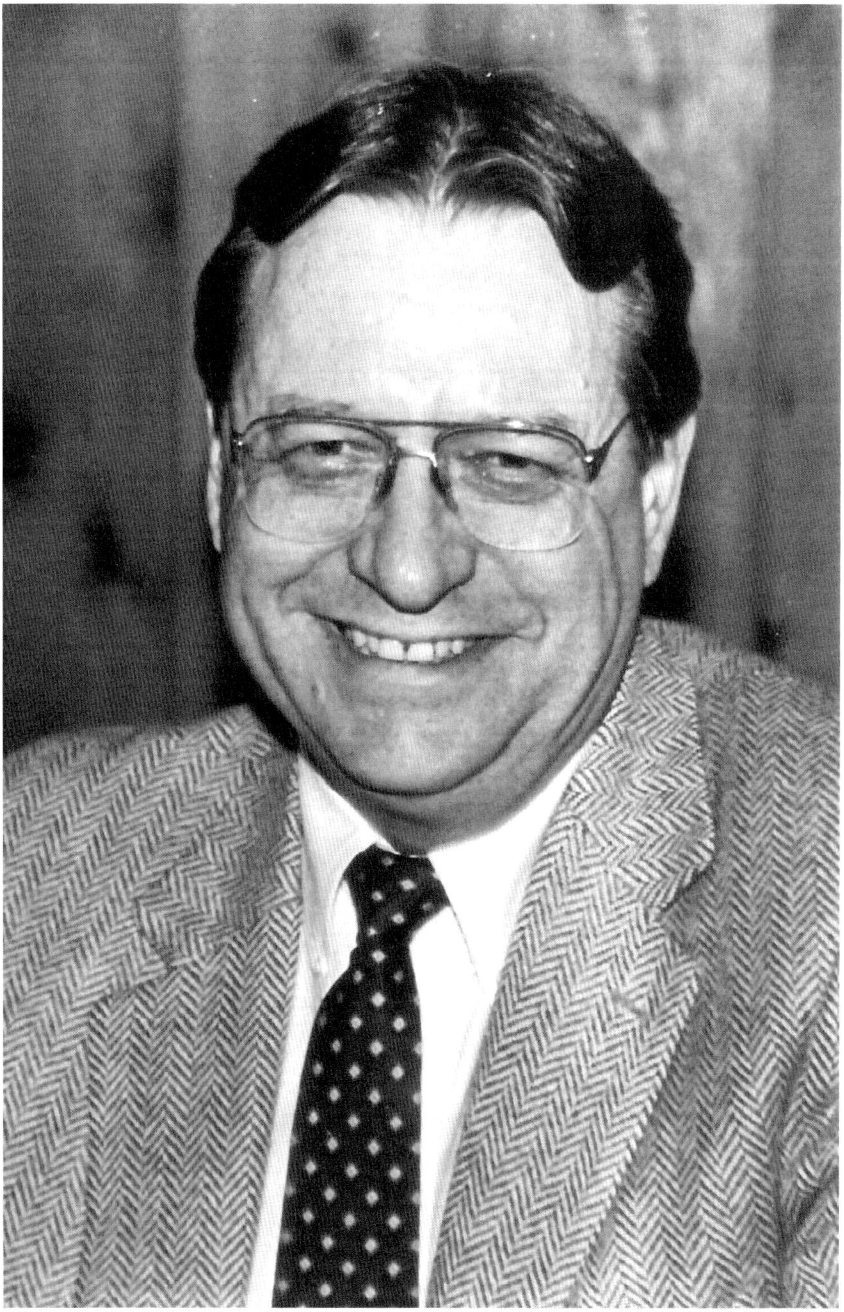

Dr. Dennis Spellman

A former captain in the US Marine Corps, Dr. Spellman was a well-known presence in St. Charles during his Lindenwood presidency and after. Interim president from 1989 to 1990 and president from 1990 to 2006, he is credited with greatly increasing enrollment at the college, launching a plan to increase building, and resolving the college's debt. While he was president, in 1997, Lindenwood College became Lindenwood University. Dr. Spellman received the St. Charles County Chamber of Commerce Lifetime Distinguished Service Award in 2000. (Courtesy of Mary Ambler Archives, Lindenwood University.)

Helen and Paul Schnare

Helen Schnare spent nearly 30 years in secondary education, mainly in St. Charles. In 1983, Helen was appointed by Gov. Kit Bond as the first woman to serve on the Missouri Highway and Transportation Commission. She and her husband, Paul, were recognized as instrumental in establishing St. Charles Community College in 1986. Paul Schnare, who helped select the site of the college, was elected as a member of the first St. Charles Community College Board of Trustees, and he and his wife established endowment scholarships for students with financial need. Both Schnares volunteered in the college library for several years. In 2009, St. Charles Community College named the college library the Paul and Helen Schnare Library. Paul died in 1997, and Helen passed in 2013. (Courtesy of St. Charles Community College.)

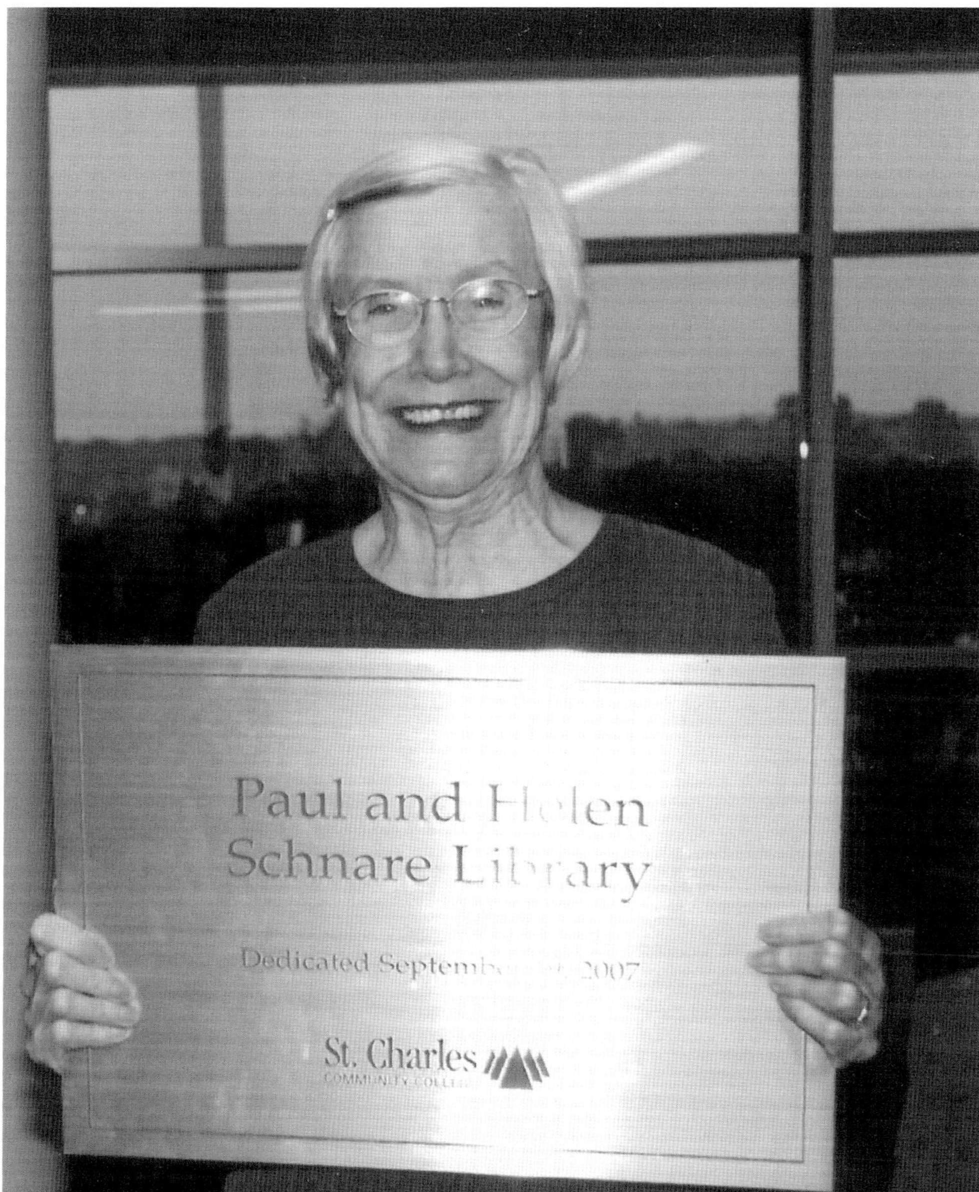

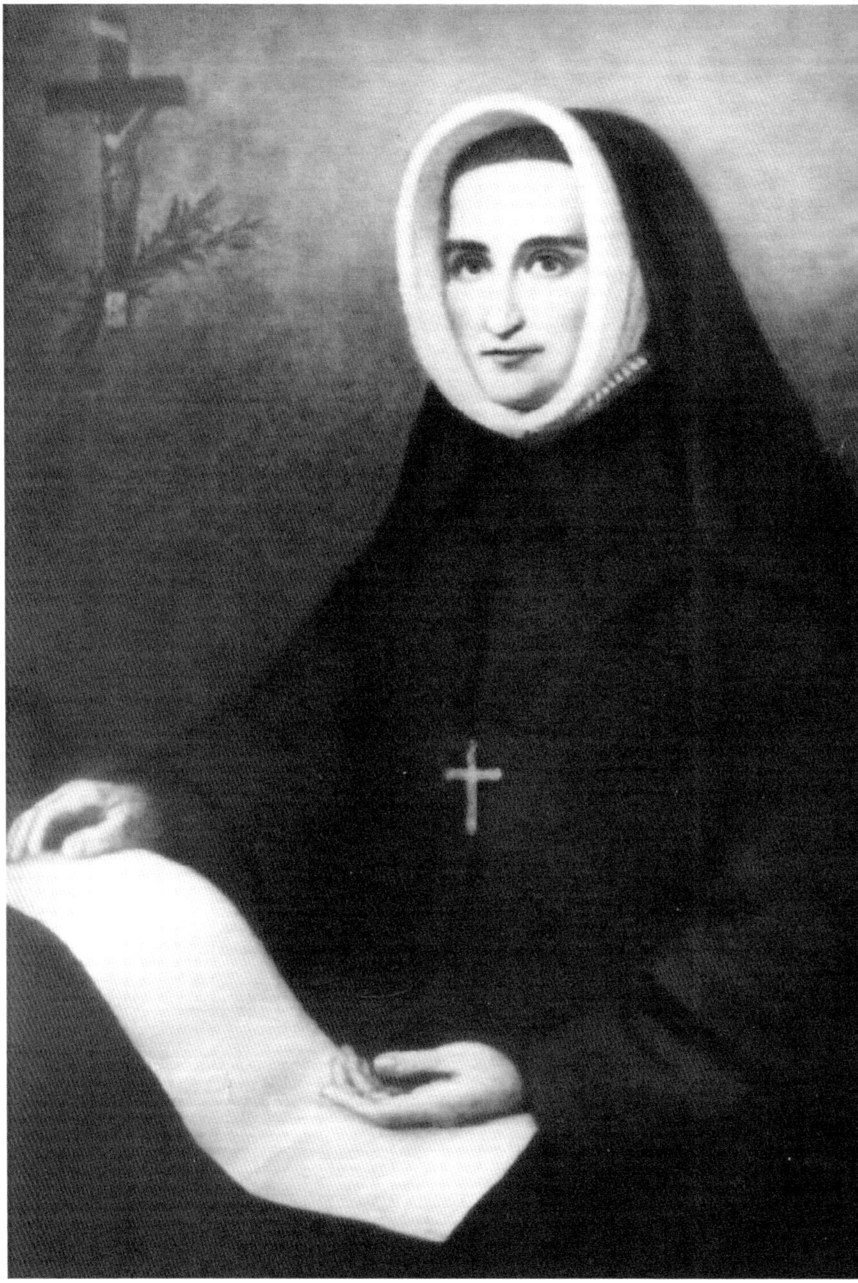

Rose Philippine Duchesne

Born in France in 1769, Rose Philippine Duchesne and four other nuns came to St. Charles in 1818. In a little log cabin, they founded the first school of the Society of the Sacred Heart in America. At the age of 72, Duchesne fulfilled a lifelong desire to serve as a missionary to Native Americans and began work with the Potawatomi Indians in Sugar Creek, Kansas. She later returned to the school in St. Charles she had founded. She died at the convent in 1852 and is enshrined in a chapel on what is today the campus of the Academy of the Sacred Heart. She was declared a saint in the Catholic Church in 1988 by Pope John Paul II. (Courtesy of Academy of the Sacred Heart.)

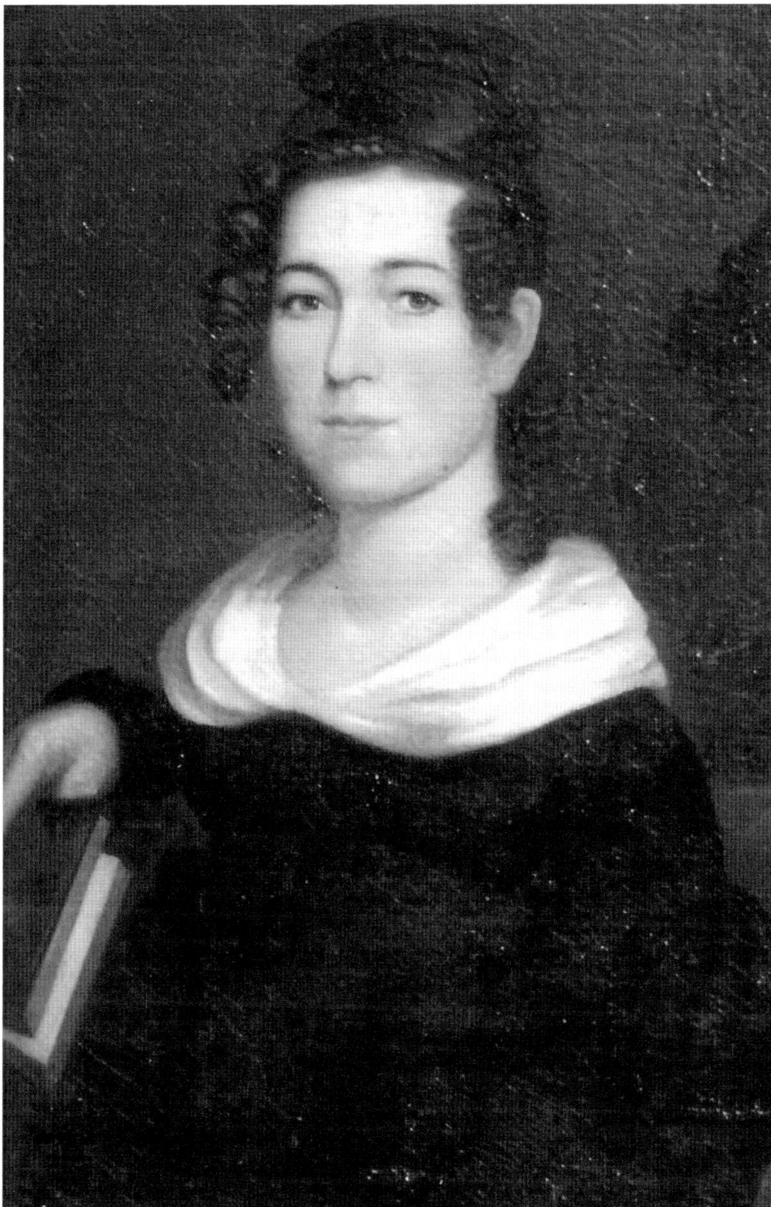

Mary Easton Sibley

Known as the founder of Lindenwood University, Mary Sibley and her husband, George Sibley, moved from Fort Osage to St. Charles in 1827 and settled on a piece of land George had acquired and named Linden Wood for the plentiful linden trees. Soon after, Mary started a small school in her home, teaching her sister, Louisa, and a few other girls, probably children of friends. In or around 1831, the Sibleys built a log cabin at Linden Wood to board 20 students and provide classroom space. Mary Sibley served as the school's president until 1856. In 1864, after the death of her husband, Mary briefly moved to St. Louis, but she moved back to St. Charles in 1869 and lived near what is now Butler Library. She died in 1878 and is buried with her husband on the campus at Lindenwood. Mary's father was Rufus Easton, Missouri's second attorney general. (Courtesy of Mary Ambler Archives, Lindenwood University.)

George C. Sibley

Soldier, explorer, and former postmaster at Fort Osage, George Sibley moved to St. Charles in 1827 with his wife, Mary Easton Sibley. Mary, who had taught children at Fort Osage, began teaching her sister and a few local children. Around 1831, George built a log cabin on the Sibleys' property, which he called Linden Wood. The cabin would house students and provide classroom space. Eventually, the school would become the Linden Wood School for Girls, which today is Lindenwood University. In 1833, George ran as a Whig for US Congress, but he pulled out of the race. Between 1839 and 1840, he served as president of the Missouri Internal Improvements Board and as a railroad commissioner. Sibley was also very active in the Presbyterian Church. He died on January 31, 1863, and is buried with Mary Sibley on the campus of Lindenwood University. (Courtesy of St. Charles County Historical Society.)

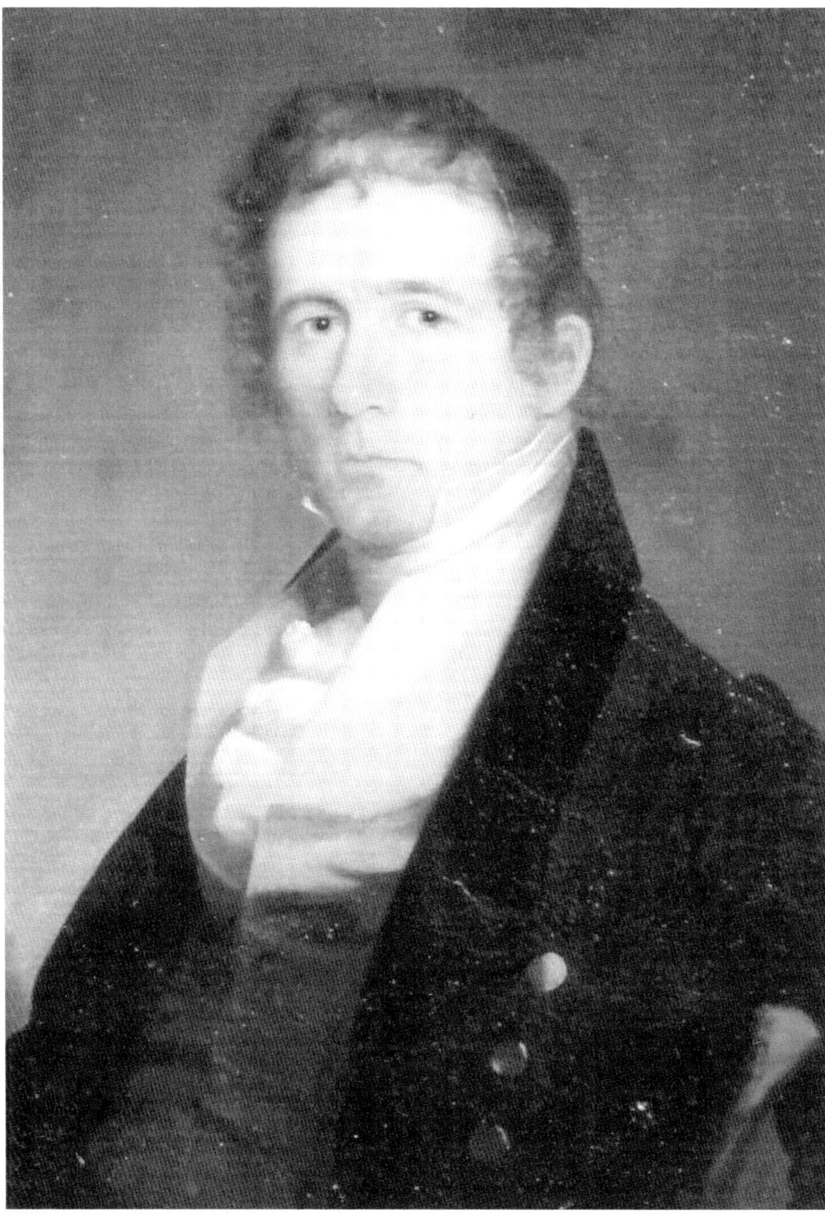

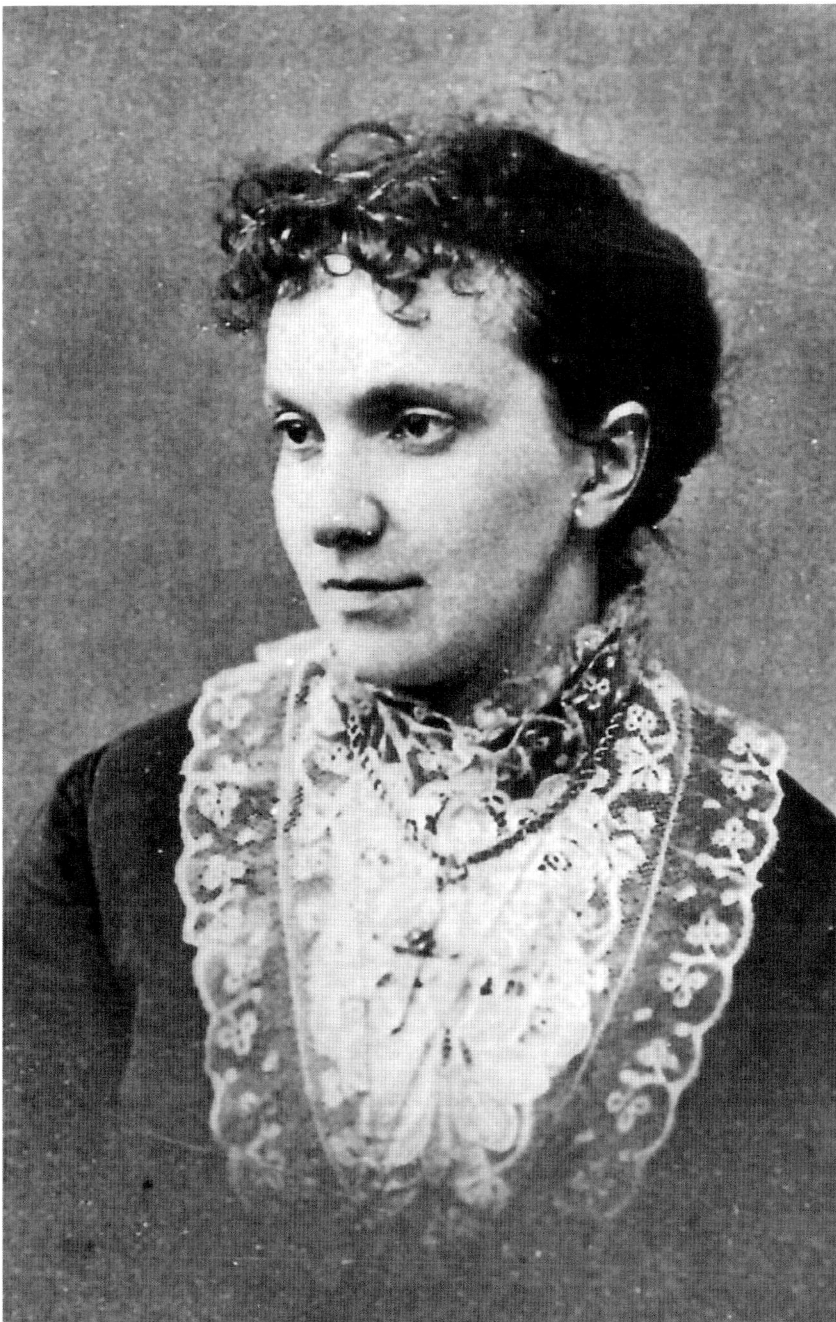

Mary E. Jewell
Mary Jewell was the only woman, besides Mary Sibley, to serve as president of Lindenwood University. Records show she had served as a teacher and principal under former president John Howard Nixon. Some historians believe Mary Jewell was the first female college president in the United States. She served as the school's president from 1876 to 1880. (Courtesy of Mary Ambler Archives, Lindenwood University.)

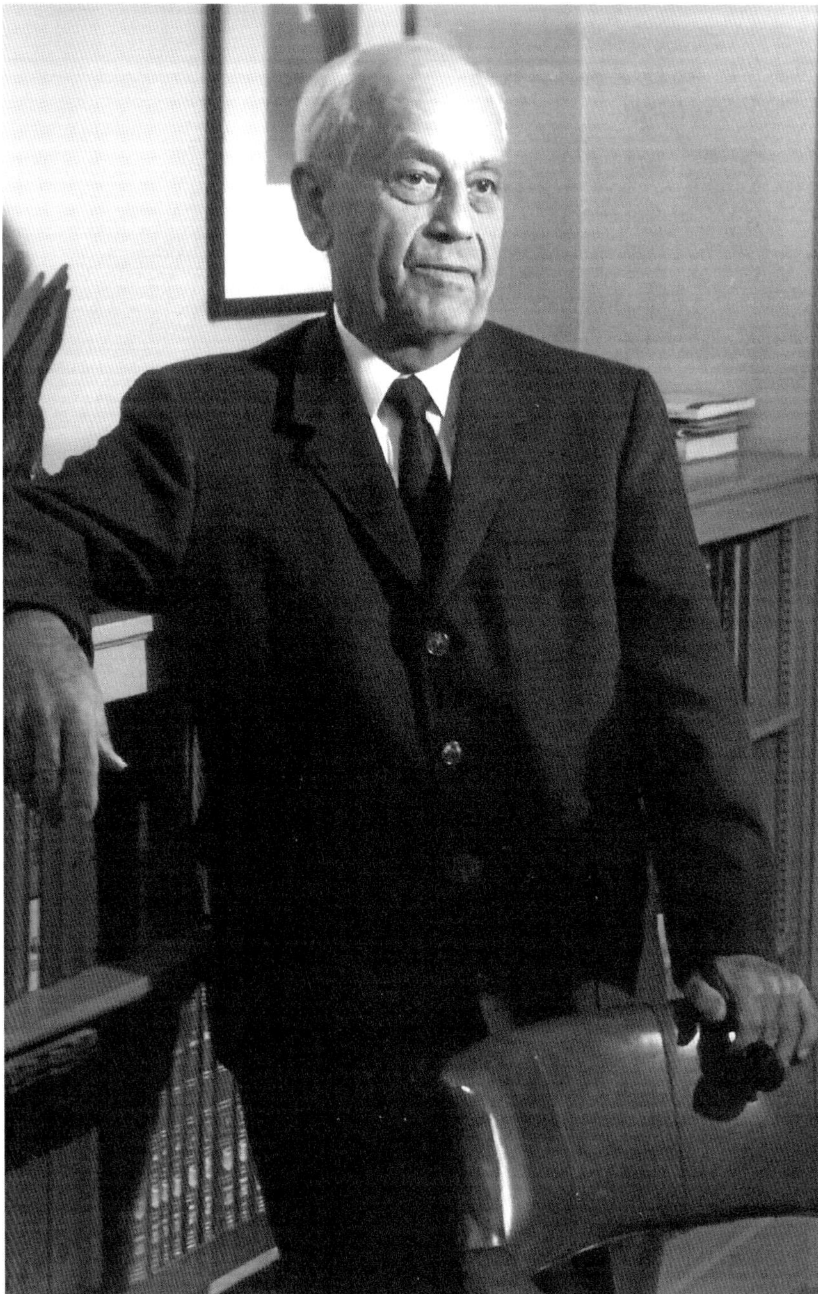

Dr. Franc McCluer

Franc "Bullet" McCluer served as Lindenwood's president from 1947 to 1966 and again from 1973 to 1974. Prior to coming to St. Charles, McCluer served as president of Westminster College in Fulton, Missouri, when Winston Churchill gave his "Iron Curtain" speech. Nicknamed "Bullet" for his debate skills, he is said to have been able to fire off arguments three times as fast as most people. In 1968, McCluer was honored with a Lifetime Distinguished Service Award from the St. Charles County Chamber of Commerce. (Courtesy of Mary Ambler Archives, Lindenwood University.)

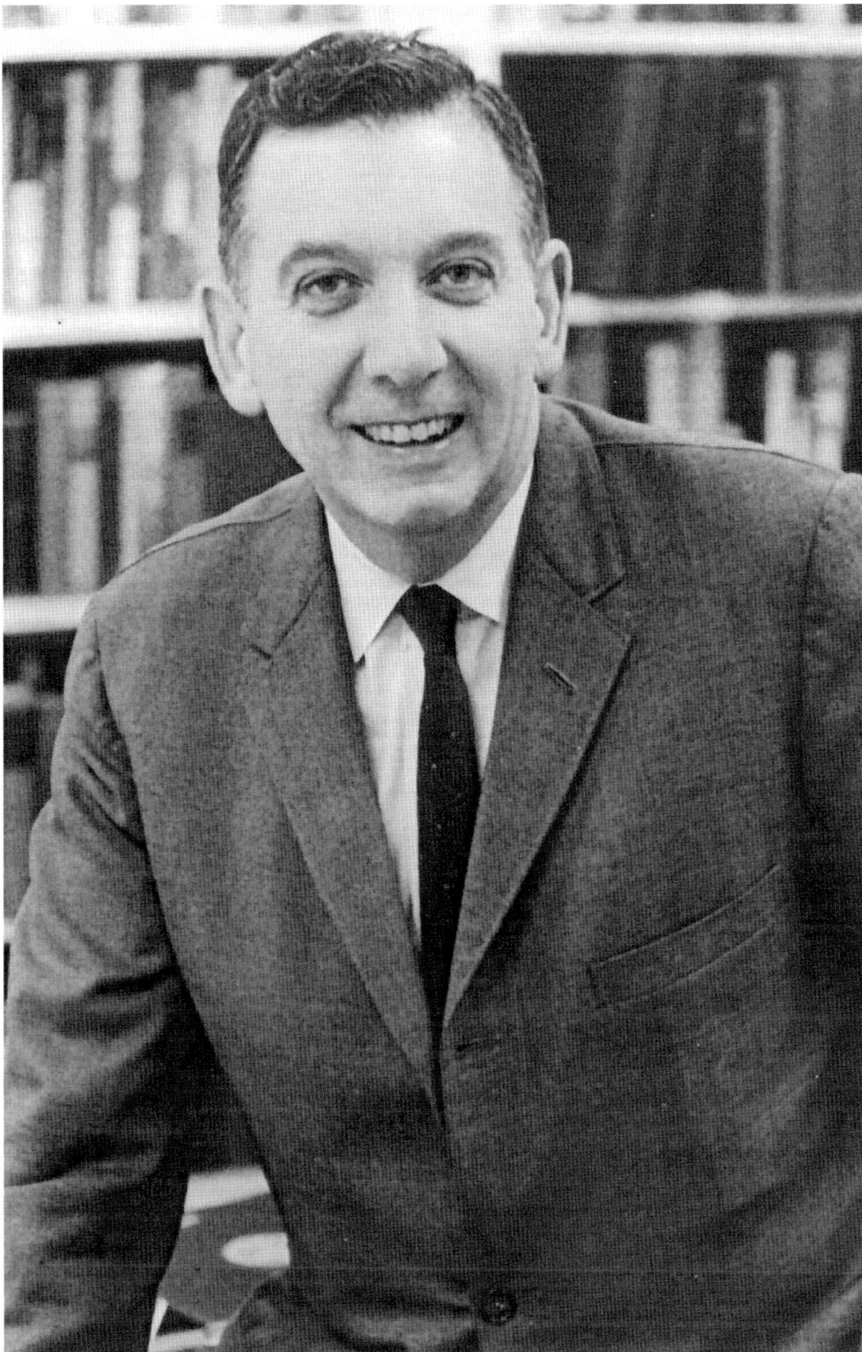

Dr. John Anthony Brown

Dr. Brown was president of Lindenwood College from 1966 to 1973. During that time, in the 1968–1969 academic year, men were officially admitted to the former women's college. While president, Dr. Brown helped convince the Missouri Legislature to provide state aid to private-college students for the first time in history. (Courtesy of Mary Ambler Archives, Lindenwood University.)

Jane Crider

Jane Crider moved to St. Charles in 1947 with her husband, Dr. Russell Crider, and her children. In 1959, Crider joined forces with Margaret Holmes to establish a home-based candle shop that employed disabled adults. In 1960, she and Holmes, along with other activists, incorporated as Boone Center, Inc., expanding their services to furniture refinishing and repair. Today, Boone Center Workshop, known as BCI since 2005, is one of the leading contract packing facilities in Missouri, employing over 300 people with disabilities. Jane Crider is a founding board member for United Services and Four County Mental Health Services, a former board member of Lindenwood University, and a recipient of the Sibley Medallion of Honor Award in 1988. She is past chairwoman of St. Charles County Mental Health Council. Crider has also served on the Eastern Regional Advisory Council and the Blue Ribbon Committee for the Missouri Department of Mental Health. Recognitions include the St. Charles County Chamber of Commerce Outstanding Citizen award in 1959, Citizen of the Years award in 1984, a St. Louis Women of Achievement award in 1987, and the St. Charles County Mental Health Hero award in 1990. (Courtesy of St. Charles County Historical Society; photograph by Michael Schlueter.)

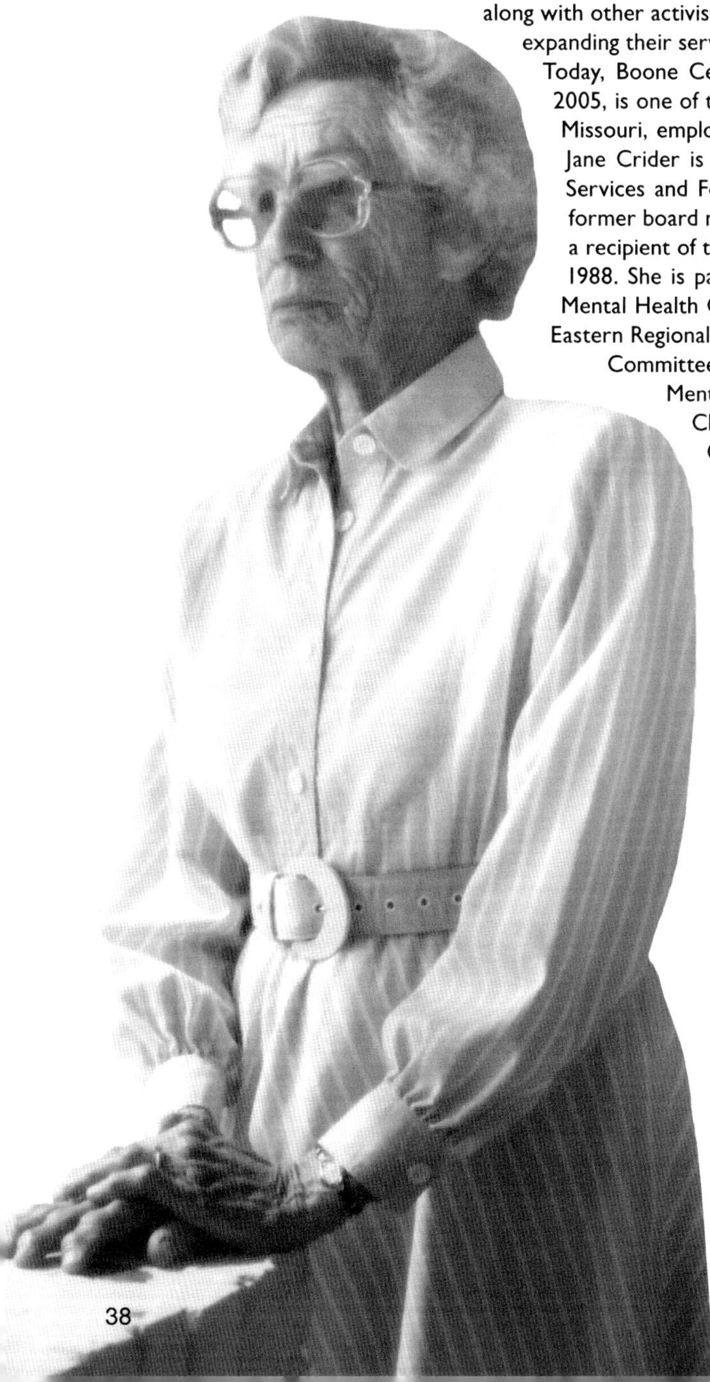

Sr. Anna Mae Marheineke

Beloved teacher and mentor to many, Anna Mae Marheineke, RSCJ, was born on December 27, 1917, in St. Charles and baptized on New Year's Day, 1918, at St. Charles Borromeo Catholic Church. She began attending the Academy of the Sacred Heart at age five in 1923 and finished high school there in 1934. After studying at Maryville College in St. Louis, she attended the Sacred Heart convent in Albany, New York. Her first assignment after leaving the convent was in Cincinnati, and she was later sent to New Orleans. Eventually, she returned to St. Louis to earn her bachelor of arts degree in sociology with a minor in education.

Sister Marheineke returned to the Academy of the Sacred Heart in St. Charles for one year in 1945 and again in 1965. There she taught for the next 40 years—a time she once called the happiest years of her religious life. In 1994, she decided it was time to hand the reins to younger teachers. She did not quit, though—she simply transitioned to helping in the library, where she could still see her beloved schoolchildren every day.

Until the end of her life, generations of former students visited and wrote to thank her for all she had taught them. "I don't expect that," she said in 2001, "and that isn't the reward I'm after. To hear a child say, 'Oh, I see! I understand.' That's the most gratifying thing. I think that's the greatest reward of teaching."

A collection of Sister Marheineke's poems, *Smile the Sun Around My Heart*, was published in 2005 by the Academy of the Sacred Heart Alumni Association. That same year, Sister Marheineke moved to Oakwood, the Society of the Sacred Heart retirement center in Atherton, California. She died peacefully on Wednesday, August 14, 2013, the eve of the Feast of the Assumption of the Blessed Virgin Mary.

"The hundreds of souls she has touched send Mother Marheineke off with love and deep thanks," wrote a former student and colleague. "Thank you, dearest Mother. Thank you from the bottom of a heart overflowing with love for you." (Courtesy of Academy of the Sacred Heart.)

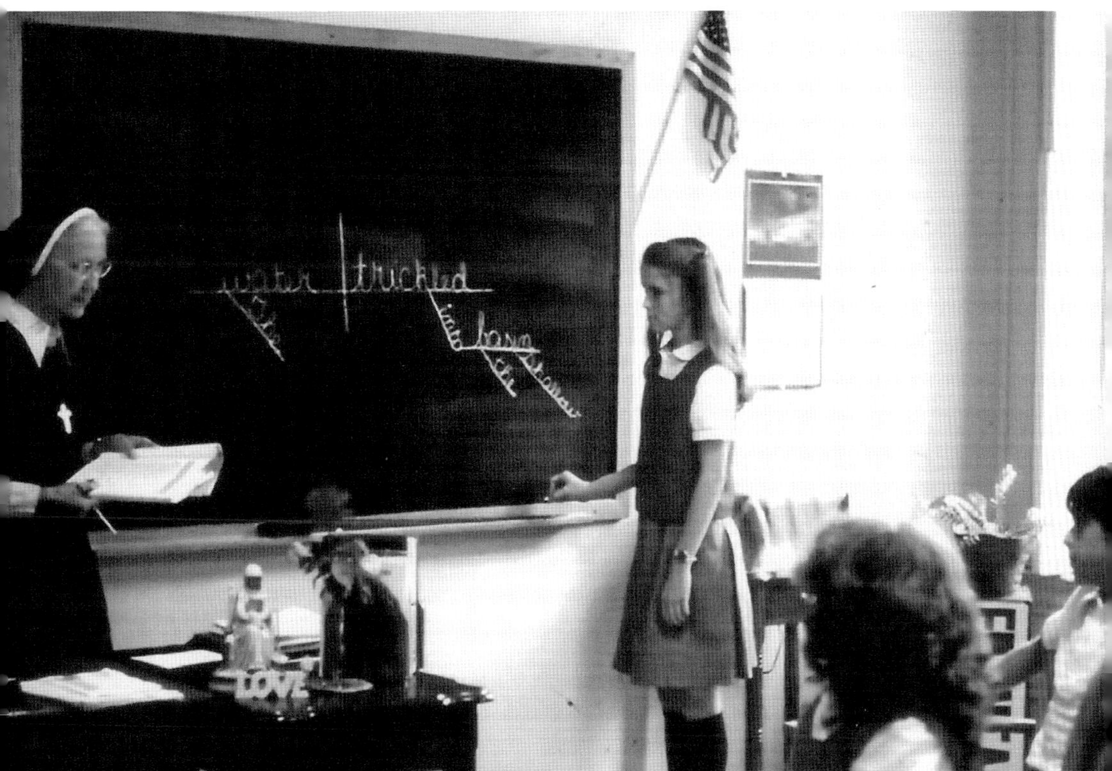

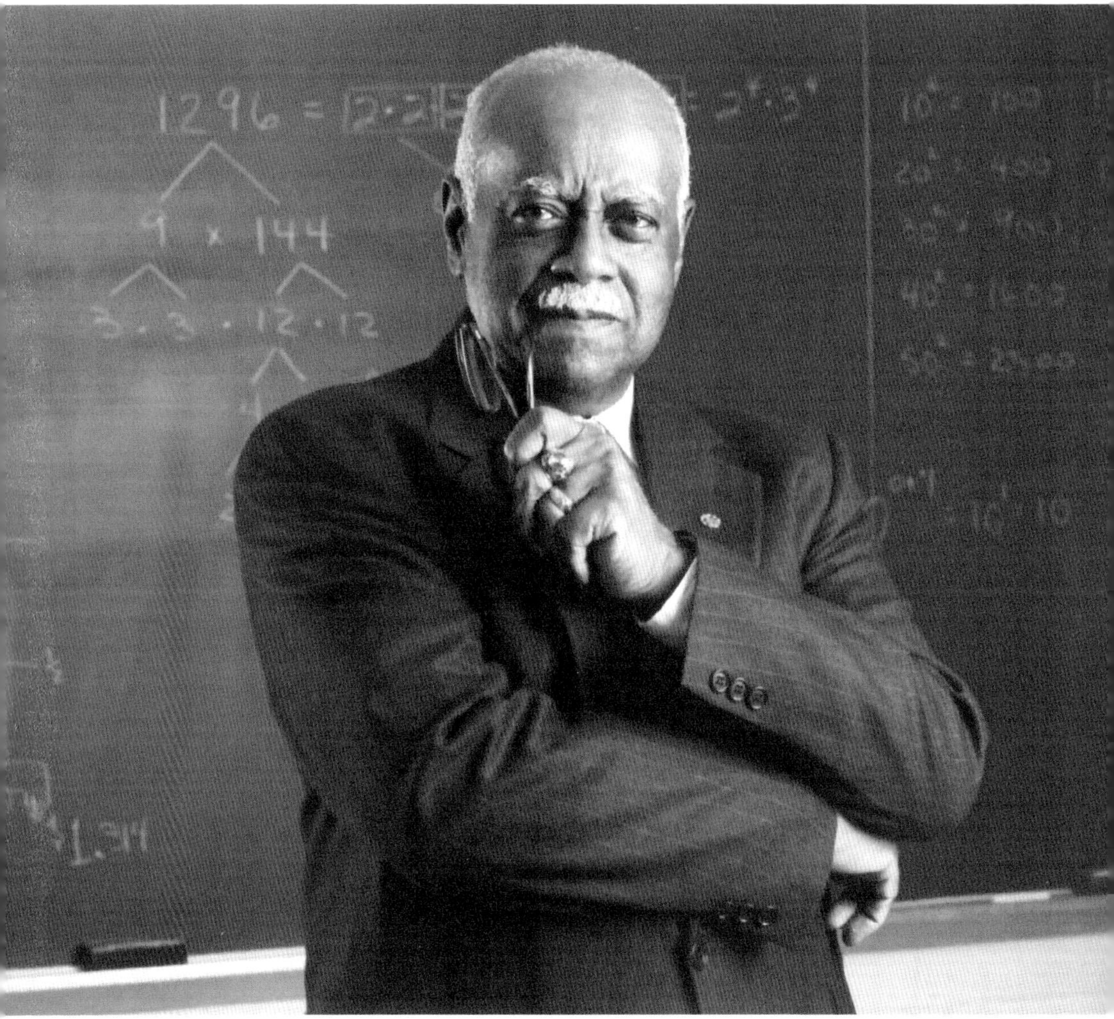

Melvin Washington

Melvin Washington's career spanned 47 years, including 40 in the St. Charles School District. He began working at Franklin High School as a teacher and coach and eventually became principal in 1943. Washington later taught math for 10 years at St. Charles High School and was appointed assistant principal at Hardin Middle School. From Hardin, he went to Jefferson Middle School as principal. Toward the end of his career, he became interim superintendent of the St. Charles School District. Later, he returned to teach at Jefferson Middle School until his retirement. The first African American elected to public office in St. Charles County, Washington was elected to the board of the St. Charles School District for two terms. He was honored in 2004 as a "Pioneer in Education" by the Missouri Department of Elementary and Secondary Education. Washington sat on many boards and advisory committees in St. Charles. A lifetime member of Kappa Alpha Psi, Washington was also a trustee and steward of the board of St. John AME, distinguished past president and lifetime member of the St. Charles Optimist Club, and a member of the Missouri Human Rights Commission. His many recognitions include the St. Charles County Chamber of Commerce Lifetime Distinguished Service Award in 1984 and the Citizen of the Years award in 2001. (Courtesy of St. Charles County Historical Society; photograph by Michael Schlueter.)

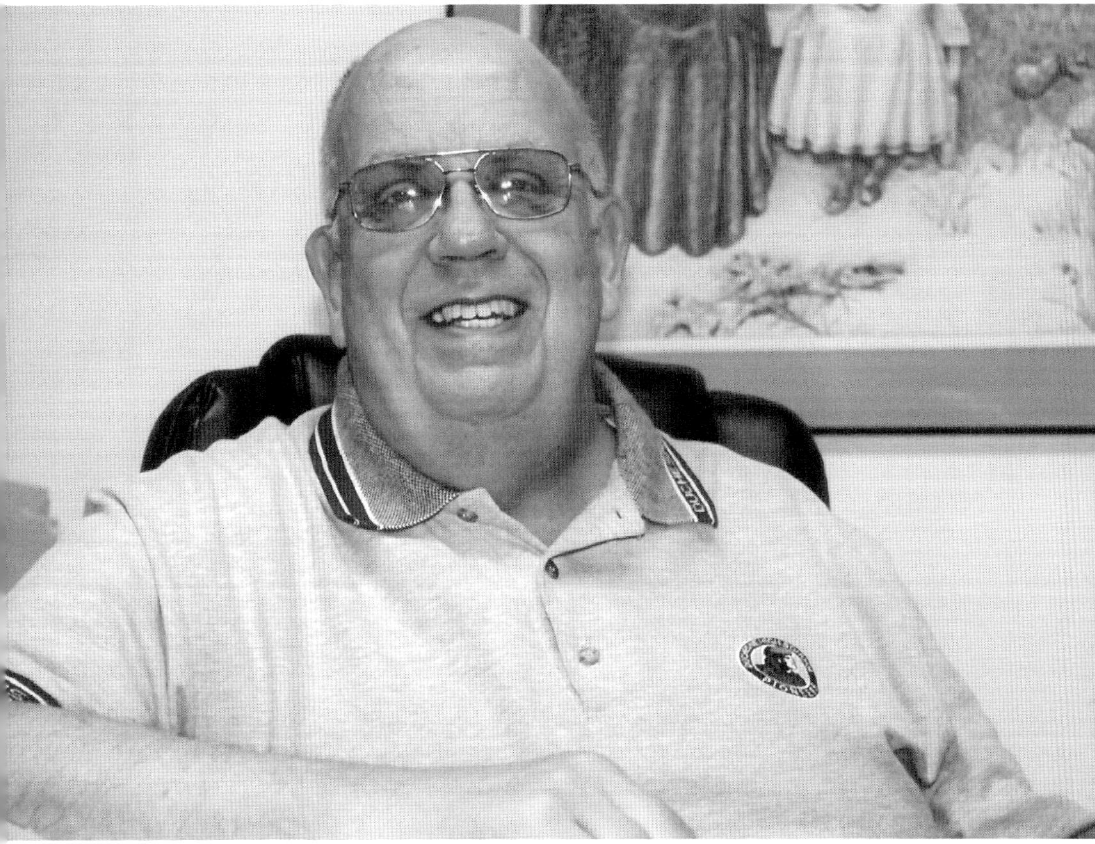

Terry Gravemann
Born and raised in St. Charles, Terry Gravemann attended kindergarten at Benton School and then was a student at St. Charles Borromeo School and Duchesne High School. After graduating from Northeast Missouri State University (now Truman State University) in 1972, he returned to St. Charles and worked for St. Charles County and the Missouri Department of Welfare, managing the Commodity Foods Distribution Program. In August 1973, Gravemann returned to Duchesne High to teach social studies and help moderate the Key Club and National Honor Society. In 1979, while still teaching, he was named part-time dean of students. In 1989, he began serving as the full-time dean, and he became the administrator/president of the school in 2002. He retired in 2012. The Legacy of Learning Tuition Assistance Fund was launched in his honor in 2012. He and his wife participate on several committees at St. Cletus Catholic Church, and Terry is on the lay advisory board of SSM Health St. Joseph Hospital–St. Charles. He is a member of St. Charles Knights of Columbus. Gravemann feels his years at Duchesne provided an opportunity for him to not only teach but to learn as well, and he established many cherished friendships. "I enjoy knowing my former students have gone on to successful careers, with many continuing to work and raise their own families in St. Charles," he said. In the early 1980s, Terry Gravemann was honored as an Outstanding Young Educator by the St. Charles Jaycees. He was also named one of the "50 over 50 Community Shapers" by *St. Charles Business Magazine* and one of the "Beyond the Best Top 50 in Business" by *StreetScape Magazine*. (Courtesy of Terry Gravemann.)

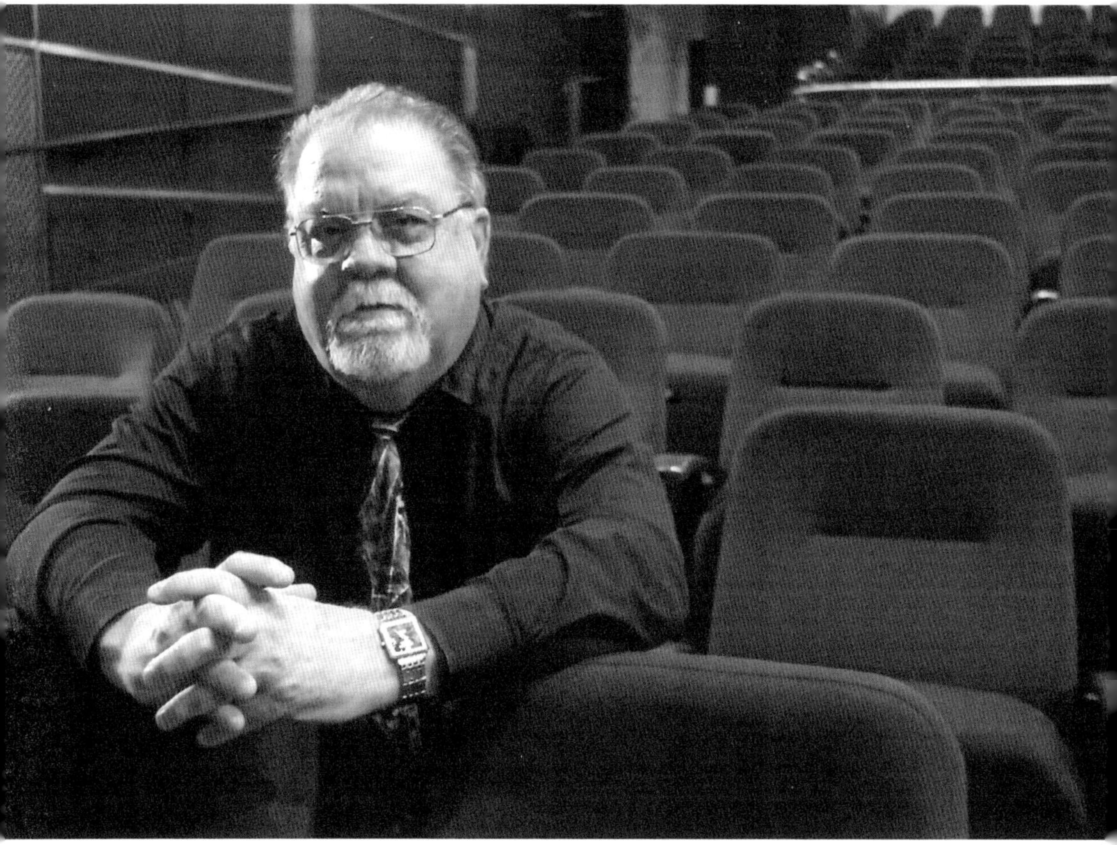

Peter Carlos

Peter Carlos, professor of digital cinema arts at Lindenwood University, has worked in film and television as a freelance producer, director, writer, and editor. He is the station manager and programmer for Lindenwood's television station, LUTV. He has also worked as a production manager, second unit director, coproducer, and script reader, and he has written or cowritten film treatments and scripts for several directors and producers. In Hollywood, Carlos worked with actors Jim Carrey, Kirsten Dunst, Steve Oedekerk, and Denise Crosby. His short film *Dad's Day* won Top Applause and Rising Star awards in national film festivals and was shown on national broadcast and cable channels. Carlos won two St. Louis Emmys, for a television spot and corporate programming. His short film *Gravity* won Best Drama in the St. Louis Filmmakers Showcase in 2010. In 2002, he was voted one of the Top 100 Multimedia Producers in America by *AV Video* magazine. His students at Lindenwood University have won two Midwest Region Student Emmys. Carlos has also published two books of poetry, *Praise the High Grass* and *Dreamfish*, and his work has been included in many literary journals. In 2014, Carlos was awarded a Fulbright Specialist Scholarship, and he will be traveling in 2016 to Paris and then to the Institut Americain Universitaire in Aix-En-Provence to study French New Wave films. (Courtesy of Lindenwood University.)

CHAPTER THREE

Prominent Citizens and Professionals

Pulling together all of the facts and accomplishments of so many prominent St. Charles citizens, professionals, and business leaders—both past and present—is overwhelming, for the simple fact that so many have done so many interesting things. It is regrettable that it is not possible to include every award, appointment, contribution, and recognition for each person highlighted in this chapter, due to space restrictions. Some St. Charles locals included in this book could have an entire volume dedicated to them alone, their accomplishments are so many and so great.

As accomplished as these legendary locals are, they are also diverse. Notable are the Jackson brothers, both doctors, who practiced medicine in St. Charles in the early 1900s, when they did not have hospital privileges at St. Joseph Hospital due to their race (although they were later recognized by the hospital). Everyone will agree that Kathryn Linnemann is legendary for having started a library with donated books in a small room at a local school, persevering even after a fire destroyed many of the books.

Notables who must also be mentioned here include Ryne Stiegemeier, who captured much of the history of St. Charles in photographs during his lifetime, and his daughter Barb, who remains involved in the preservation of the historic district. Mary Lou Ahmann's devotion to civic duty and community service earned her recognition by the St. Charles County Chamber of Commerce in 1983 as the first female Citizen of the Years.

Who could forget David Flavan's Noah's Ark Restaurant, with its mechanized animals? Or Pio Pedrucci, who once owned the restaurant that bears his name and that is now run by his son-in-law Ernest Dempsey?

Unfortunately, as this book was going to print, the authors were still learning the names of truly notable locals and legends, enough to fill this book and a dozen more—people like William Randolph Weber, Douglas Boschert, Paul Niedner, Ray Harmon, and John Hannegan. What an amazing group of people it is who call St. Charles their home.

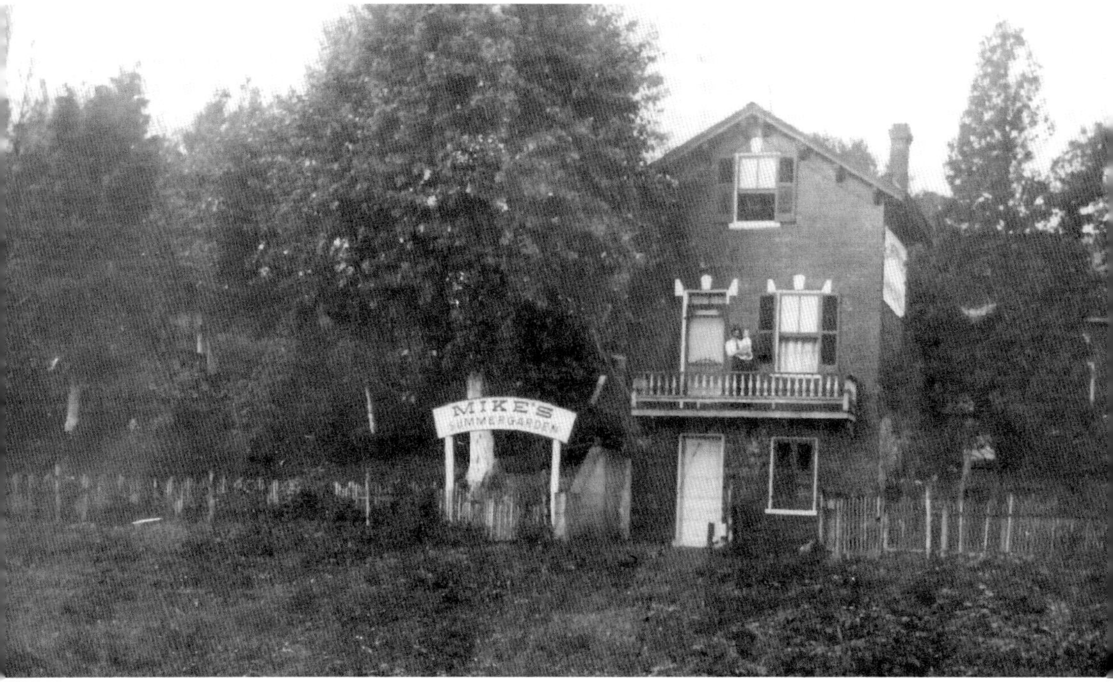

Wepprich Family

The popular Wepprich's Wine Garden opened at 1219 South Main Street in 1900, but a photograph in 1908 sports the name M.S. Wepprich's Winehall. Michael S. Wepprich owned the winery, and Concord wine was made onsite at that time. The winery had its own vineyards on slopes above the garden until the 1960s, producing about 2,500 gallons of wine from its own Concord grapes. The business stayed in the Wepprich family until 1973, and it was owned and operated in later years by Dorothy Wepprich. Later, it became the St. Charles Vintage House Restaurant and Wine Garden, which is now closed. Michael and his son Albert Wepprich are pictured here in 1908. (Courtesy of St. Charles County Historical Society.)

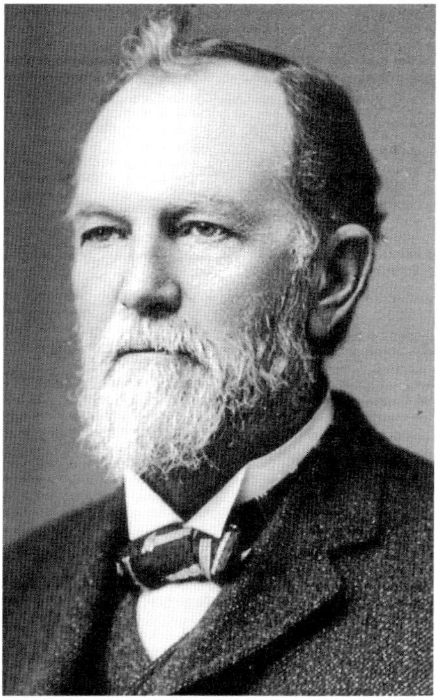

Dr. John Henry Stumberg

John Stumberg was born in St. Charles in 1838. He served with the 29th Missouri Infantry as a surgeon during the Civil War. In 1887, he was one of 13 doctors who helped organize the St. Charles County Medical Society. When the new brick St. Joseph Hospital opened in 1891, Dr. Stumberg was on staff. It is said he was the first doctor in town to own a microscope, at a time when laboratory research was in its infancy and a diagnosis was usually based on symptoms alone. Dr. Stumberg served on the board of directors at Lindenwood College from 1877 to 1903. Pictured below is St. Joseph Hospital (today SSM Health St. Joseph Hospital–St. Charles) in 1904. (Both, courtesy of SSM Health Archives.)

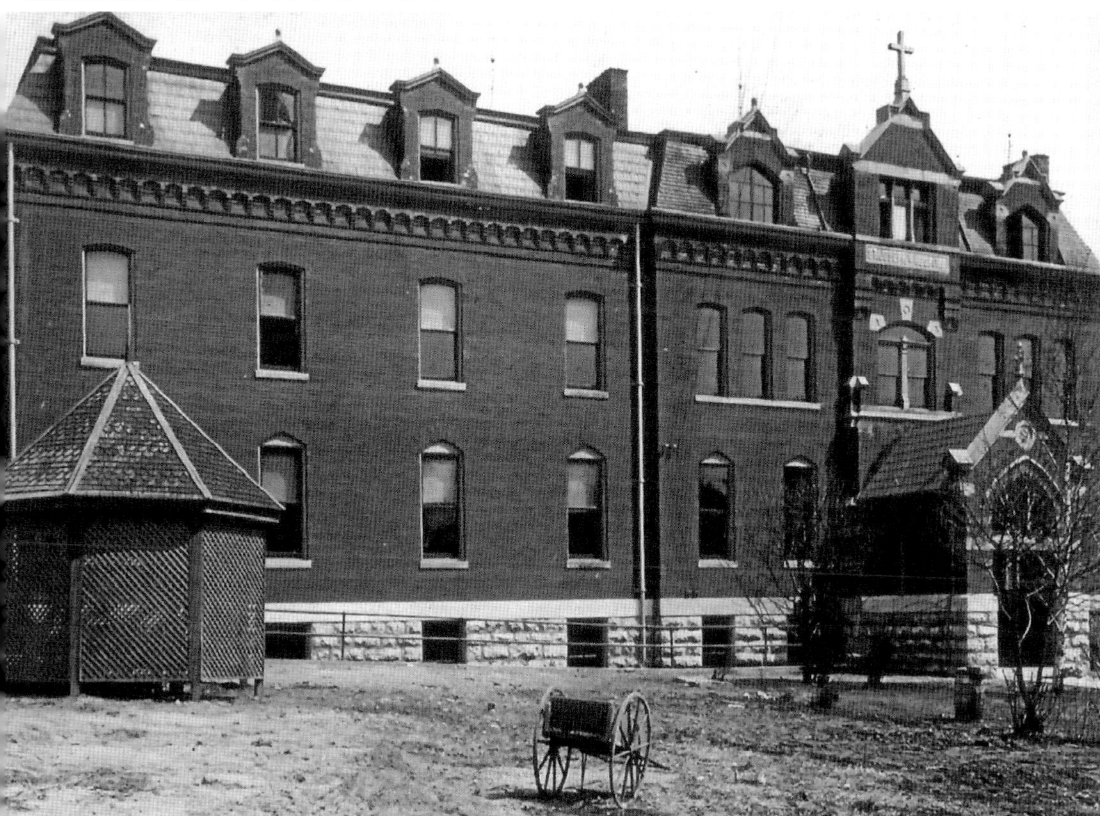

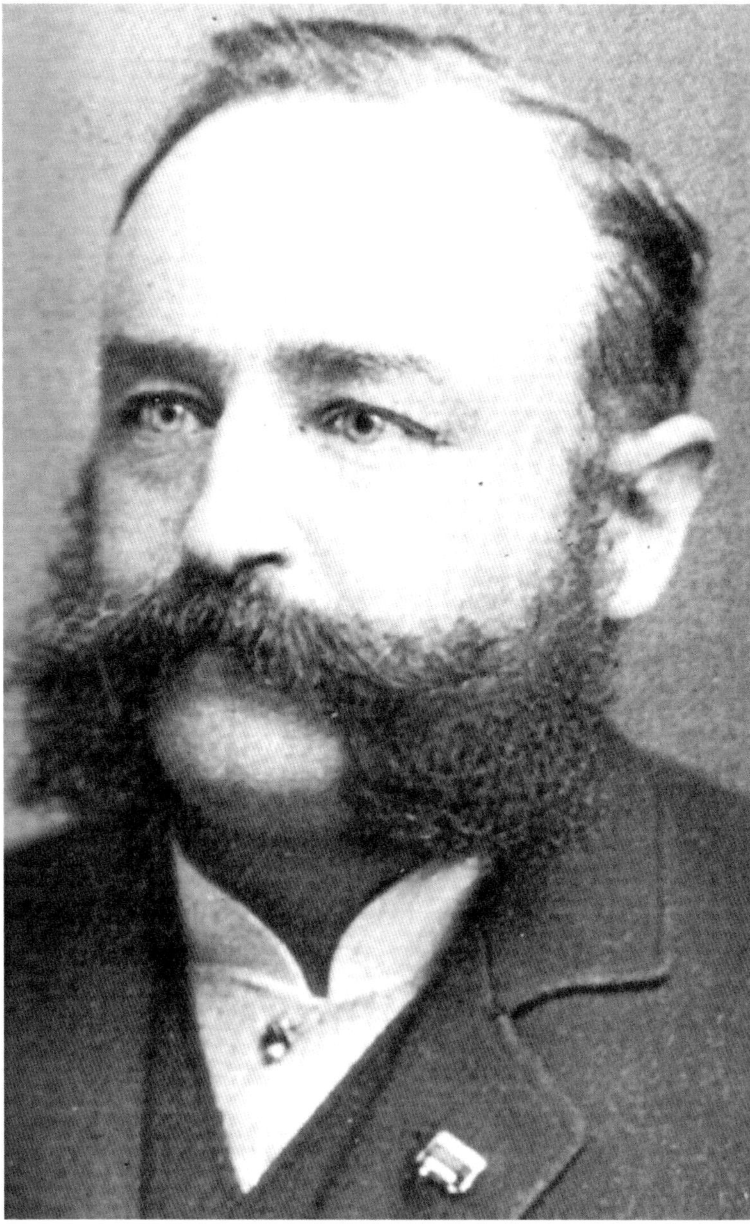

Dr. Benjamin Geret

Dr. Geret played an early and important role in the development of SSM Health St. Joseph Hospital–St. Charles. A native of Bavaria, he served as a doctor in the Bavarian army during the Franco-Prussian War. When he arrived in St. Charles in 1872, Geret opened a general practice at 200 Clay Street. The first hospital on Chauncey Street was not set up to handle surgery; when a patient urgently needed a gall bladder removed, Dr. Geret improvised, padded a table with blankets, boiled instruments on a gas burner, and performed the first surgery in the history of the hospital. When the new hospital was being built across from St. Peter Church in 1890, Geret donated an adjoining lot, which, incidentally, had been the burial ground for the victims of the 1833 cholera epidemic in St. Charles. (Courtesy of SSM Health Archives.)

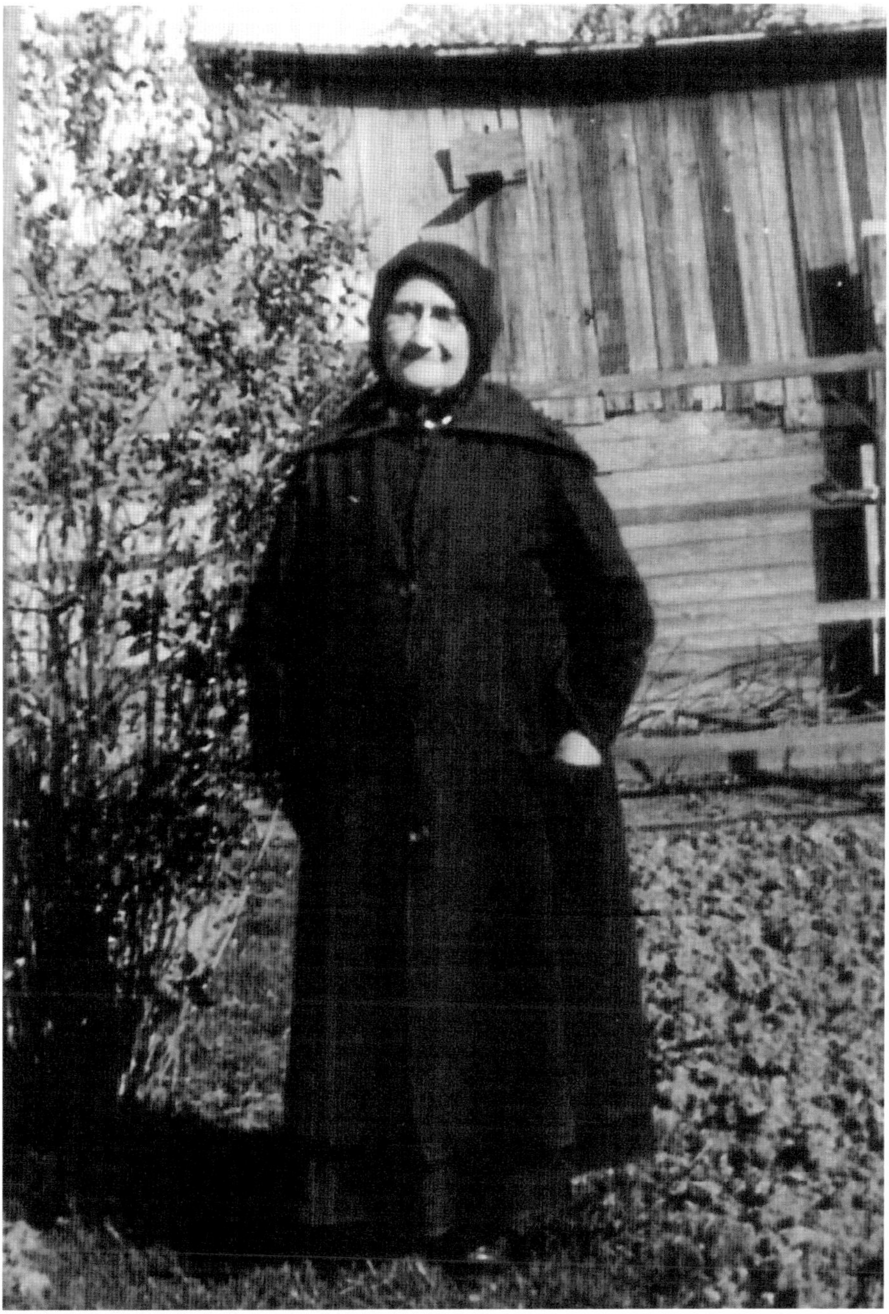

Sophie Hupe
Born about 1848, Sophie Hupe had many jobs during her life in St. Charles, working as a clerk, running a millinery shop, and partnering in the hotel business. She is best known for her work as a midwife, a role she took on at about age 51, after her husband had died. She was well respected in the community, and according to historical accounts, her services were recommended by doctors in the area. Many knew her fondly as "Grandma Hupe." In 1924, she suffered a stroke, and on May 26, 1929, she died at what was then the Carmelite Home on Clay Street. (Courtesy of St. Charles County Historical Society.)

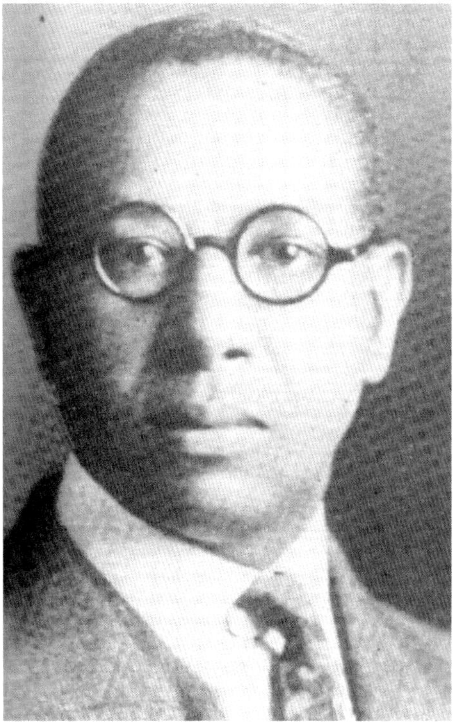

Dr. Thomas Jonathan Jackson

Born in 1882 in Ruston, Louisiana, Thomas Jackson graduated from Meharry Medical College in Nashville in 1905. He was in general practice in St. Charles at Perry and Main Streets. His brother Benjamin Jackson joined him in his practice in 1917. Dr. Jackson, according to recorded accounts, was widely respected and well liked in St. Charles. His family home was at 915 North Sixth Street. He died on February 16, 1928, of hypertension and chronic nephritis. Unfortunately, because Dr. Jackson and his brother were African Americans, they were not able to practice at St. Joseph Hospital. The hospital did recognize their contributions in later years. (Courtesy of SSM Health Archives.)

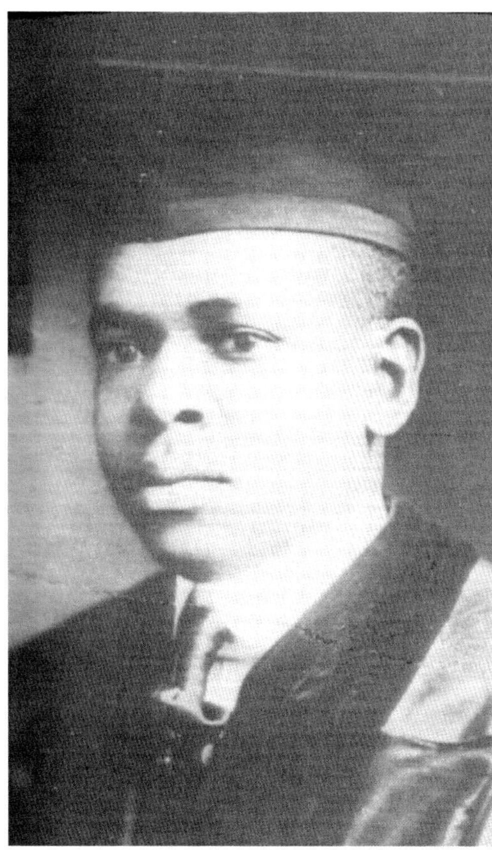

Dr. Benjamin Jackson

Benjamin Jackson was born in Oklahoma in 1894 and graduated from Meharry Medical College in 1917. Shortly after, he moved to St. Charles to practice medicine with his brother Thomas Jackson. Dr. Jackson served in World War I with the 92nd Division. He lived with his family at 1718 Gallaher Avenue in St. Charles. He died on May 6, 1928, of tuberculosis. (Courtesy of SSM Health Archives.)

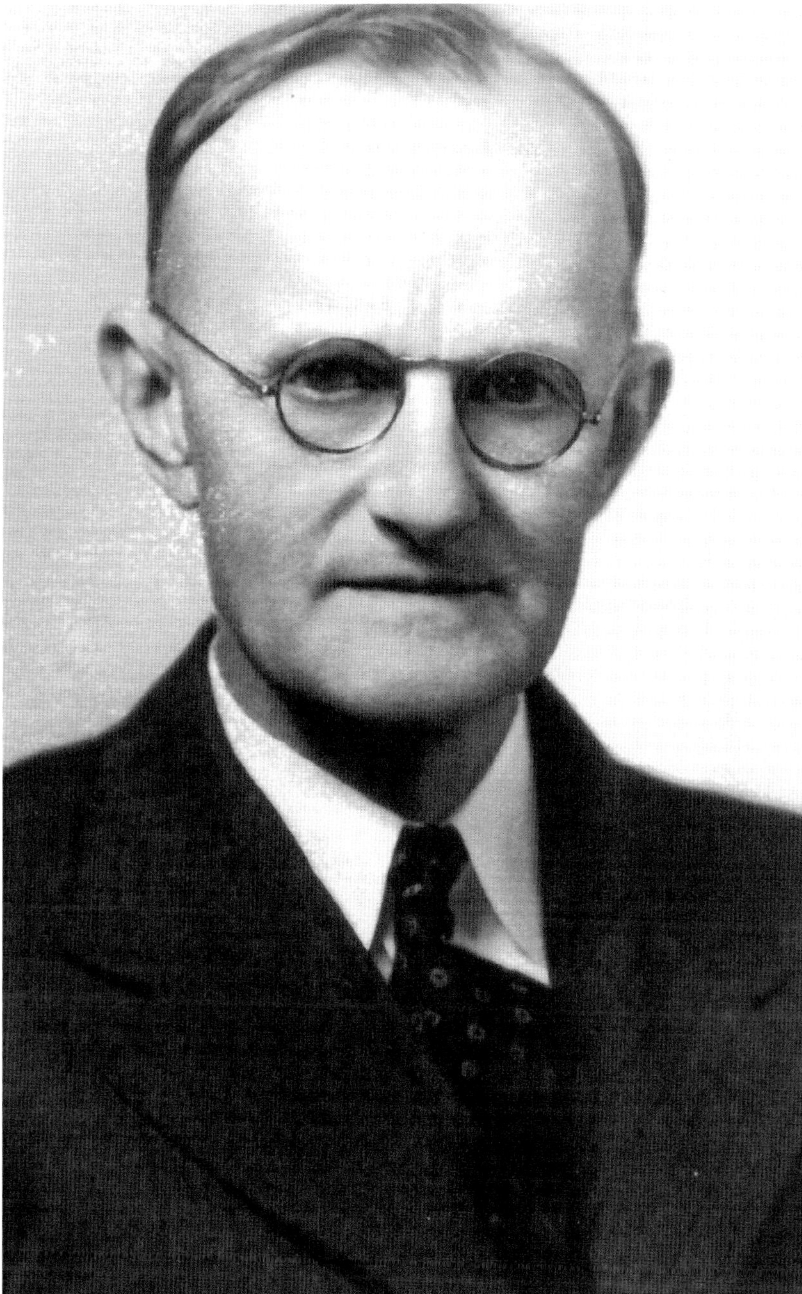

Dr. B. Kurt Stumberg

B. Kurt Stumberg, son of Dr. John Henry Stumberg, was the first chief of staff at St. Joseph Hospital when the new brick building opened across from St. Peter Church in 1891. Dr. Stumberg had served on the board of Lindenwood College for more than 30 years and was the college physician for many of those years. At the time of his death, he was chairman of the finance committee. He had served as a doctor in both the Spanish-American War and World War I. He was the father of H. Kriete Stumberg (see page 77). (Courtesy of St. Charles County Historical Society.)

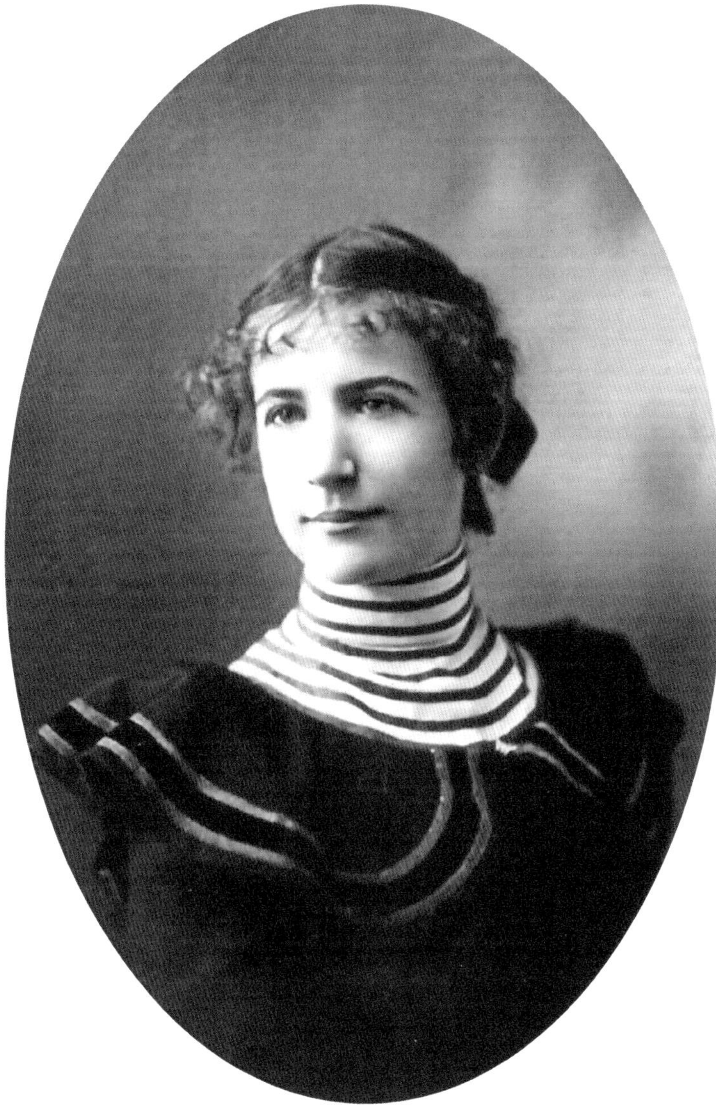

Aimee Marie Louise Becker

Aimee Becker, known as Miss Aimee B, was born in St. Charles in 1890. Her great-grandparents, the Martens, were from Prussia, and the Beckers were from Germany. The families were among the first to settle along the Missouri River in what is today St. Charles. In 1865, Francis Marten built a house at 837 First Capitol Drive, formerly Clay Street, and the house remained in the Marten-Becker family until 1982. Aimee Becker, described as a lady of refinement and a gracious hostess, attended Lindenwood College and graduated in 1908 with a degree in tennis and tea! She was an active member of Immanuel Lutheran Church, a civic leader, and a philanthropist. In 1982, Becker bequeathed the Marten-Becker House to the St. Charles County Historical Society, of which she was a charter member. Sherry Pfaender and Judy Howell later purchased the house from the society and opened Miss Aimee B's Tea Room. Aimee Becker passed away in 1984 at age 94. In January 2014, locals Brie and Zack Smithey purchased the wonderful home and business from Pfaender and Howell. The Smitheys proudly serve delicious homemade recipes for breakfast and lunch and love to share their hospitality daily. (Courtesy of Brie Smithey.)

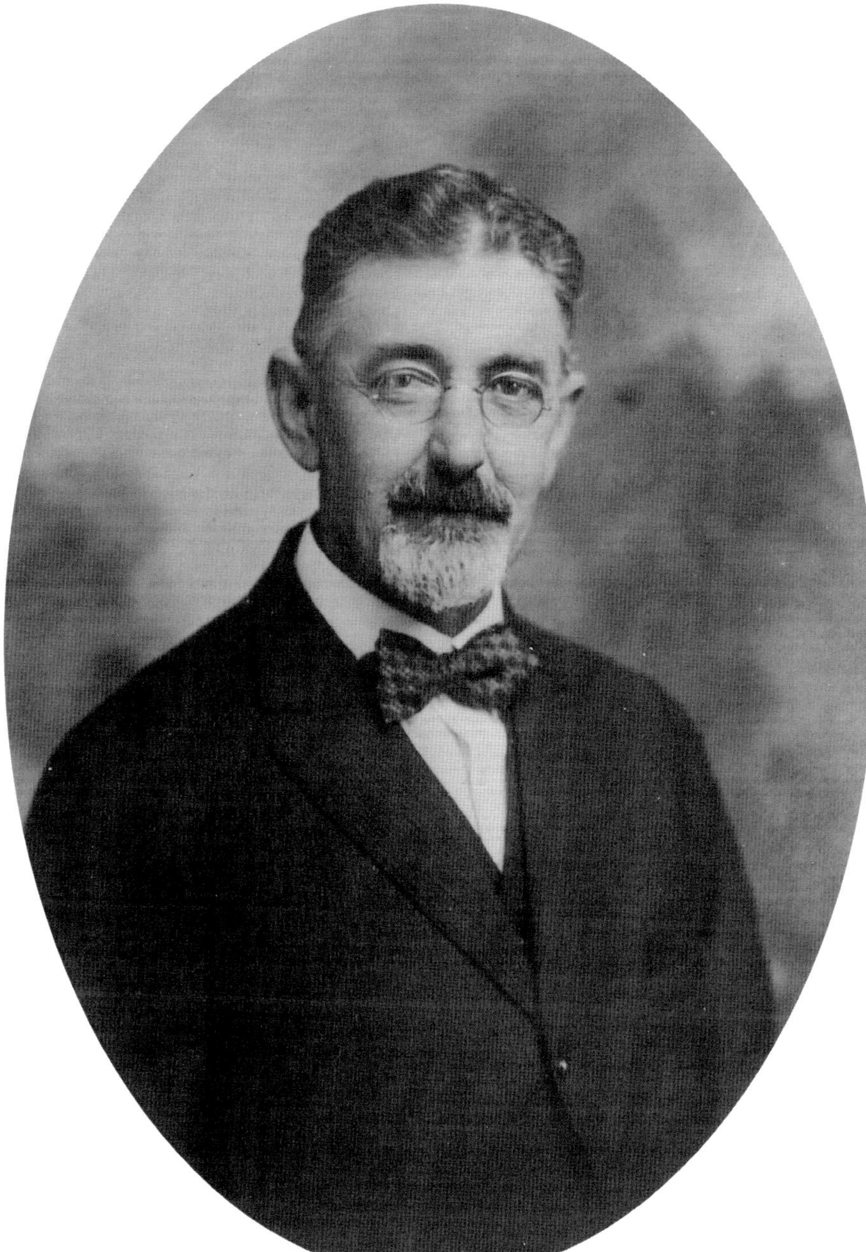

John J. Buse

John Buse spent more than 40 years gathering material and researching the history of St. Charles. His collection included writings from newspapers, books, and memories from fellow citizens, as well as his own. His son and grandson preserved his collections, which provided a detailed portrait of the development of St. Charles for almost half a century. The book *In His Own Hand: A Historical Scrapbook of St. Charles County, Missouri*, with photography by Rudolph Goebel, was published in 1998. Buse, seen here about 1900, worked at the St. Charles Car Company (later the American Car & Foundry Company) until his death in 1933. (Courtesy of St. Charles County Historical Society.)

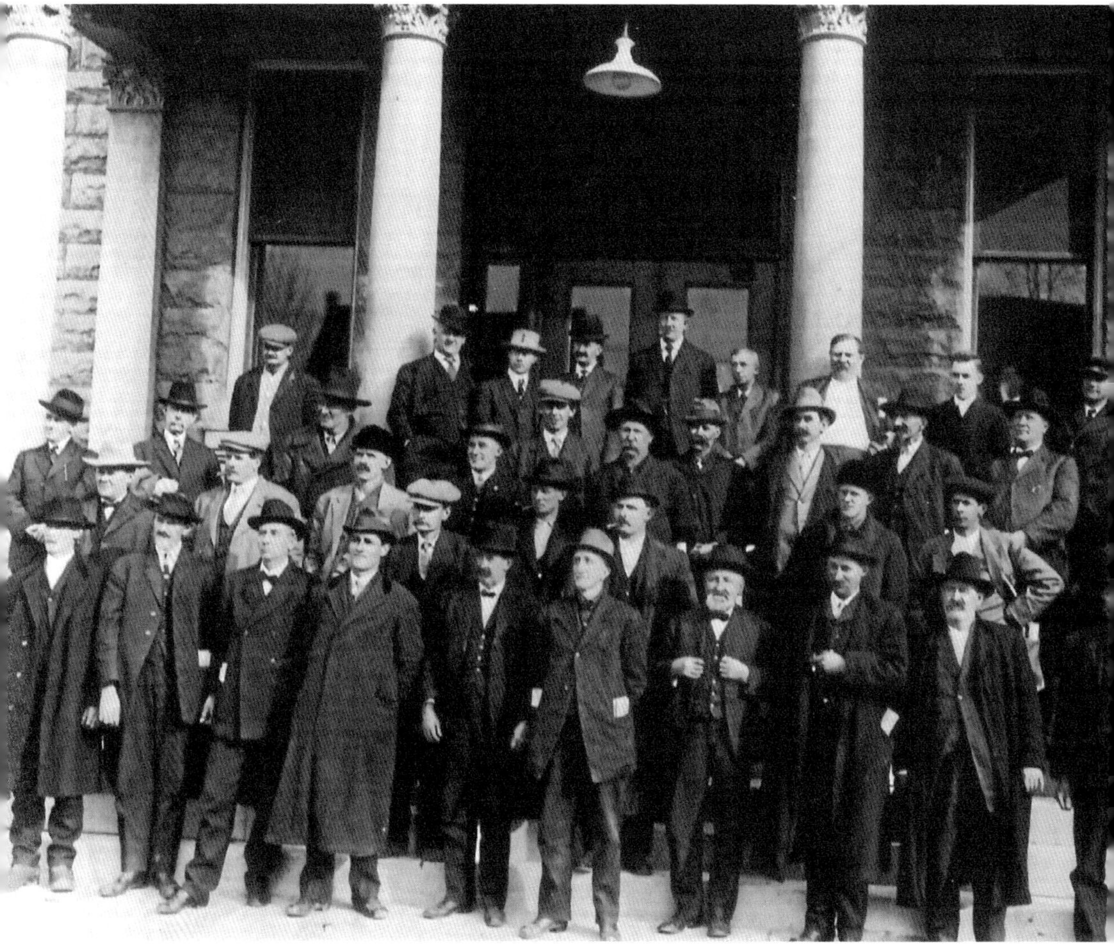

Theodore C. Bruere

The son of a prominent St. Charles attorney and politician who bore the same first name, the younger Bruere was elected to the office of prosecuting attorney of the county in 1894 and held that post for eight consecutive terms. Upon his retirement, he had prosecuted more murderers than all of the other incumbents of the office combined. Bruere is identified as being part of this group of St. Charles County court officials on May 3, 1915. His exact place in the photograph is not known. (Courtesy of St. Charles County Historical Society.)

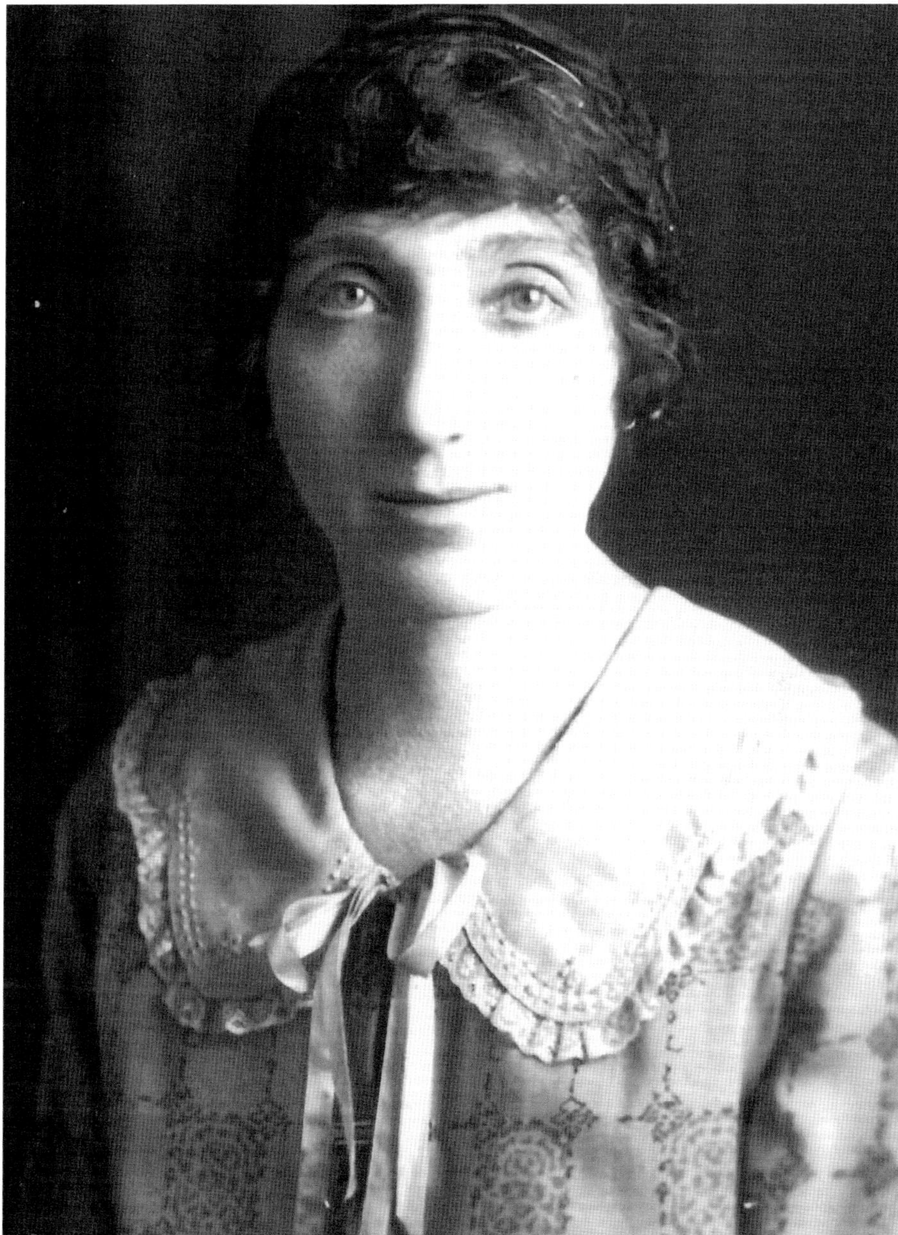

Leona Ehrhard

Leona Ehrhard was born in St. Charles in 1888. Her family, from Alsace, France, lived on Monroe Street. She attended St. Charles Borromeo School and the Academy of the Sacred Heart, then received a music degree from Lindenwood College in 1914. Some of her original music was published, and she became an affiliated teacher of the National Academy of Music. Ehrhard taught piano from her home to as many as 50 students per term. She also played the organ for St. Charles Borromeo Church and St. Peter Church for over 50 years. She was known by many for the Christmas pageants she directed and for her baskets of homemade Christmas cookies. Ehrhard is featured in Cleta Flynn's 2014 book *Through a Woman's Eyes.* (Courtesy of St. Charles County Historical Society.)

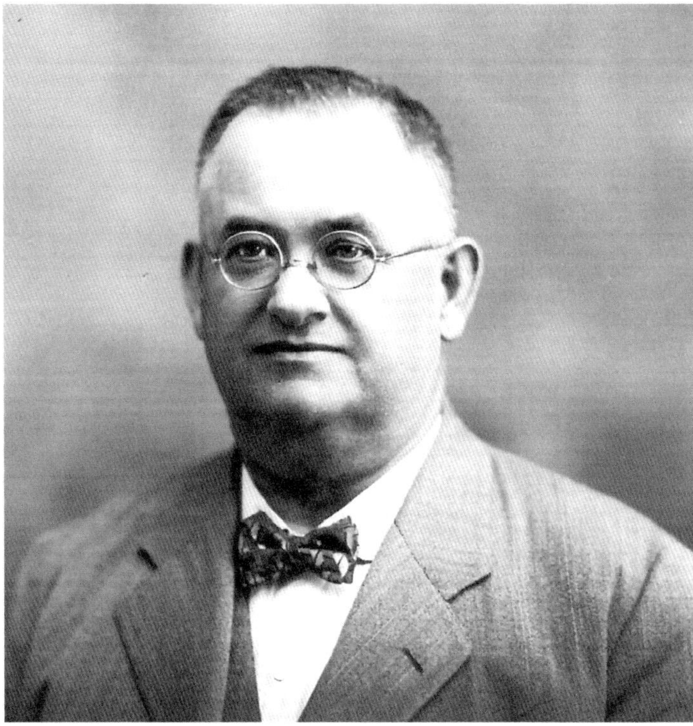

Dr. Benedict Peter Wentker

Benedict Wentker, a prominent St. Charles physician and surgeon, was born in Minnesota in 1874. He moved to St. Louis and graduated from Beaumont Medical College, which is now part of St. Louis University, in 1900. He later moved to St. Charles, where he became known as "the baby doctor," because he delivered most of the area's children in subsequent years, with the help of midwife Sophie Hupe (see page 47). Dr. Wentker's home at 709 North Fourth Street (below) later became the rectory of St. Charles Borromeo Catholic Church. Wentker is in the back seat of the automobile. (Both, courtesy of St. Charles County Historical Society.)

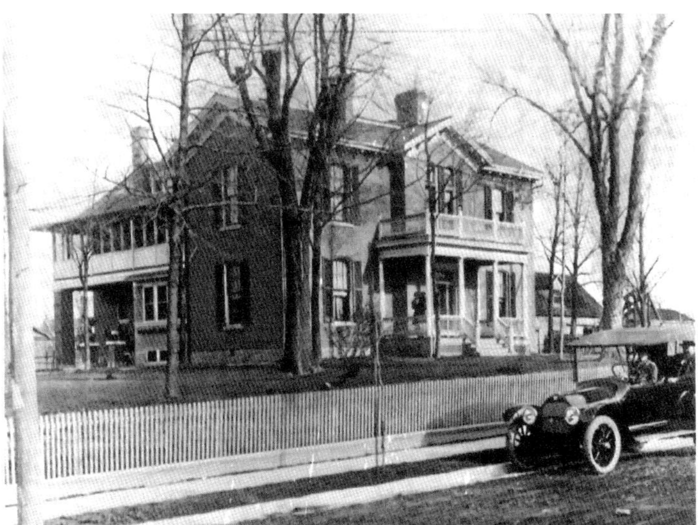

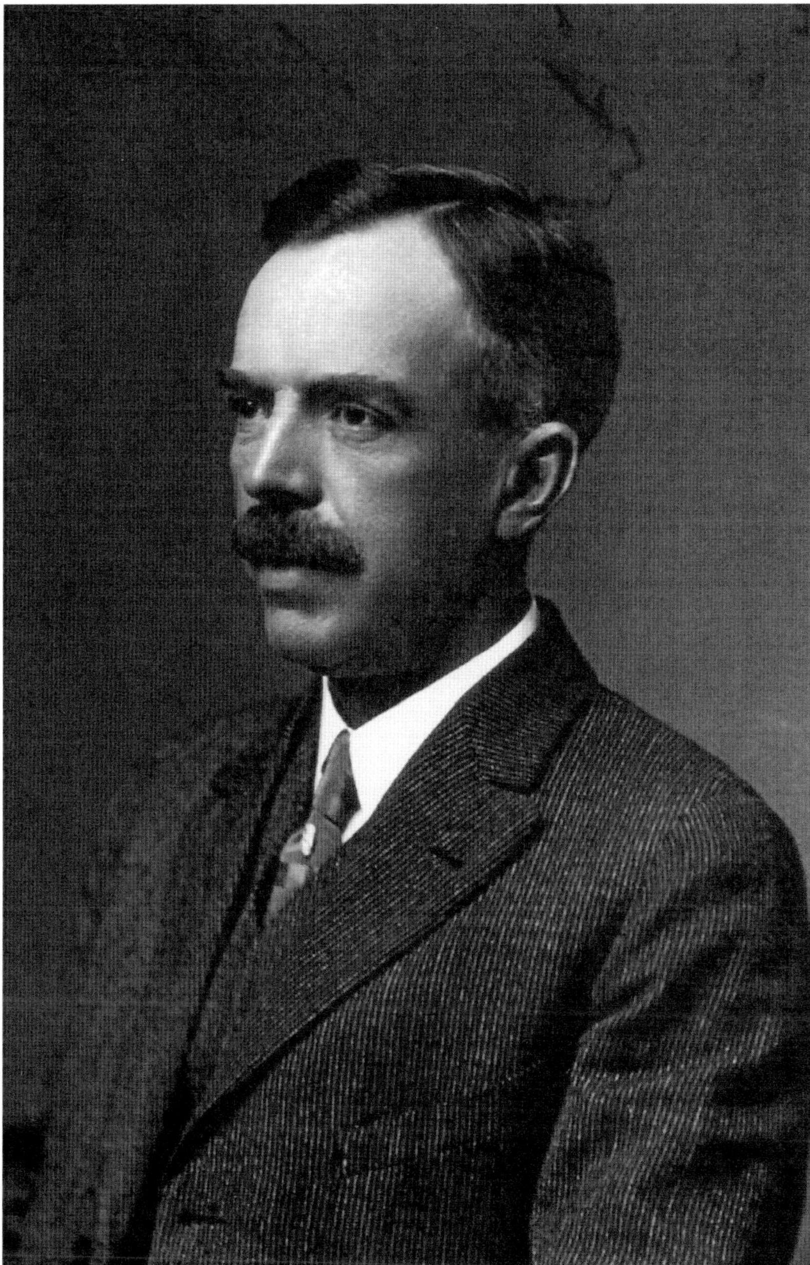

Benjamin Linton Emmons

Benjamin Linton Emmons V (1861–1942) opened the first abstract company in St. Charles County in 1884. The office was located in the Moose Building/Odd Fellows Hall. Emmons was also considered a local historian, and a collection of his materials related to the history of St. Charles is housed at the Missouri History Museum. His father, Benjamin Linton Emmons IV, born in 1810, was the St. Charles postmaster and circuit clerk. His grandfather, Benjamin Linton Emmons III, was born in 1777 in Vermont and died in St. Charles in March 1850. He reportedly is the founder of the first Masonic lodge in St. Charles. (Courtesy of St. Charles County Historical Society.)

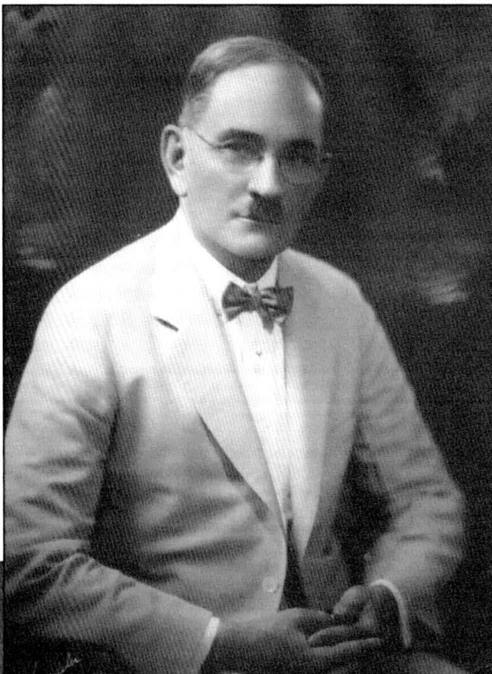

Henry G. Rauch

In the early 1900s, Henry G. Rauch, with his brother Julius, began the St. Charles Electric Express Company to haul freight between St. Charles and St. Louis. He later organized Rauch Lumber and Rauch Truck Lines. Rauch Lumber (below) became a St. Charles landmark after its founding in 1917. The people in the photograph are not identified. Rauch Memorial Hall at Lindenwood University is named for Henry G. Rauch, his son Frank, and his grandson Henry P. Rauch. (Left, author's collection; below, courtesy of Lucy Rauch.)

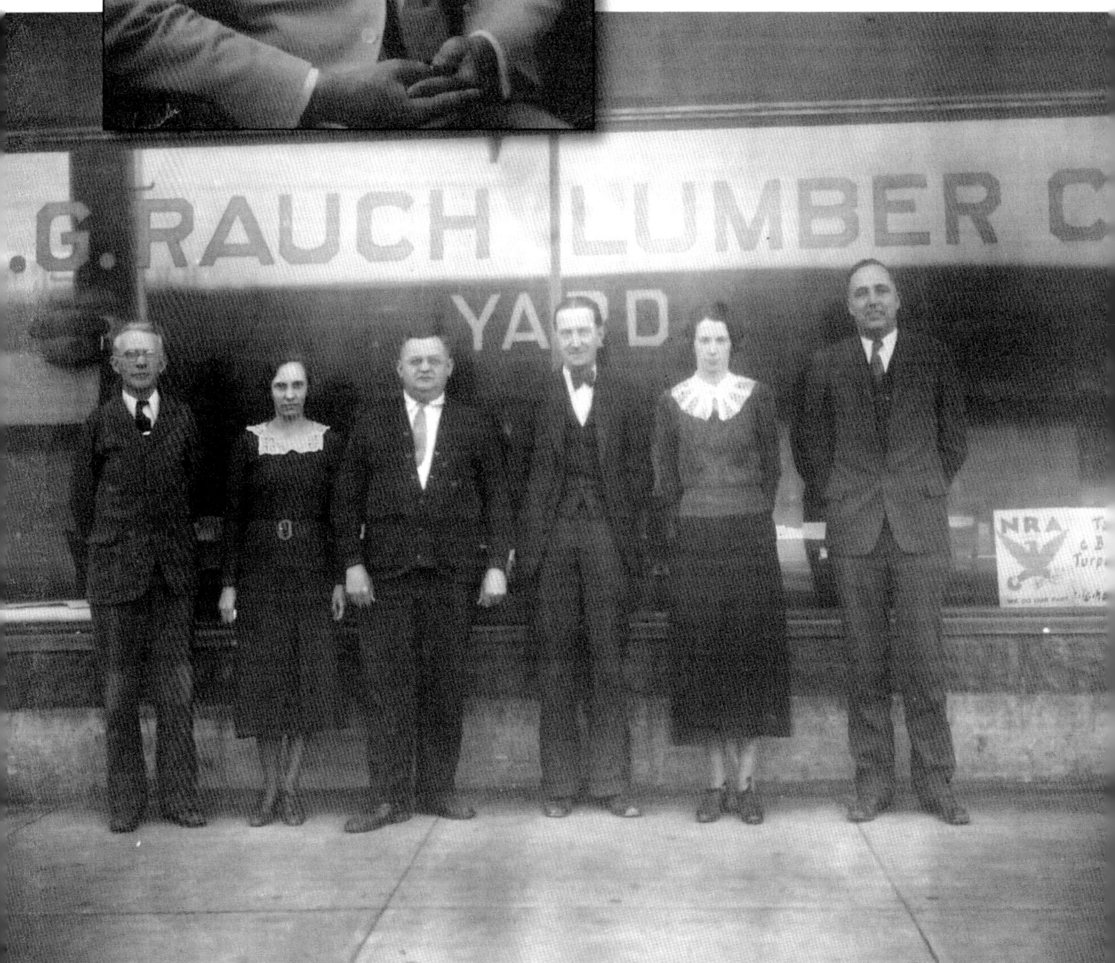

Frank B. Rauch

A quiet philanthropist who donated to many civic causes, Frank Rauch was deeply involved in the St. Charles Borromeo Church community. His company, begun by his father, H.G. Rauch, was one of St. Charles's leading suppliers of lumber and building supplies. Frank Rauch was the first chair of the advisory board at St. Joseph Hospital and belonged to the Knights of St. Gregory. In 1959, he was named St. Charles Man of the Year (the award was later called Citizen of the Years). (Courtesy of Lucy Rauch.)

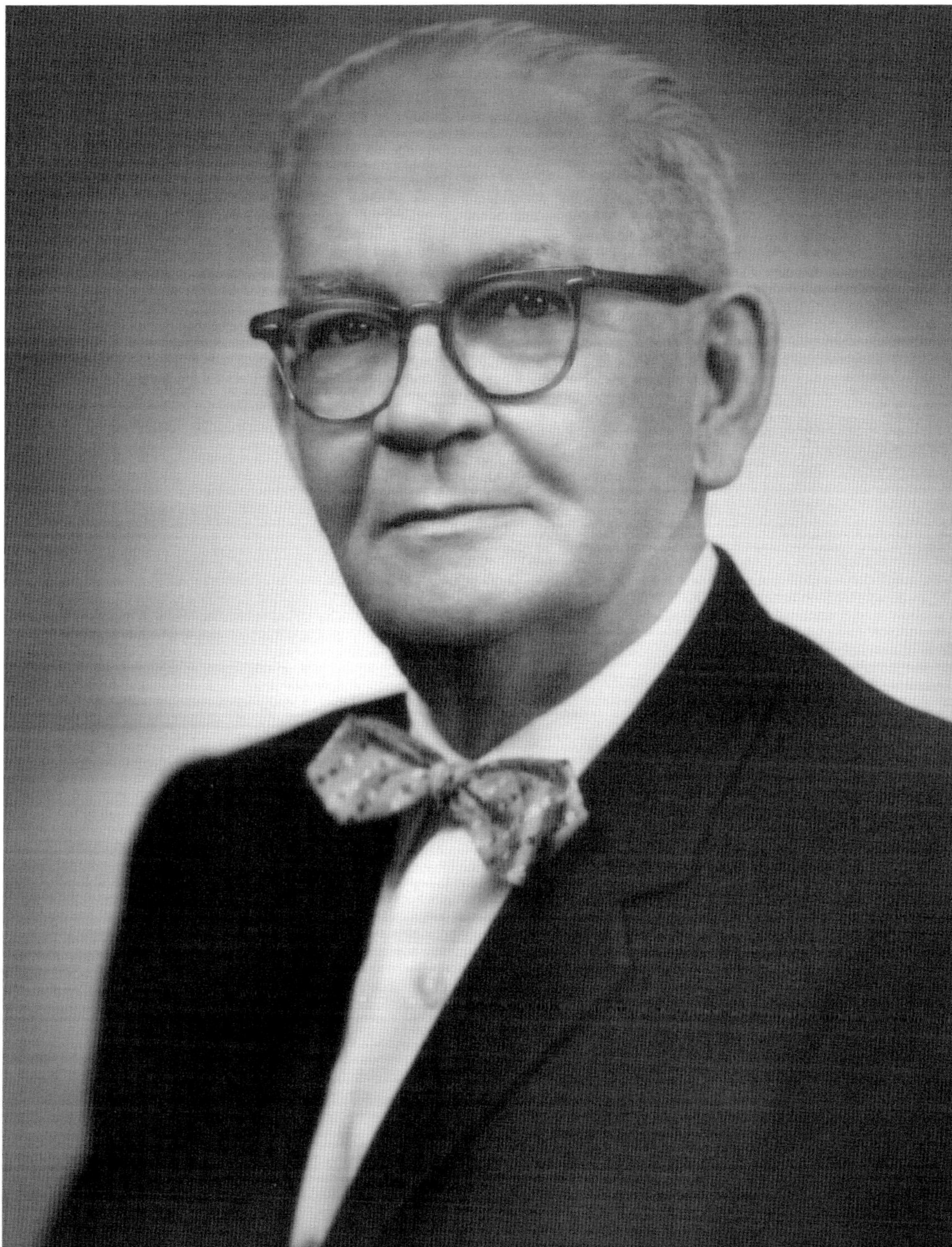

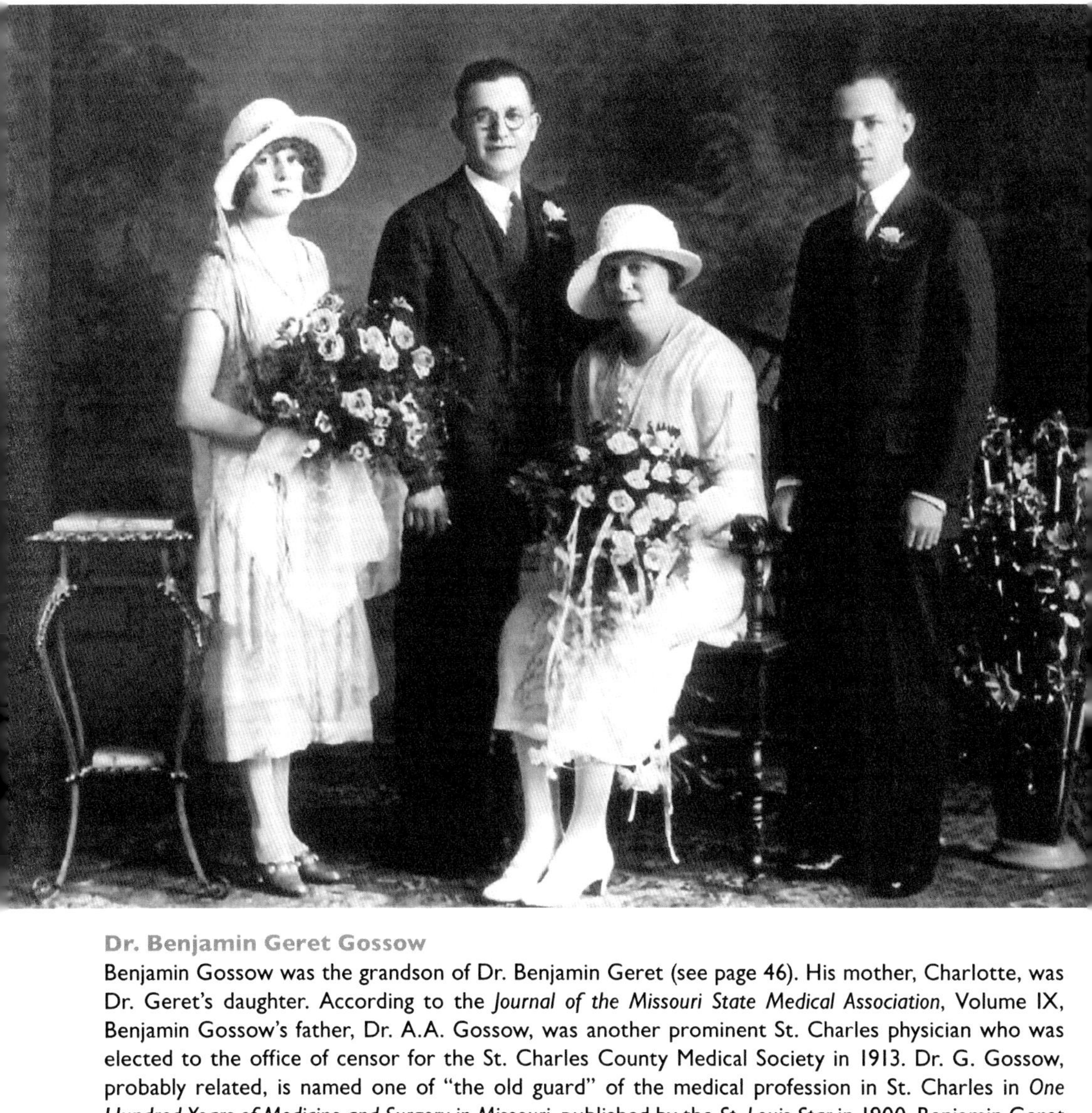

Dr. Benjamin Geret Gossow

Benjamin Gossow was the grandson of Dr. Benjamin Geret (see page 46). His mother, Charlotte, was Dr. Geret's daughter. According to the *Journal of the Missouri State Medical Association*, Volume IX, Benjamin Gossow's father, Dr. A.A. Gossow, was another prominent St. Charles physician who was elected to the office of censor for the St. Charles County Medical Society in 1913. Dr. G. Gossow, probably related, is named one of "the old guard" of the medical profession in St. Charles in *One Hundred Years of Medicine and Surgery in Missouri*, published by the *St. Louis Star* in 1900. Benjamin Geret Gossow is listed on the St. Louis University register of students for 1918 as a pre-med student. He and Marie Moerschel are shown here at center on their wedding day, June 9, 1925. Their attendants are Matilda Moerschel and Ralph Rechtern. (Courtesy of St. Charles County Historical Society.)

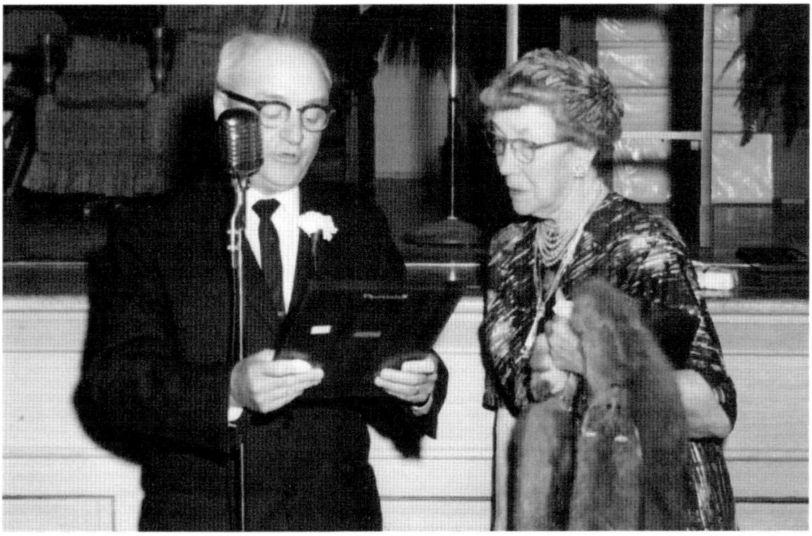

Kathryn Linnemann

"Miss Kathryn," as local residents knew her, taught piano to students in her home on Jefferson Street, but she had a vision of opening a library for St. Charles. She began the library in her own home, but in 1914, the St. Charles School Board gave her a small room at Jefferson School near her home to grow the library, using books her friends donated. For her services, her only compensation was the joy she found in watching people, especially children, reading the books. Linnemann often took flowers to sick neighbors and delivered books to bedridden children. On Valentine's Day, 1918, a fire destroyed the little library and several of the books. Although Miss Kathryn continued to operate in a small shed with the books she had salvaged, eventually, a library board was formed, and a tax was passed in 1928. A new building was purchased on Jefferson Street in 1930 to accommodate the library's growth. Linnemann served as head librarian for over 40 years. She is pictured above on April 23, 1963, receiving an award from Mayor Henry Vogt for 50 years of service. The below photograph shows the library sign around 1950. Since 1982, after consolidation with the county library district, the Kathryn Linnemann branch has been located on Elm Street. (Both, courtesy of St. Charles County Historical Society.)

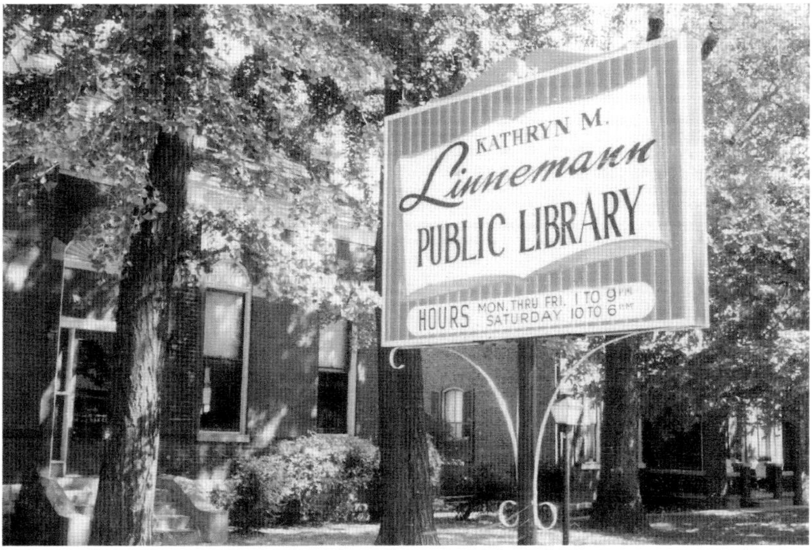

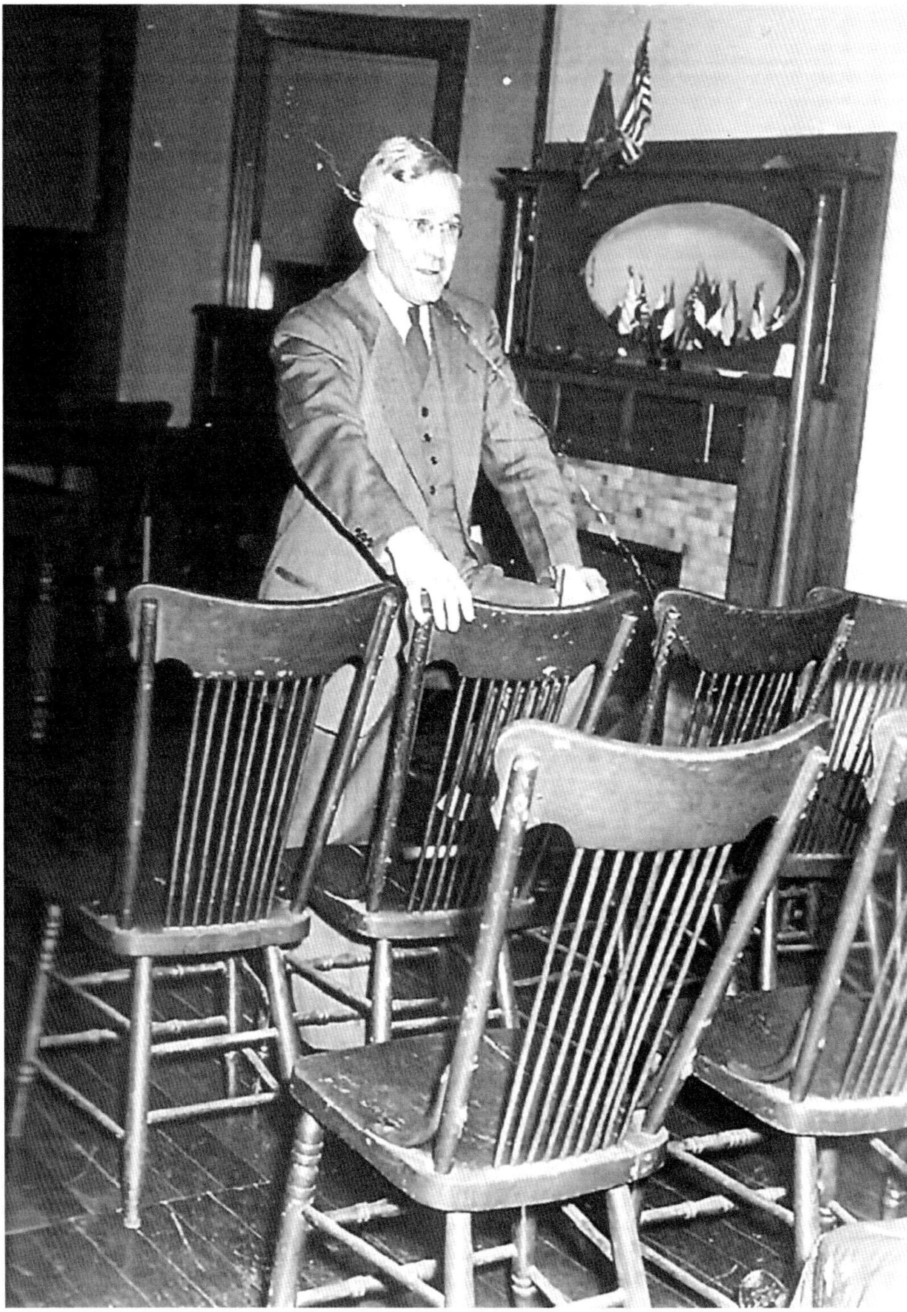

Homer Clevenger

A World War II veteran, Dr. Clevenger later became a professor and chairman of the history department at Lindenwood University, where he taught from 1941 to 1968. During that time, Clevenger served as mayor of St. Charles (1945–1952). He was also a member of the committee appointed by the St. Charles Community Council to form a county historical society in 1956 and later became the St. Charles County Historical Society's first president. In 1969, Dr. Clevenger was named Man of the Year by the St. Charles County Chamber of Commerce. (Courtesy of St. Charles County Historical Society.)

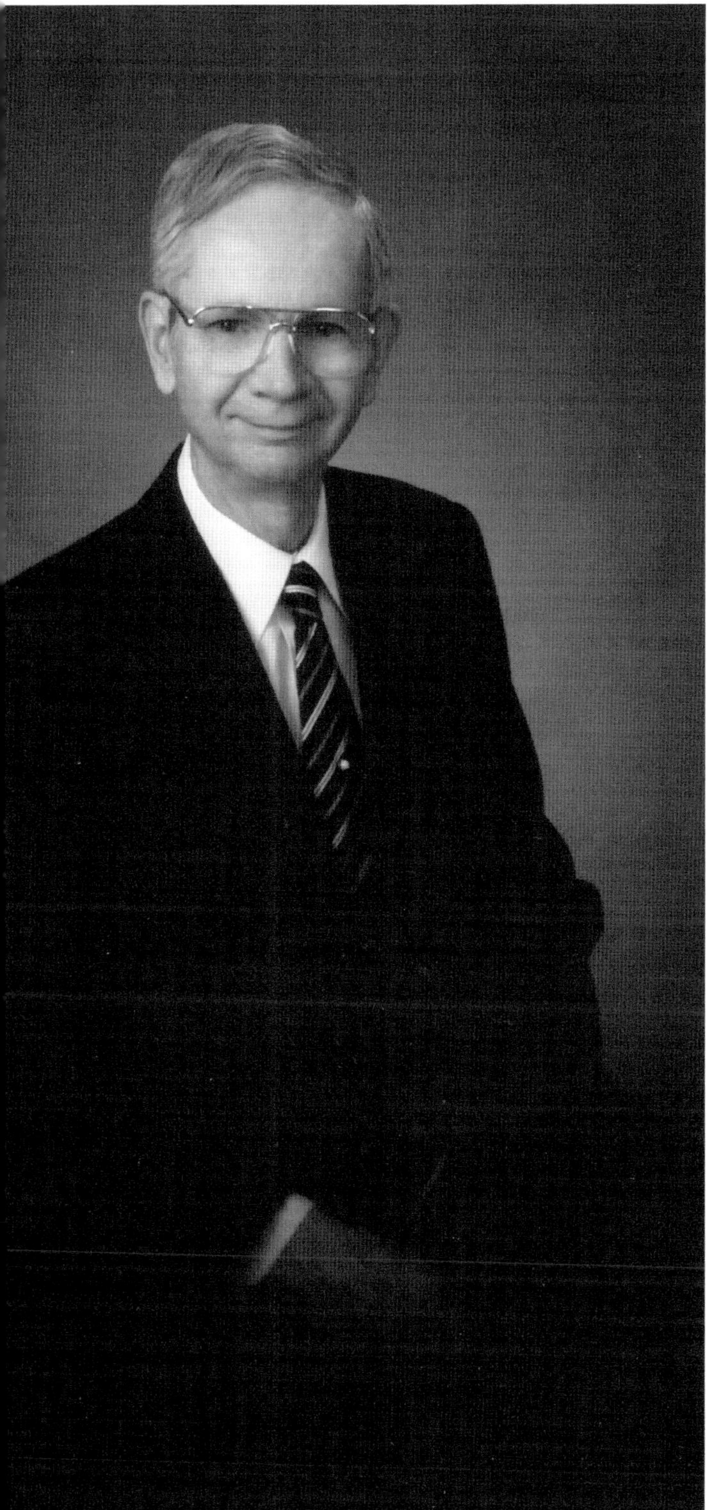

Henry P. Rauch
A veteran of World War II and a graduate of St. Louis University, Henry Rauch was president and chief executive officer of Rauch Lumber Company from 1972 until 1987. Among his many community contributions, Rauch was chairman of the United Way, a charter member and first secretary of the St. Charles Jaycees, and president of the St. Charles Library Board, helping to start the library's bookmobile program. Rauch was president of the St. Charles County Chamber of Commerce and a chairman of the Lay Advisory Board of St. Joseph Hospital, the St. Charles Chapter of the American Red Cross, and the board of directors of Commerce Bank. In 1979, he was named Man of the Year by the chamber of commerce. (Courtesy of Lucy Rauch.)

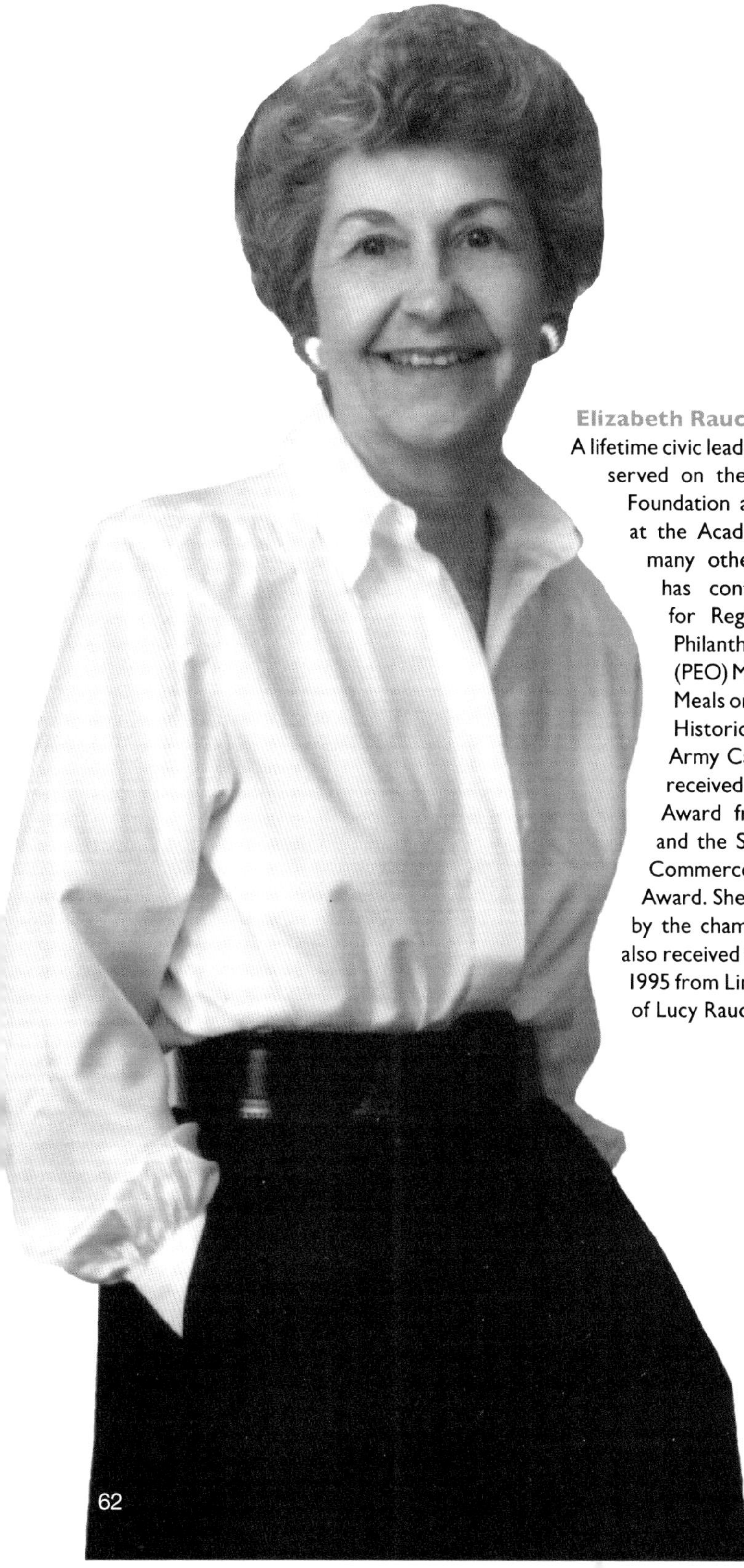

Elizabeth Rauch

A lifetime civic leader in St. Charles, Elizabeth Rauch served on the board of St. Joseph Hospital Foundation and founded the Mother's Club at the Academy of the Sacred Heart. The many other organizations to which she has contributed include the Alliance for Regional Community Health, the Philanthropic Educational Organization (PEO) Missouri Chapter, the United Way, Meals on Wheels, the St. Charles County Historical Society, and the Salvation Army Capital Campaign. In 1984, Rauch received the prestigious Clara Barton Award from the American Red Cross and the St. Charles County Chamber of Commerce Lifetime Distinguished Service Award. She was named Citizen of the Years by the chamber of commerce in 1992. She also received the Sibley Medallion of Honor in 1995 from Lindenwood University. (Courtesy of Lucy Rauch.)

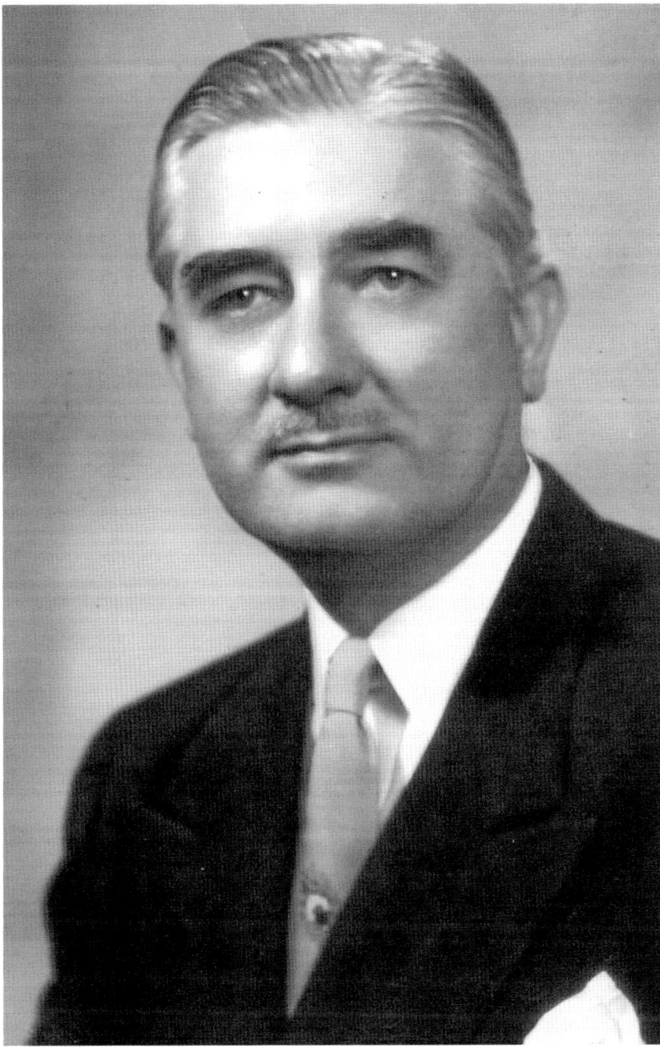

Arthur Baue

The Baue Funeral Home chapel at 620 Jefferson Street is dedicated to its founder, Arthur C. Baue, for his commitment to the St. Charles community. Baue and Clarence Hackmann founded the Hackmann-Baue Funeral Home in St. Charles in 1935. After Hackmann's death in 1950, the funeral home was renamed Arthur C. Baue Funeral Home. Arthur Baue was president from 1935 to 1968.

Lisa Baue, Arthur's granddaughter, said that Arthur believed people should dedicate their time and efforts to helping their community and those less fortunate and that every family deserves a dignified service, regardless of financial means. Among the many organizations for which Baue served as a member or leader are the Salvation Army of St. Charles County, St. Charles Community Council, St. Charles County Historical Society, the Local Community Chest Campaign (now the United Way), St. Charles Kiwanis Club, Daniel Boone District Boy Scouts of America of St. Charles County, and Immanuel Lutheran Church. Baue's many recognitions include the Salvation Army's William Booth Award for Outstanding Contributions to the Betterment of Humanity. In addition, he was the secretary of the Missouri Funeral Directors Association and was appointed to the State Board of Embalmers, serving as president in 1957. He was a member of the board of directors of National Selected Morticians from 1951 to 1954. (Courtesy of Baue Funeral Homes.)

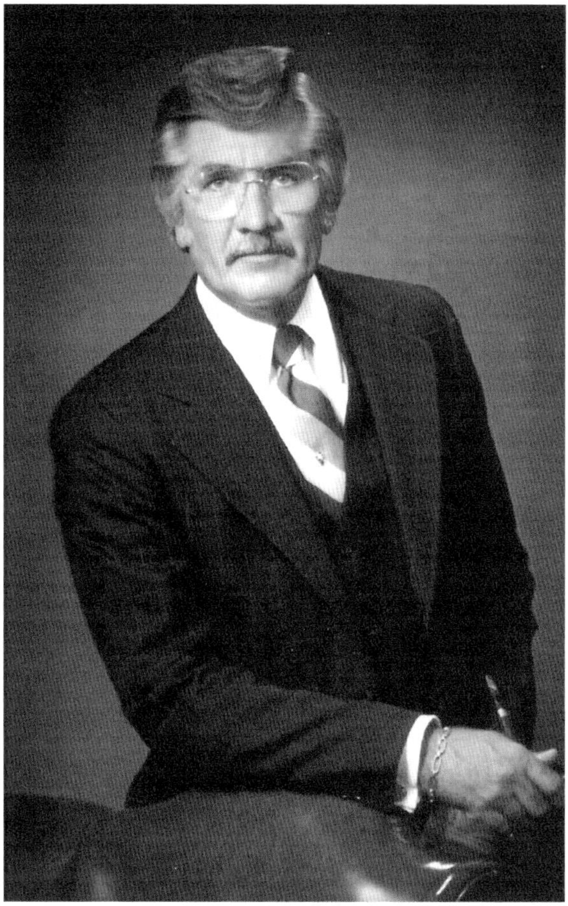

David C. Baue

The Baue Funeral Home chapel at 3950 West Clay Street is dedicated to its second president, David C. Baue. He saw the need to expand services to include cemetery and grief-support care for families in the St. Charles community. David was the second-generation owner of the company. During his tenure as president, he expanded the business to the O'Fallon community and joined his longtime friend and business associate Jerry Davis in growing the Baue Davis Funeral Home. He also joined with Fred Newman in the ownership and expansion of St. Charles Memorial Gardens, the only cemetery in the memorial gardens model "serving all faiths" in the region. Baue was a member of the St. Charles Jaycees, the St. Charles Rotary Club, and the St. Charles County Chamber of Commerce. An avid outdoorsman and sports fan, he sponsored many county sports leagues, from baseball to bowling to a girls' fast-pitch competitive team called the Baue Blues. He was inducted into the St. Charles County Sports Hall of Fame in 1985.

David Baue was president of the Order of the Golden Rule, an international funeral service organization (1978 and 1979), president of the Missouri Funeral Directors Association (1979 and 1980), and chairman of the Missouri State Board of Funeral Directors and Embalmers for three terms. He was a member of the faculty and the board of trustees of the National Foundation of Funeral Service from 1960 to 1982. He also sat on the board of overseers of Lindenwood College, the Boy Scout Eagle Board of Review, St. Charles County YMCA Board of Directors, the advisory board of Forest Park Mortuary College, and the board of directors of National Selected Morticians. Baue was past chairman of St. Charles Community Council and the United Way Fund Campaign. David Baue was named Man of the Year by the St. Charles County Chamber of Commerce in 1987. (Courtesy of Baue Funeral Homes.)

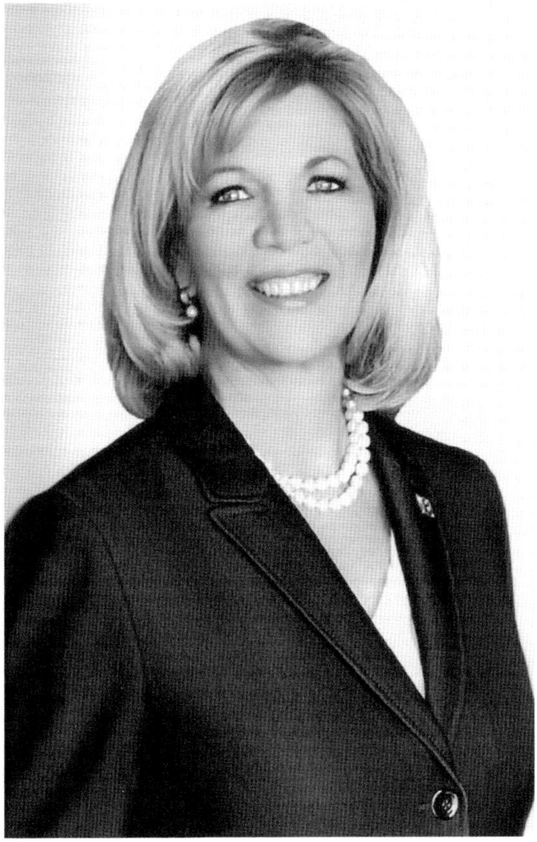

Lisa A. Baue

Lisa Baue is the third-generation funeral director in her family business. She joined the firm in 1979 and became the owner, president, and chief executive officer of Baue Funeral Homes after her father's death in 1987. Lisa, along with her staff, has grown the family business to three locations and established St. Charles County's first onsite crematory, a flower and gift shop, three reception centers, and an 80-acre cemetery and cremation park. She has also expanded the company to include a pet cremation and tribute company; a counseling center, the Center for Hope and Healing; and a new monument service company. Baue and its affiliates serve over 1,800 families per year.

Lisa Baue was instrumental in developing the company's antidrug and anti-drinking campaign, which received commendations from the US Drug Enforcement Administration's midwest division. Her company was given the St. Peters Chamber of Commerce Pacesetter Award and the Healthy Communities 2000 Award for "outstanding contribution to the health of our community."

Lisa Baue's numerous recognitions include the International Academy of Nobel Achievement Award (1984), the Young Careerist for the Missouri State Business and Professional Women's Organization award (1986), the Athena Award (1993), the Heroes Award for Mental Health (1988) presented by the St. Charles County Mental Health Council and Crider Center for Mental Health, and the St. Louis Women of Achievement award (1998). She was the 2000 honoree of the Youth in Need Celebration of Youth event and received the 2005 Leadership Award from the Dove Foundation, the 2007 Lifetime Distinguished Service Award from the St. Charles County Chamber of Commerce, the 2010 *St. Louis Business Journal* Business Woman of the Year award, the 2011 Winning Women Regional Economic Development award in the St. Charles Region, a 2012 recognition in *Small Business Monthly* as one of the Top 100 St. Louisans to Know, and the 2014 St. Charles County Chamber of Commerce Citizen of the Years award. (Courtesy of Baue Funeral Homes.)

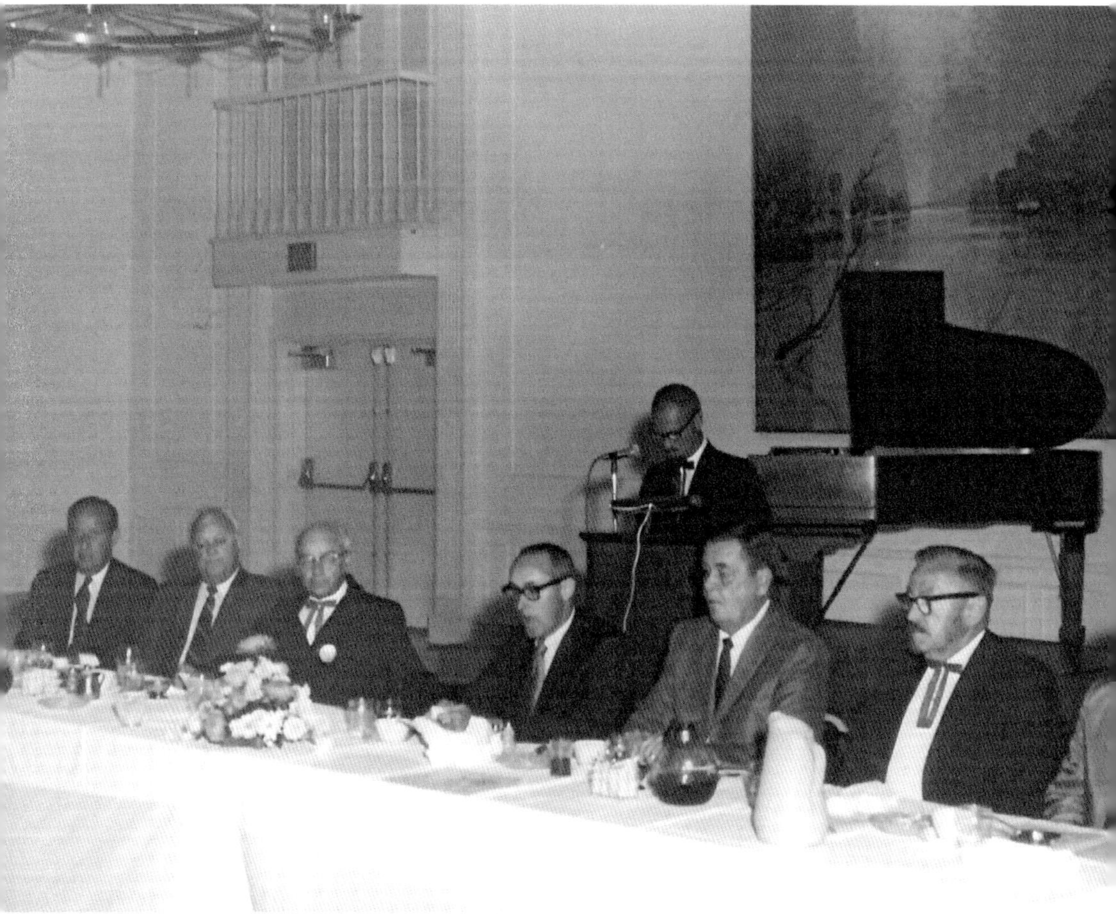

Charles Hafer

Charlie Hafer opened his first grocery store at 911 North Second Street in 1946. With Ernie Hedges, he opened the first Hedges and Hafer Supermarket in 1951. It was the first in St. Charles to offer self-service meat. Elected to the St. Charles County Amateur Sports Hall of Fame, Hafer was also a member of the St. Charles County Chamber of Commerce and Exchange Club. He enjoyed playing guitar and formed the String Busters with his friend Archie Opitz, playing for senior events in town. Hafer is identified as the man at the microphone in this undated photograph. (Courtesy of St. Charles County Historical Society.)

Ralph Borgmeyer

Ralph Borgmeyer was the founder and a charter member of the Society of Our Lady of the Way, a Missouri domestic nonprofit corporation established in the 1950s. He is credited with building the shrine to the Virgin Mary that stands near Interstate 70 and Mid Rivers Mall Drive. Borgmeyer got the idea to build a shrine when a fellow church member suggested that, since roadside shrines are not as common in the United States as in Europe, America is not as Christian-minded. Borgmeyer felt that was not true. His idea really took root when his young son Bill died from a black widow spider bite. He decided to build the shrine in his son's memory. With the help of other volunteers, Borgmeyer erected the shrine near the intersection of Highway 79 and Interstate 70. In November 1987, a new shrine was installed on donated land along Suemandy Drive in St. Peters after the old site was razed to make way for the highway interchange. In 1970, Borgmeyer was named Man of the Year by the St. Charles County Chamber of Commerce. He is seen here at left with Grover Parker in 1965, when Parker also was named Man of the Year. (Courtesy of St. Charles County Historical Society.)

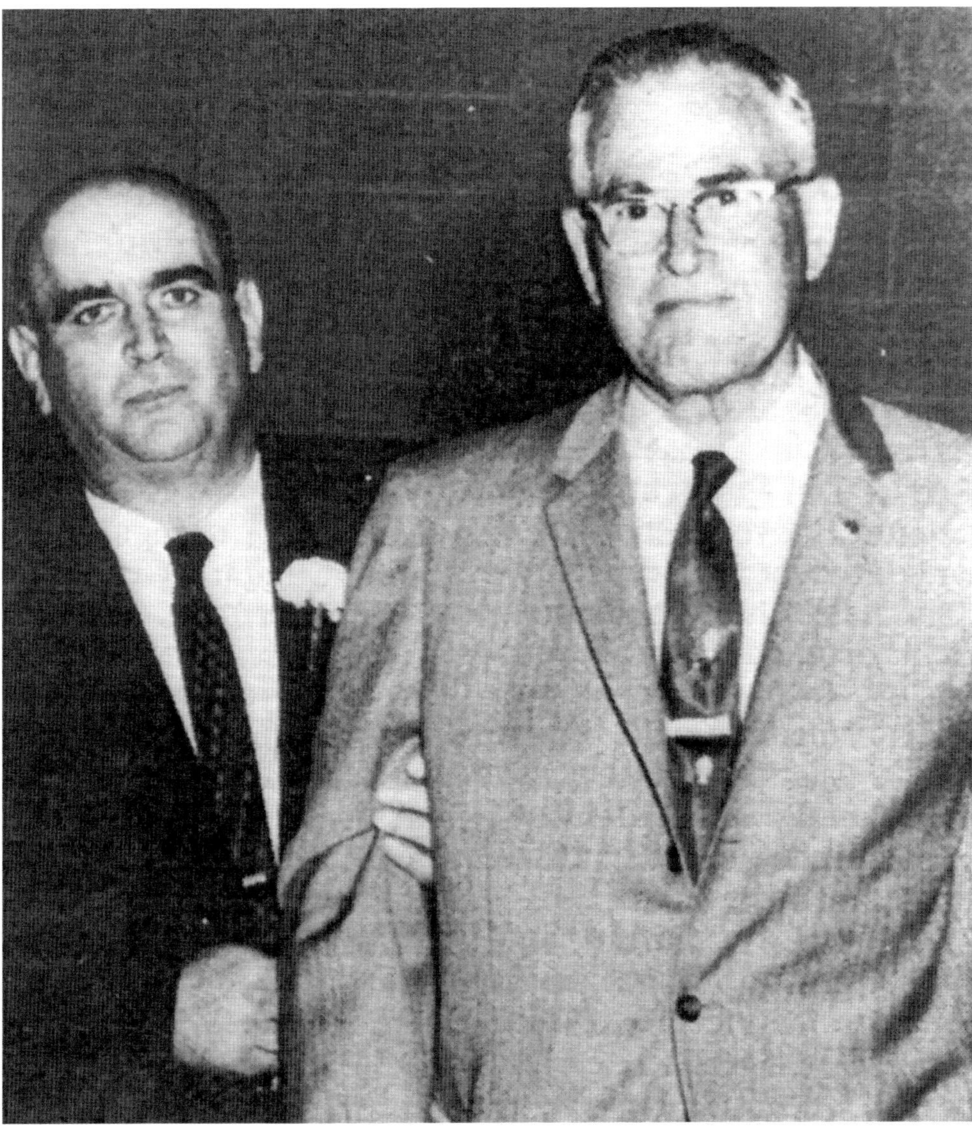

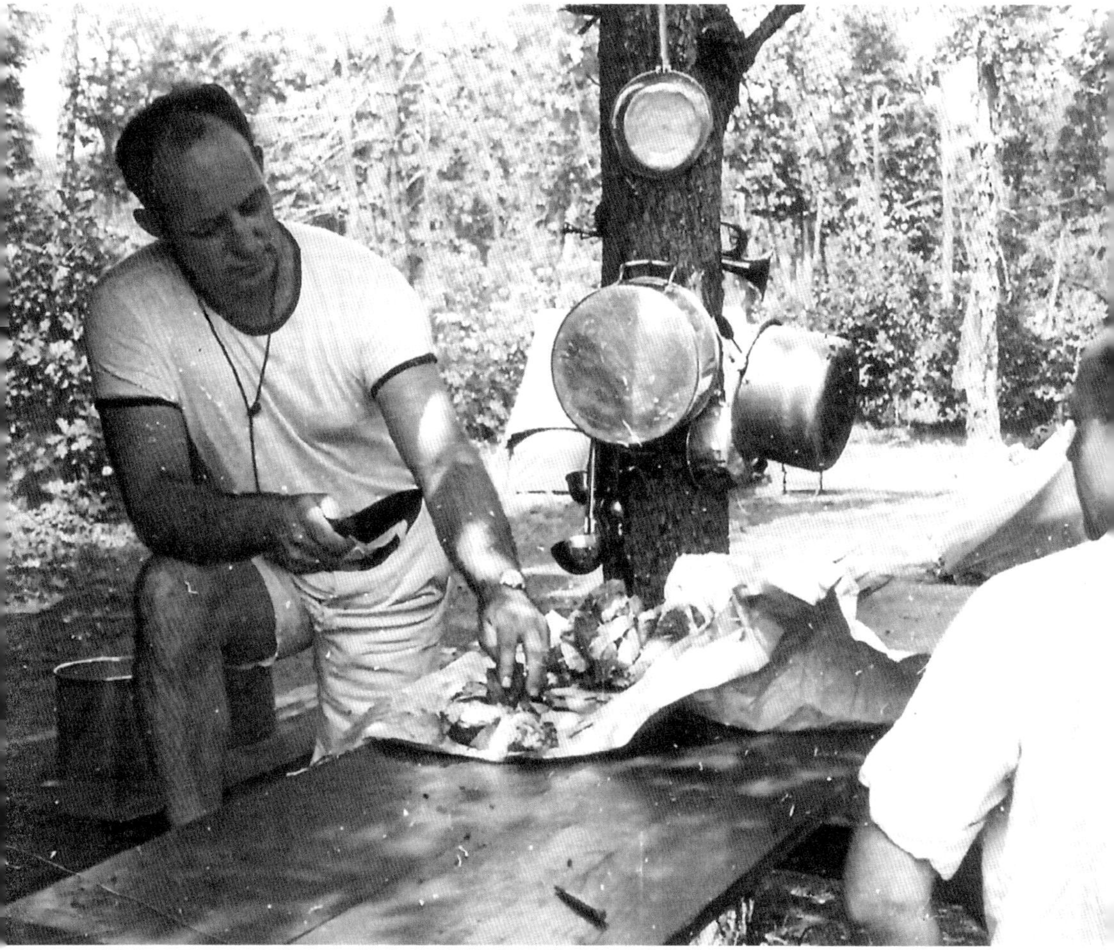

Dr. Paul Blessing

Paul Blessing was a well-respected dentist in St. Charles for 37 years. A graduate of St. Louis University, Dr. Blessing served the community as a Lions Club president, director and football coach for the Boys Club, a lifetime Navy League member, and a member of the Exchange Club, the Knights of Columbus Council of St. Charles, and the American Dental Association. In 1960, the St. Charles County Chamber of Commerce presented Blessing with the Man of the Year award. (Courtesy of St. Charles County Historical Society.)

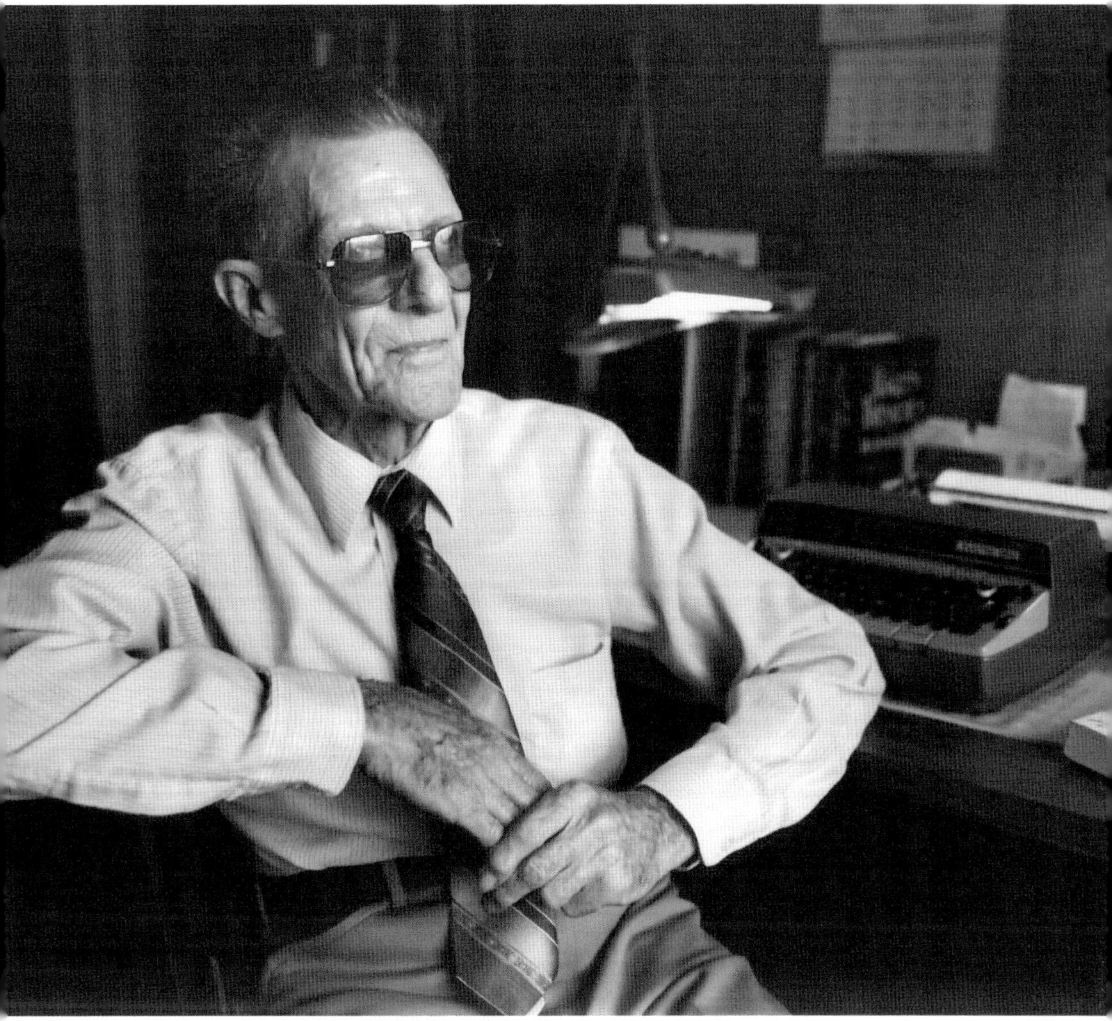

George Feltz

After retirement from a career in the defense industry, including at McDonnell Douglas Aircraft, George Feltz studied archaeology and anthropology at Southern Illinois University–Edwardsville (SIUE) and Washington University. In 1968, he and his wife worked with a South Dakota–Minnesota team on the site of an ancient Indian village. In 1973 and 1974, Feltz directed an archeological salvage excavation in St. Charles County sponsored by SIUE, excavating three distinct time periods: Late Archaic, Early Woodland, and Middle Woodland. Feltz served on the board of the St. Charles County Historical Society for several years, with continued interest in local history and historic preservation. (Courtesy of St. Charles County Historical Society; photograph by Michael Schlueter.)

Henry J. Elmendorf

As former chairman of the Missouri–St. Louis Metropolitan Airport Authority, Henry Elmendorf was instrumental in keeping Lambert Field in St. Louis. While general manager for the Jim Meagher Chevrolet dealership in St. Charles, he was credited with helping to bring the General Motors assembly plant to St. Charles County. A longtime civic leader, Elmendorf served on the board of directors for Lindenwood College and St. Joseph Hospital and on the lay advisory board for Duchesne High School. He was active at St. Charles Borromeo Church and in many Catholic organizations. In 1980, the St. Charles County Chamber of Commerce named him Citizen of the Years. (Courtesy of St. Charles County Historical Society; photograph by Michael Schlueter.)

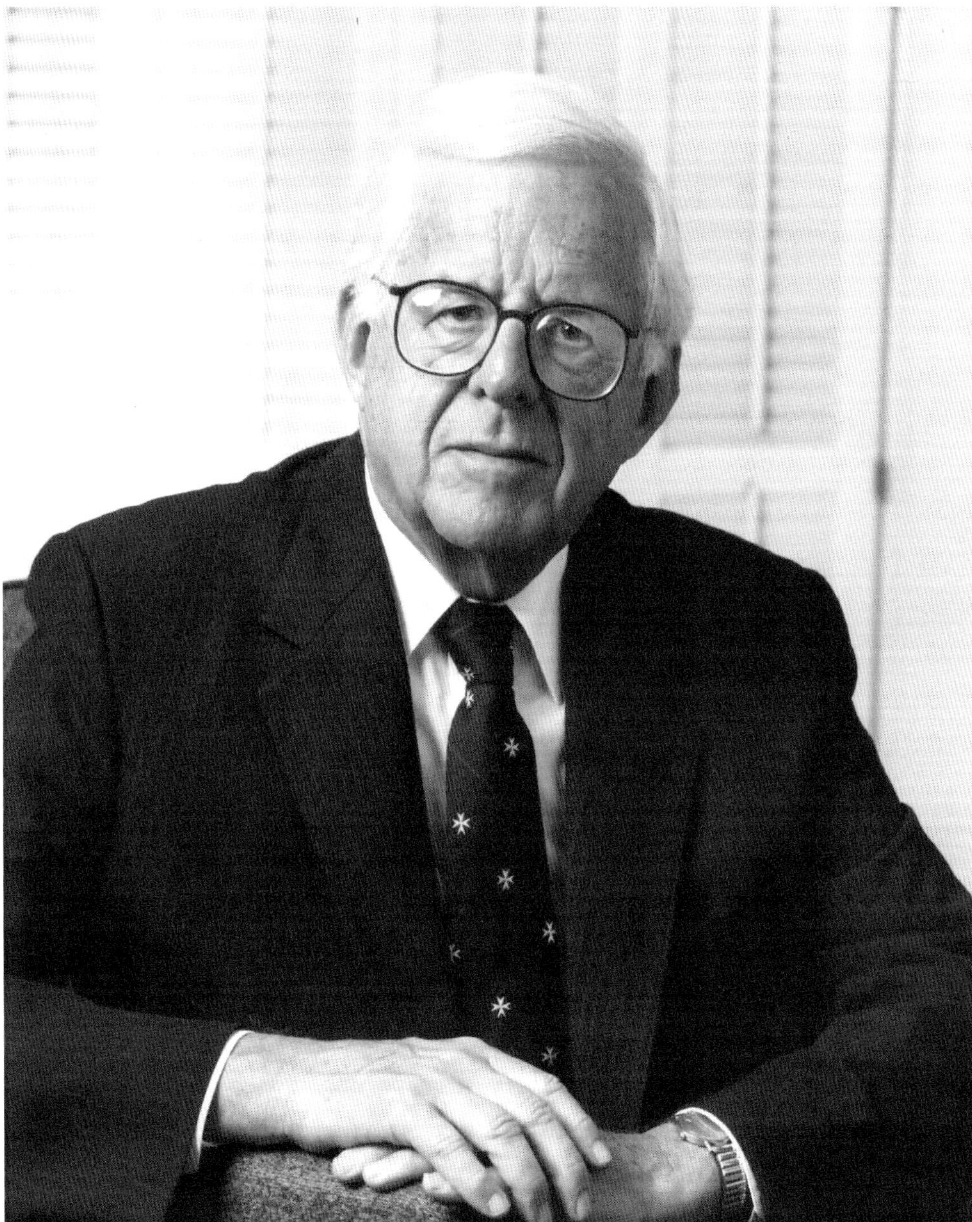

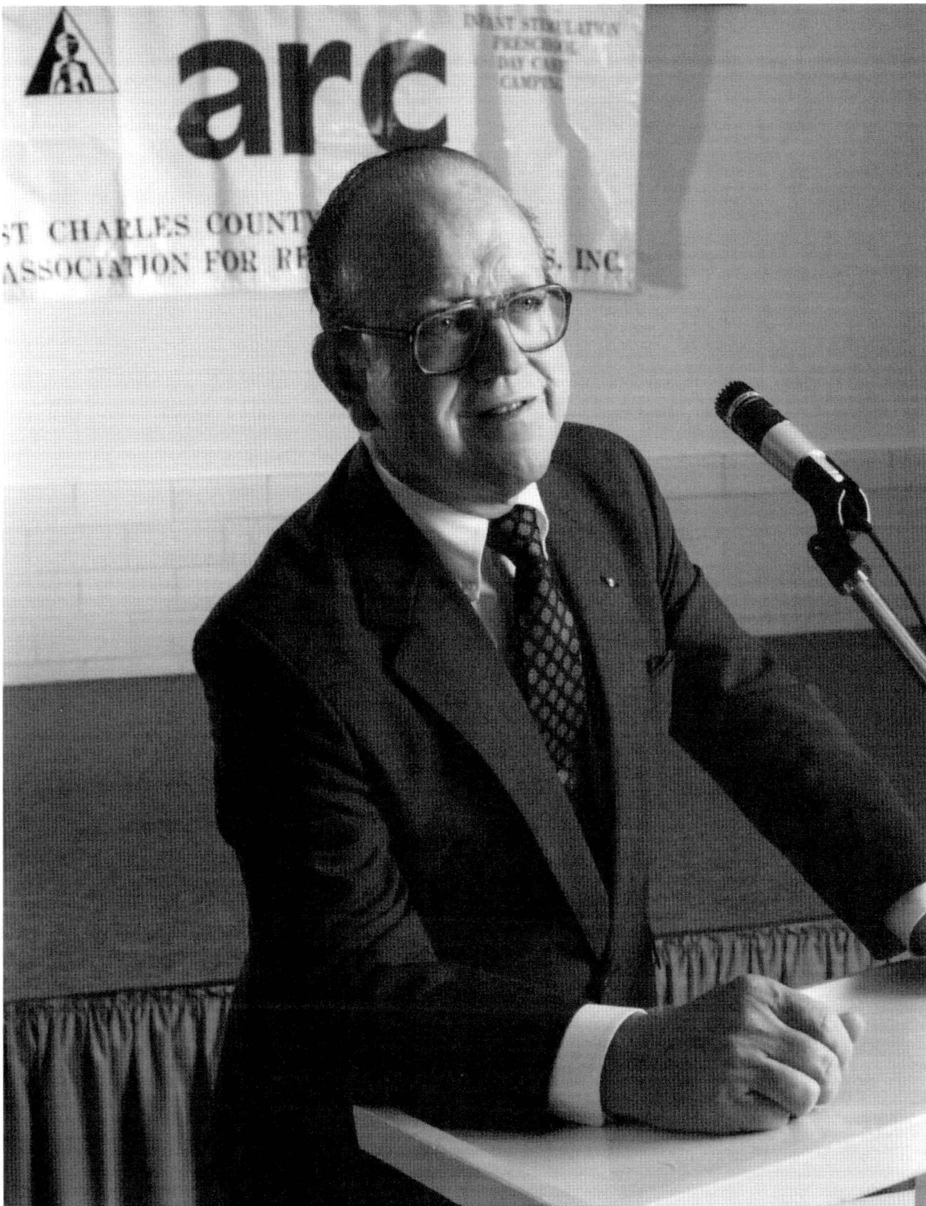

James M. Fitz

A graduate of Washington University, Fitz served in the Korean conflict and then made his career at the St. Charles Gas Company (now Laclede Gas Company). He was a longtime member of the First Baptist Church of St. Charles as well as a tireless volunteer for organizations including St. Joseph Hospital, the YMCA, Lindenwood University, Rotary International, the St. Charles County Chamber of Commerce, Industrial Development Authority of St. Charles County, Economic Development Commission/City of St. Charles, St. Charles County Economic Development Council, the Regional Chamber and Growth Association, St. Charles Community Progress, and Crime Stoppers. In 1977, he was named Citizen of the Years by the St. Charles County Chamber of Commerce. (Courtesy of St. Charles County Historical Society; photograph by Michael Schlueter.)

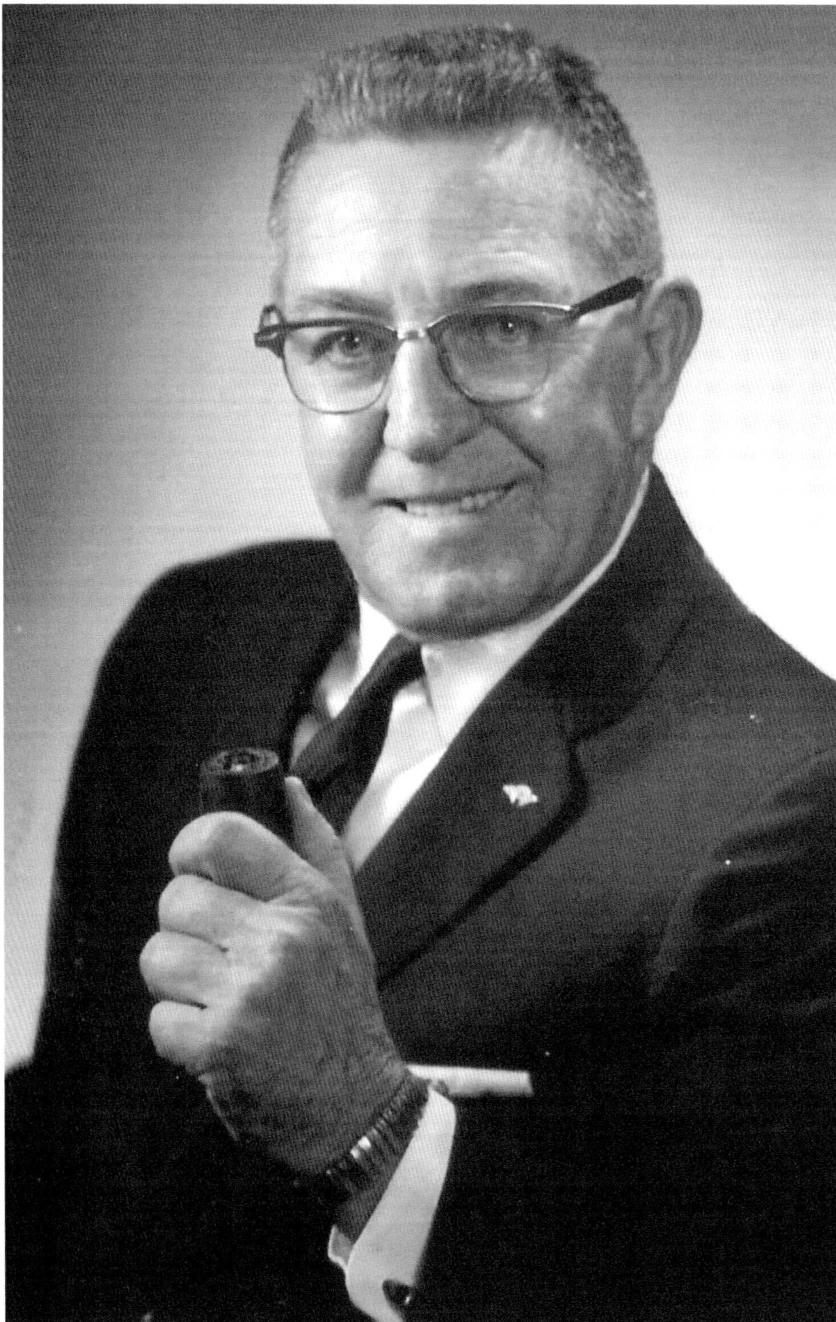

Ted Schoetker

Schoetker founded his company, Ted Schoetker Heating & Air Conditioning, in St. Charles in the 1960s. Jerry Kelly, of Jerry Kelly Heating & Air Conditioning, credits Schoetker as his mentor, having worked for him for 12 years before Schoetker passed away in 1977. The St. Charles County Chamber of Commerce named Ted Schoetker Citizen of the Years in 1974 in recognition of his contributions to civic organizations and the community. (Courtesy of St. Charles County Historical Society.)

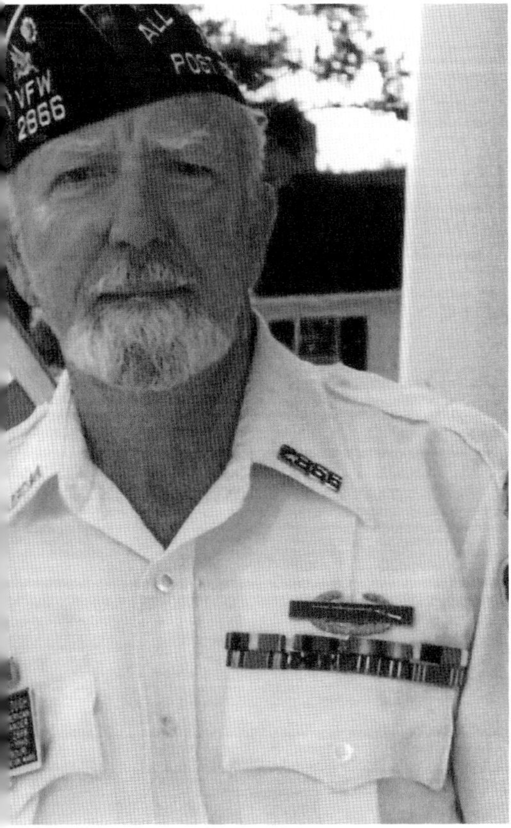

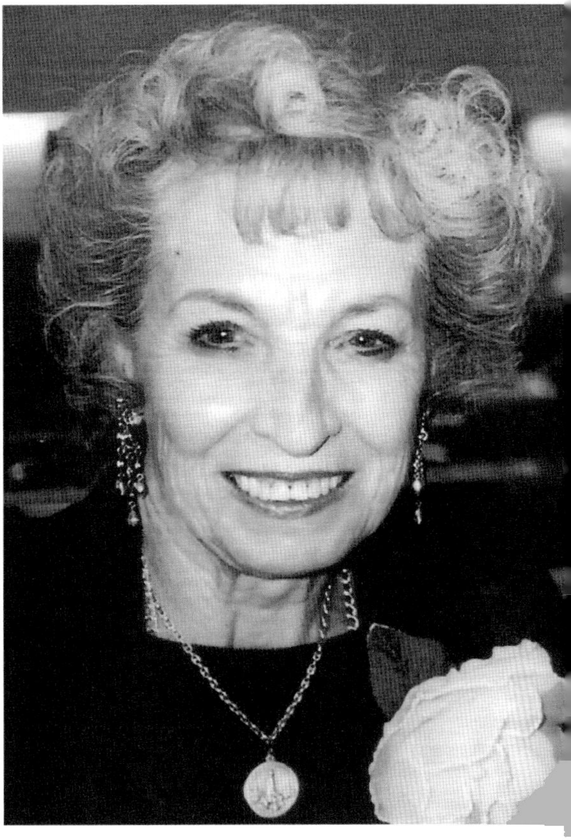

Dr. Joseph F. Keough and Belle Keough
Joseph "Doc" Keough and his wife, Belle, came to St. Charles in 1950 for postgraduate work at Logan Chiropractic College. Both World War II veterans, the couple met at Palmer Chiropractic School and later married. Doc worked part-time at American Car & Foundry in the early years. The couple had eight children, many of whom learned to play a musical instrument. The Keough Trio (which eventually included four members) played at retirement homes and county fairs. In 1963, Doc helped form the Daniel Boone Chorus, which later became the Ambassadors of Harmony, devoting 40 years to the group. He also sang tenor in the Quadri'pals.

After 35 years as a chiropractor, Doc retired, and he and Belle became active in the local VFW Post 2866 in St. Charles. Doc was elected quartermaster of the post. Belle is remembered for making her own wheat bread by hand, buying the grain from local farmers and grinding it in a mill to make the flour. (Both, courtesy of Sean Keough.)

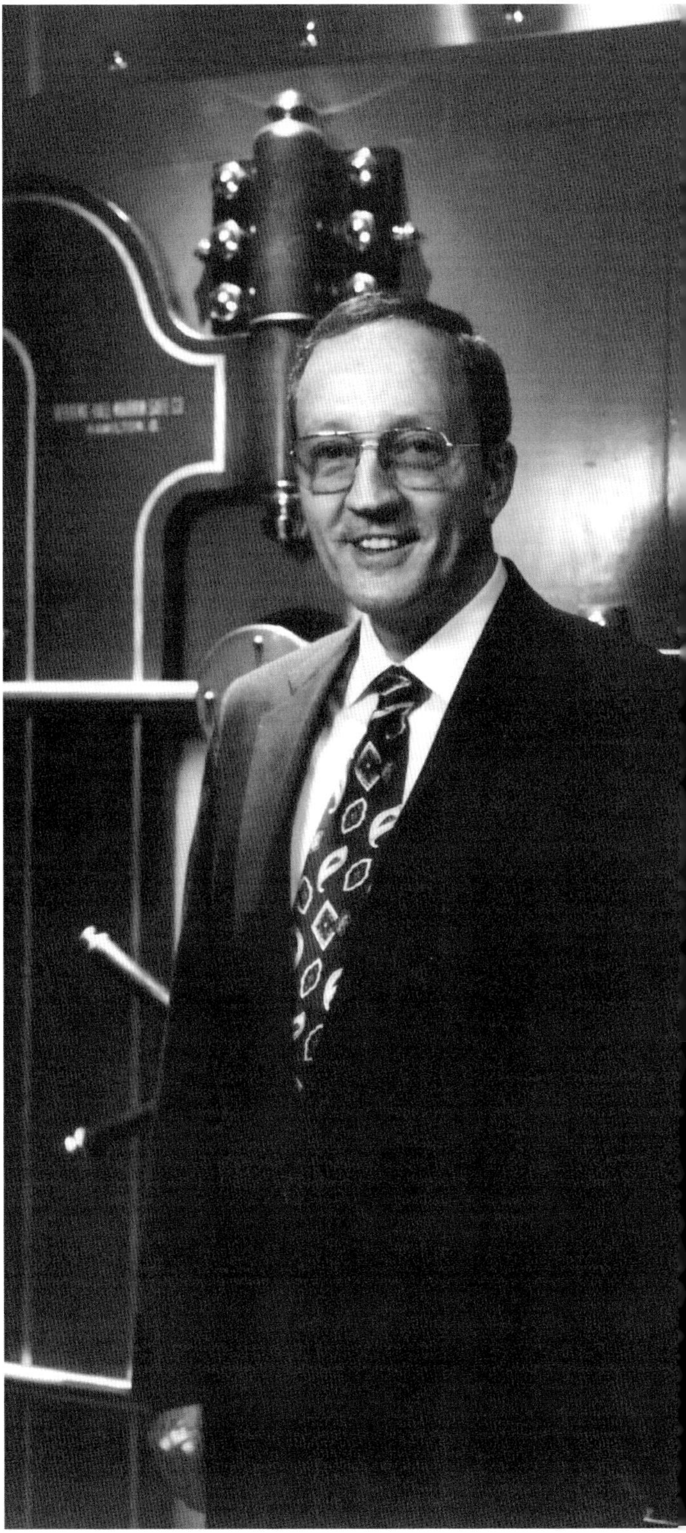

Thomas Boschert

In 1956, Thomas Boschert joined the First National Bank of St. Charles County as a filing clerk, eventually working his way up to president in 1980. He remained in that position when the institution was purchased by Landmark Bank in 1984, and he became executive vice president for Magna Bank of St. Charles County when Landmark was purchased in 1991. A member of the Army National Guard, Boschert was called to active duty in 1961 during the Berlin crisis. Among the many organizations in which Boschert has been involved are the St. Charles City Park Board, the City Library Board, the Salvation Army Board, and others. He is a member and past president of the St. Charles County Chamber of Commerce. He received the 1987 Lifetime Distinguished Service Award and was named the 1991 Citizen of the Years by the St. Charles County Chamber of Commerce. (Courtesy of St. Charles County Historical Society.)

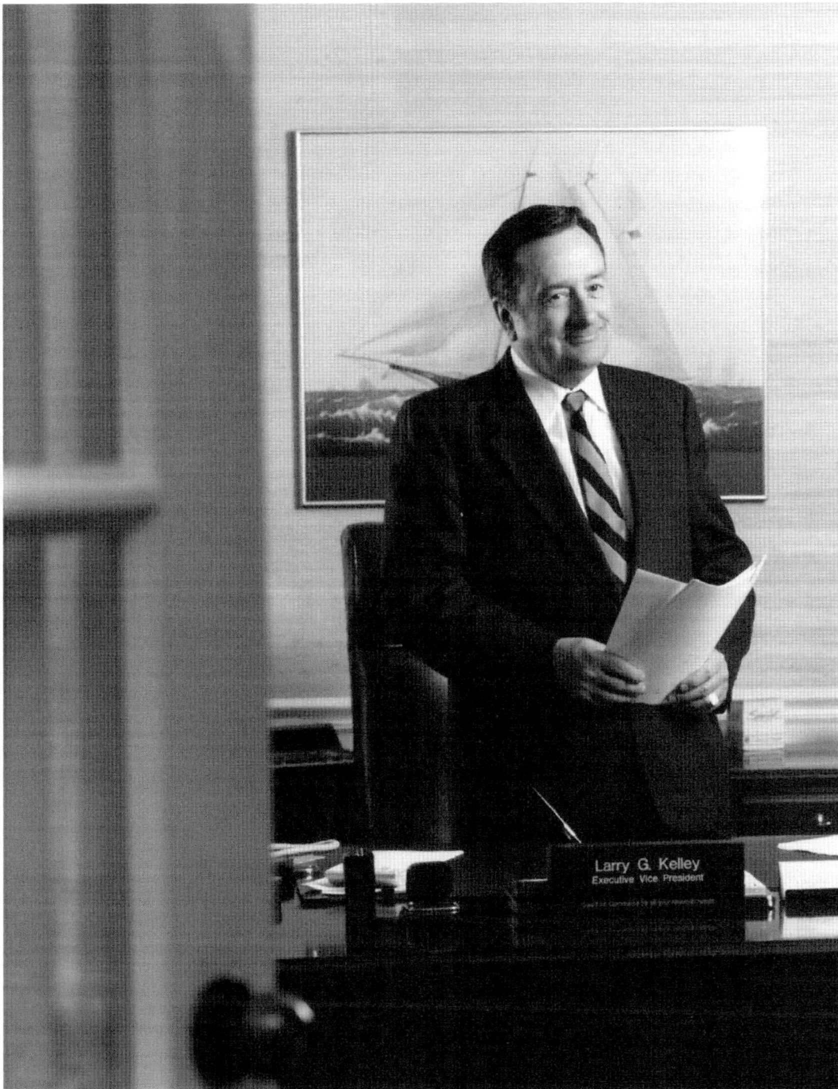

Larry Kelley

Larry Kelley was named president, chairman of the board, and chief executive officer of Commerce Bank of St. Charles County in mid-1976, and he promptly moved to St. Charles to begin involving himself in the community. Since then, he has been a civic leader through his participation in the St. Charles County Chamber of Commerce, the United Way Tri-County Campaign, the Lindenwood College Board of Overseers, and many more organizations. He cofounded St. Charles Community Progress, chairing the group from 1989 to 1992. Kelley has been a member of the St. Charles County Regional Chamber and Growth Association (RCGA) Advisory Board and the board of directors of the St. Charles County Economic Development Council. He has also volunteered his time with the Emmaus Home, Boy Scouts of America, Crime Stoppers, Salvation Army, and dozens of other organizations. From 1989 to 1992, he chaired a committee of Concerned Citizens for Health-Care Assistance for the Needy Residents of St. Charles County. Kelley was named Executive of the Year by the St. Charles chapter of Professional Secretaries International in 1981 and a Citizen of the Years by the St. Charles County Chamber of Commerce in 1989. (Courtesy of St. Charles County Historical Society; photograph by Michael Schlueter.)

Edward J. Pundmann Jr.

Ed Pundmann was president and a co-owner of Pundmann Ford, the auto dealership his father founded in 1925. Pundmann was a civic leader, sitting on the boards of the St. Charles Rotary Club, the St. Charles County Chamber of Commerce, Boone Center Workshop, Family and Children's Services of Greater St. Louis, St. Charles Jaycees, and many others. He was very involved in St. Charles government and church activities, earning the 1986 Citizen of the Years and the 2002 Small Business Person of the Year Award from the St. Charles County Chamber of Commerce and the 1989 Governor's Award for Economic Development. He also received several awards from Ford Motor Company. (Courtesy of St. Charles County Historical Society; photograph by Michael Schlueter.)

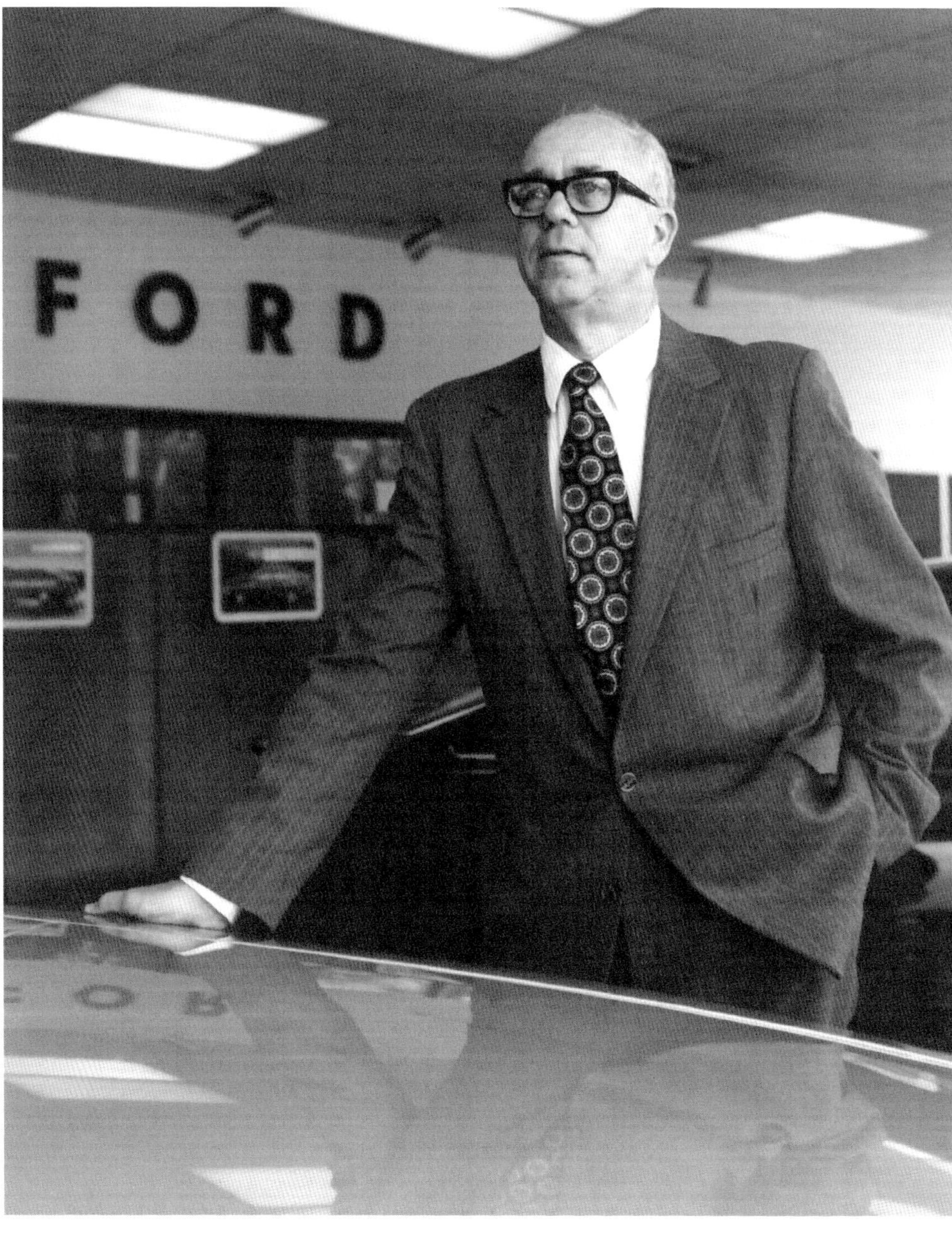

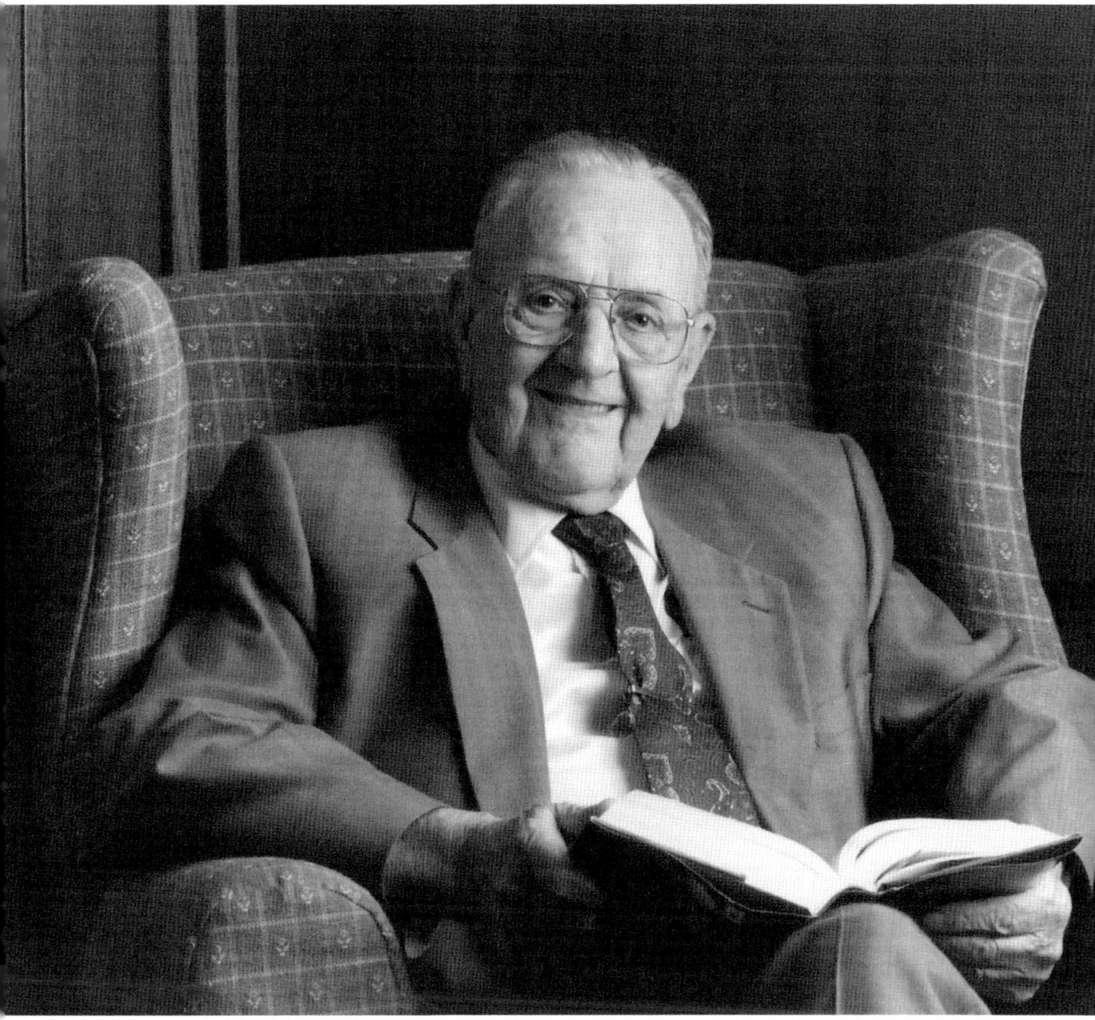

Henry Kriete Stumberg

H. Kriete Stumberg, son of Dr. B. Kurt Stumberg, was a successful attorney and a prosecutor before and after serving in the US Army during World War II. He was discharged with the rank of captain, later becoming chairman of the first St. Charles County Charter Commission in the 1970s. He is recognized as one of the founders of the St. Charles County Chamber of Commerce and the St. Charles County Historical Society. As president of the St. Charles School District board, he helped establish the Lewis and Clark Vocational Technical School. Stumberg was named Man of the Year in 1975. He was married to Cordelia Buck Stumberg (see page 78) for 58 years until his death in 1999. (Courtesy of St. Charles County Historical Society; photograph by Michael Schlueter.)

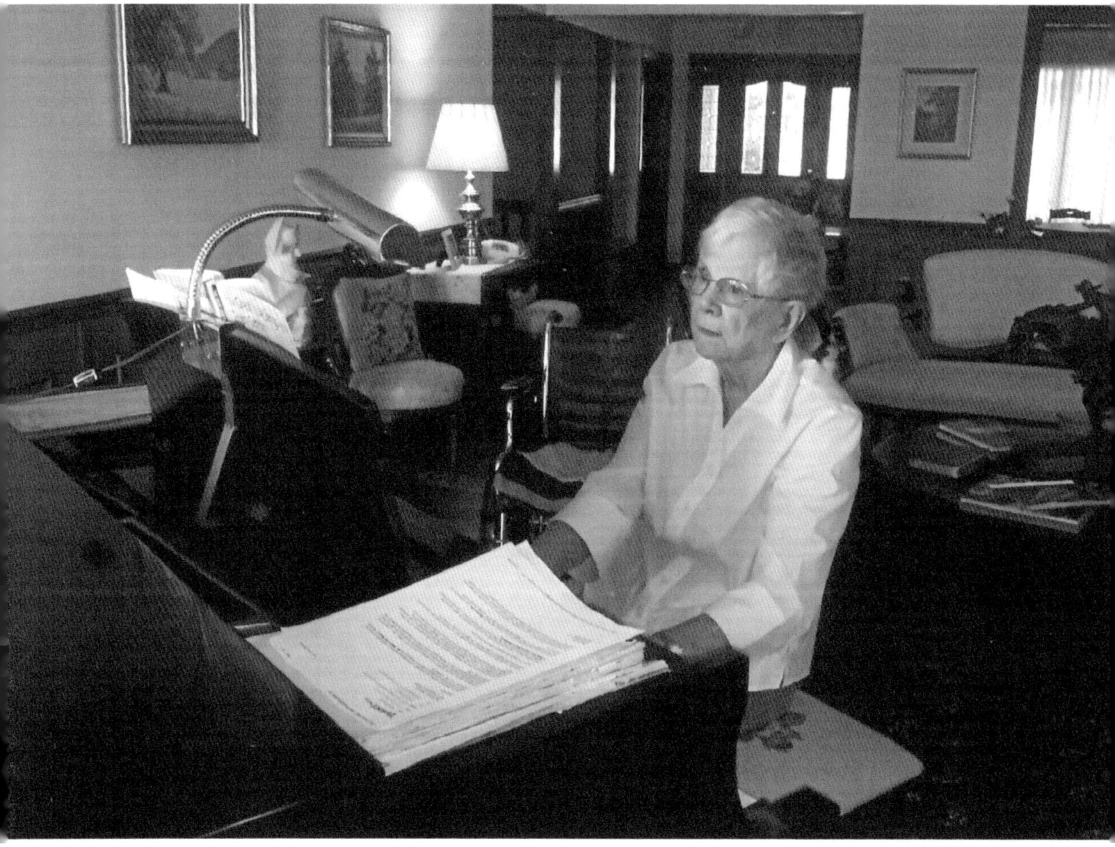

Cordelia Buck Stumberg

Cordelia Stumberg was born in October 1919 in Little Rock, Arkansas. At a very early age, her parents recognized her musical gift and bought her a piano. She performed often for others during her schooling, including one memorable event in 1936, when she played for the singing of the national anthem during Pres. Franklin Roosevelt's visit to her high school. Later that year, Cordelia rode the train to St. Louis and then a bus to St. Charles to attend Lindenwood College. She graduated in 1940 with a bachelor of music degree and, in 1971, earned a master's degree from SIU-Edwardsville. Among other accomplishments, Stumberg is the founder of the St. Charles Choral Society (Missouri Choral Society), a former board member of the First State Bank and the Crescendo Concert Series, and a winner of the 1988 St. Charles County Chamber of Commerce Lifetime Distinguished Service Award. (Photograph by author.)

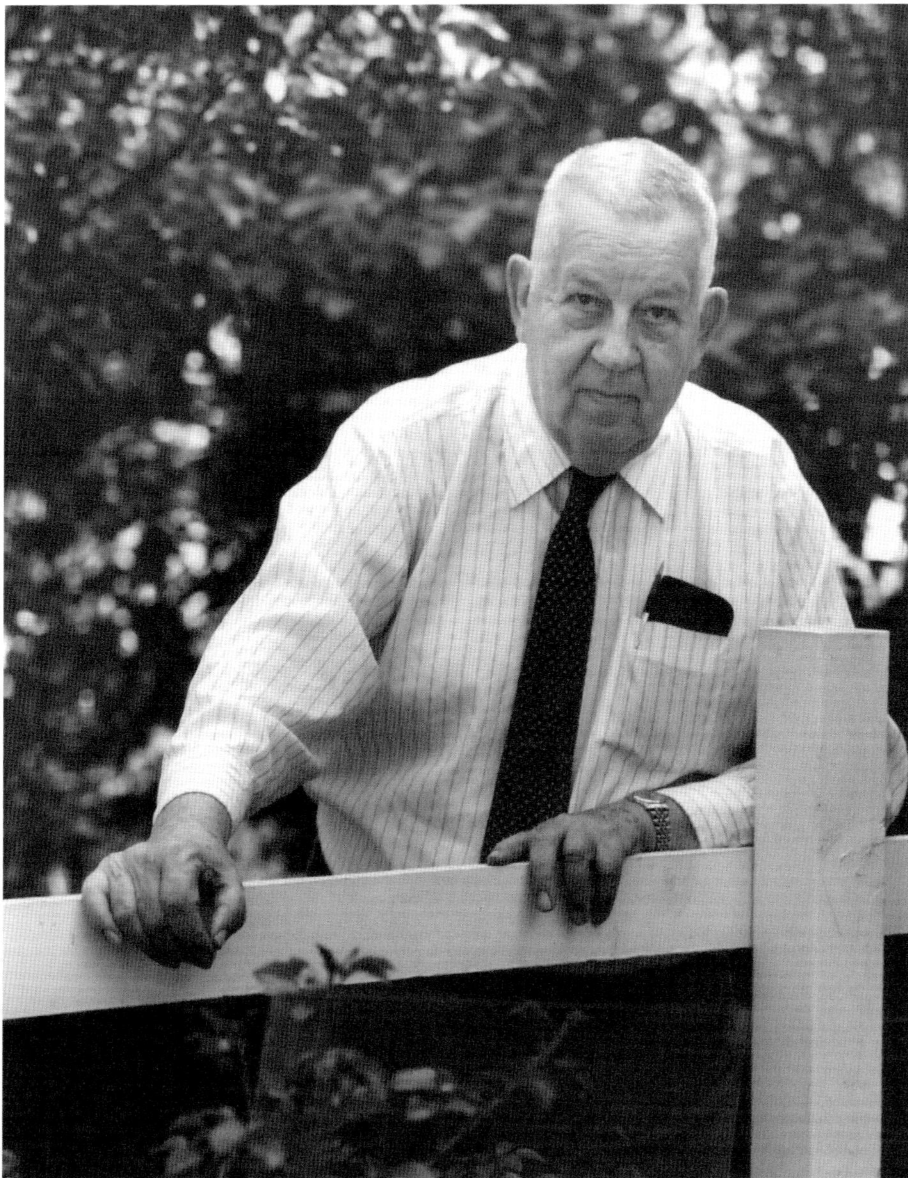

John Bruere Becker

John Becker served as an officer in the US Navy on a submarine chaser in the southwest Pacific during World War II. Afterward, he worked for three large architectural firms from 1946 to 1981. Becker's many contributions to the St. Charles community include helping to organize Little League Baseball as an Optimist Club member, an organization for which he also served as president. He was also president of the Boys and Girls Club of St. Charles, a charter member of the St. Charles County Historical Society, a volunteer at St. Joseph Hospital, a member of the St. Charles City Board of Adjustment, the city Building Officials and Administrators (BOCA) Board and Architectural Review Board, and the American Red Cross, and president of St. Charles Borromeo School PTA. Becker received the St. Charles County Chamber of Commerce Citizen of the Years award in 1988. (Courtesy of St. Charles County Historical Society; photograph by Michael Schlueter.)

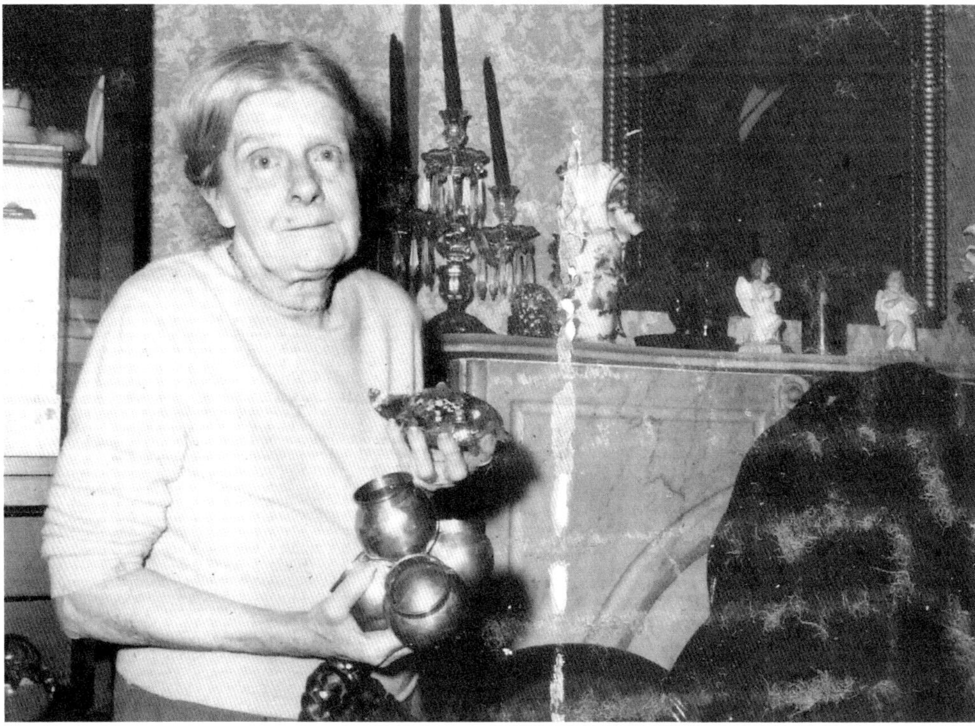

Edna McElhiney Olson
Edna Olson studied history at Lindenwood College. After a career as an interior decorator, Olson opened an antiques shop at 407 South Sixth Street and, later, another one at 900 North Second Street. She was a founding member of the St. Charles County Historical Society and its first archivist. She contributed many writings to the historical society over the years. Her book *Historical St. Charles, Missouri* was published in 1967. (Courtesy of St. Charles County Historical Society.)

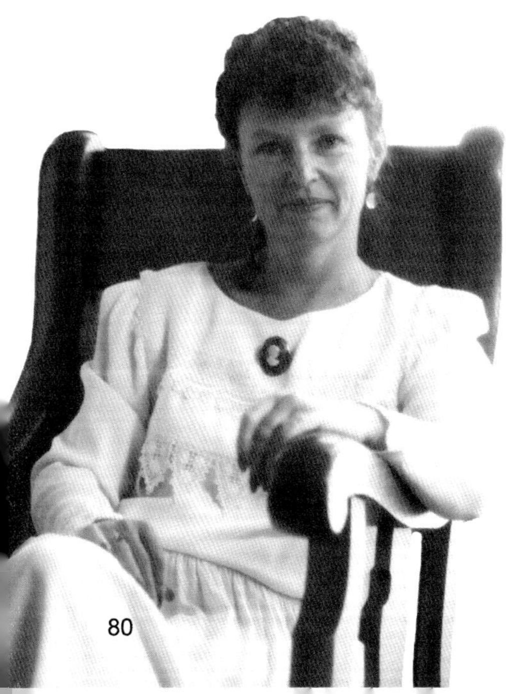

Sue Schneider
Sue Schneider's family has a long history in St. Charles, dating back more than 150 years. She credits her family's sense of community and volunteer spirit for her own involvement in working to preserve and promote the historic district of St. Charles. With others, Schneider helped found Youth in Need, and she served as its director for 12 years. She was also chosen to help explore forms of county government and recommend a proposed charter to county voters in 1992, which passed with a healthy majority. She remains involved in the preservation of St. Charles history. (Courtesy of St. Charles County Historical Society; photograph by Michael Schlueter.)

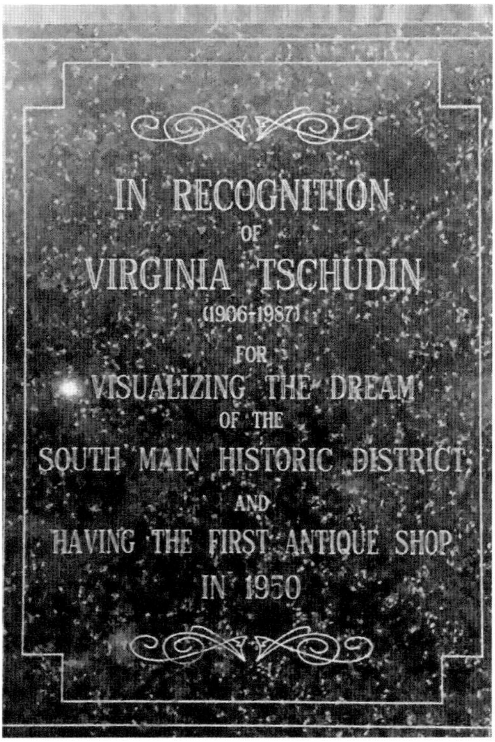

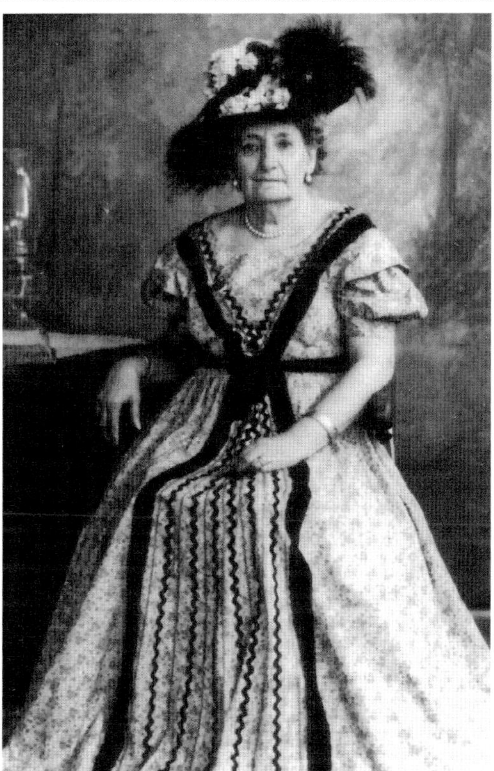

Virginia Musterman Tschudin
Virginia Tschudin was one of the first antiques dealers and shop owners to buy property and establish a business on Main Street during the early restoration of the historic district. She was dubbed "First Lady of South Main" by many. Her last shop, House of Yesterday, was located at 519 South Main Street, and a plaque was installed at the home in her honor. It recently resurfaced and is pictured above. (Above, photograph by author; below, courtesy of Gina Christine and Bruce Musterman.)

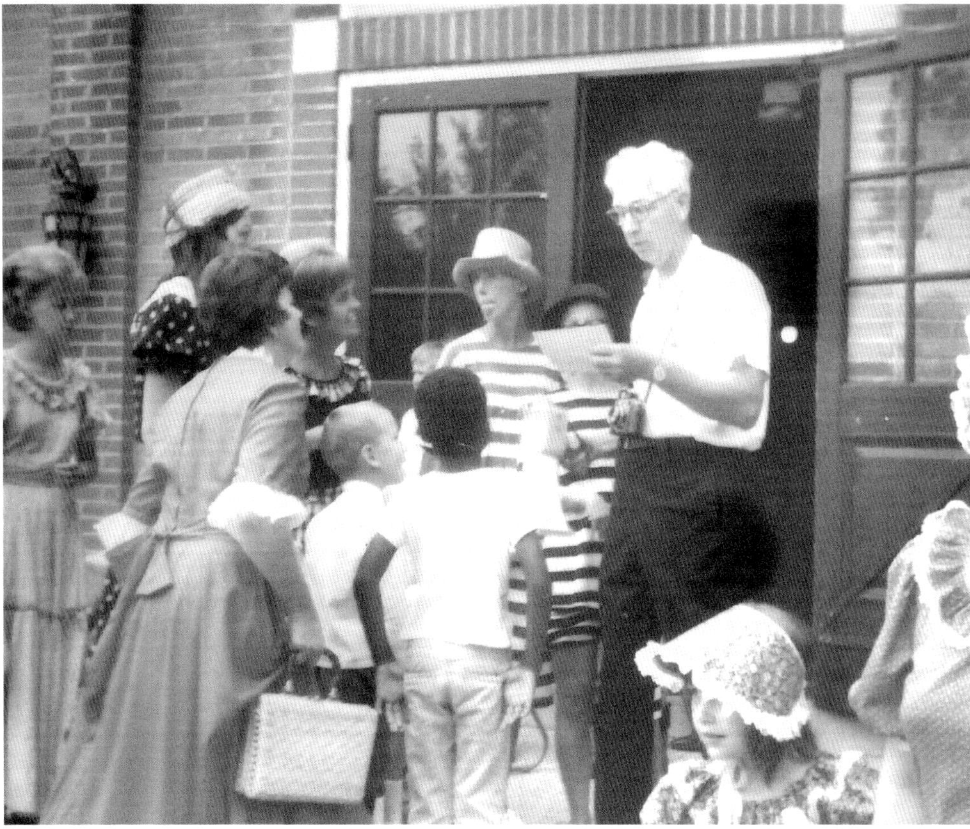

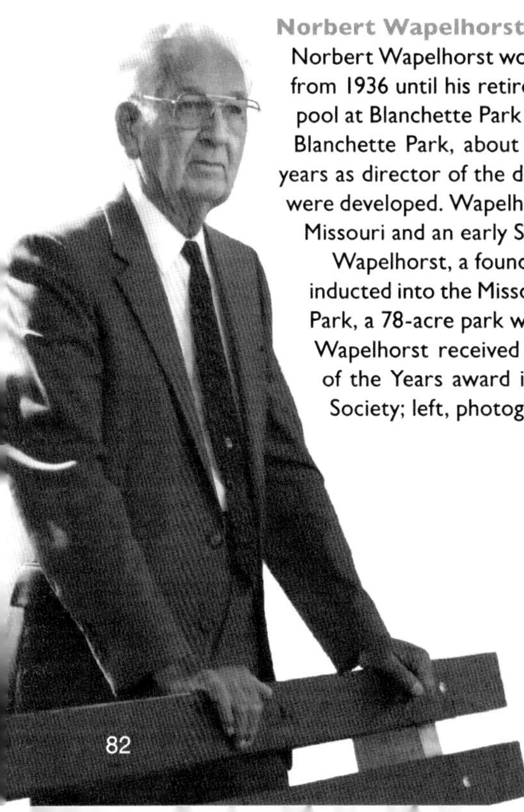

Norbert Wapelhorst

Norbert Wapelhorst worked for the St. Charles Parks and Recreation Department from 1936 until his retirement in 1979, beginning as a construction foreman on the pool at Blanchette Park when St. Charles had a population of about 11,000 people. Blanchette Park, about 42 acres at that time, was the city's only park. In his 41 years as director of the department, two aquatic centers, 18 parks, and a cemetery were developed. Wapelhorst designed McNair Park, named for the first governor of Missouri and an early St. Charles resident, and supervised its construction.

Wapelhorst, a founder of the St. Charles Park and Recreation Foundation, was inducted into the Missouri Recreation and Parks Hall of Fame in 2009. Wapelhorst Park, a 78-acre park with a pool, trail, and sports facilities, is named in his honor. Wapelhorst received the St. Charles County Chamber of Commerce Citizen of the Years award in 1981. (Both, courtesy of St. Charles County Historical Society; left, photograph by Michael Schlueter.)

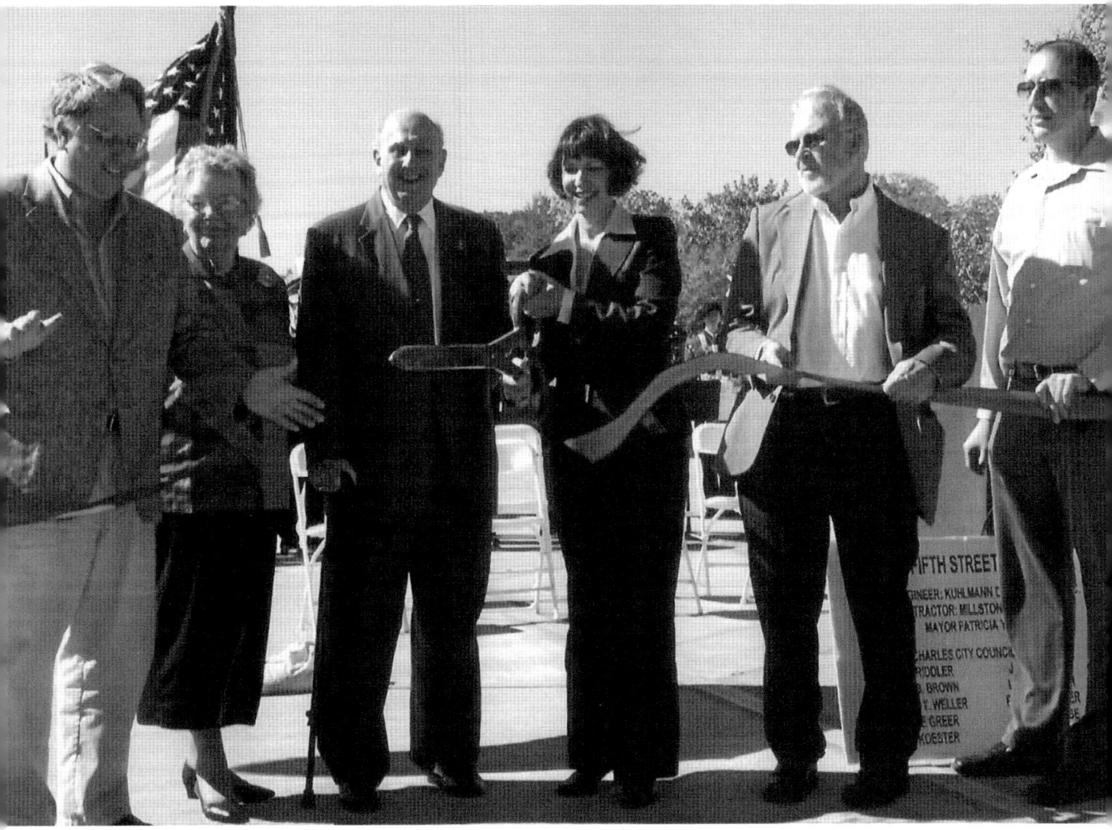

Mel Wetter

Mel Wetter was born in 1929 and attended school at St. Peters. He was an insurance salesman by trade and a successful business owner. According to his son, he was always interested in the welfare of the city of St. Charles and sat on several committees before being elected mayor in 1983. Because of Mel Wetter's dedication and service to St. Charles, especially the Frenchtown area, the Fifth Street extension was named Mel Wetter Parkway. He was named Citizen of the Years by the St. Charles County Chamber of Commerce in 2005, but of all his accomplishments, his family says he is proudest of having started the preliminary plans for the Highway 370/Discovery Bridge. This photograph was taken in the spring of 2006 at the ribbon-cutting ceremony for the Mel Wetter Parkway. Mel's wife, Kathleen, is second from left, Mel is third from left, and Mayor Patti York is fourth from left. (Courtesy of the St. Charles County Chamber of Commerce.)

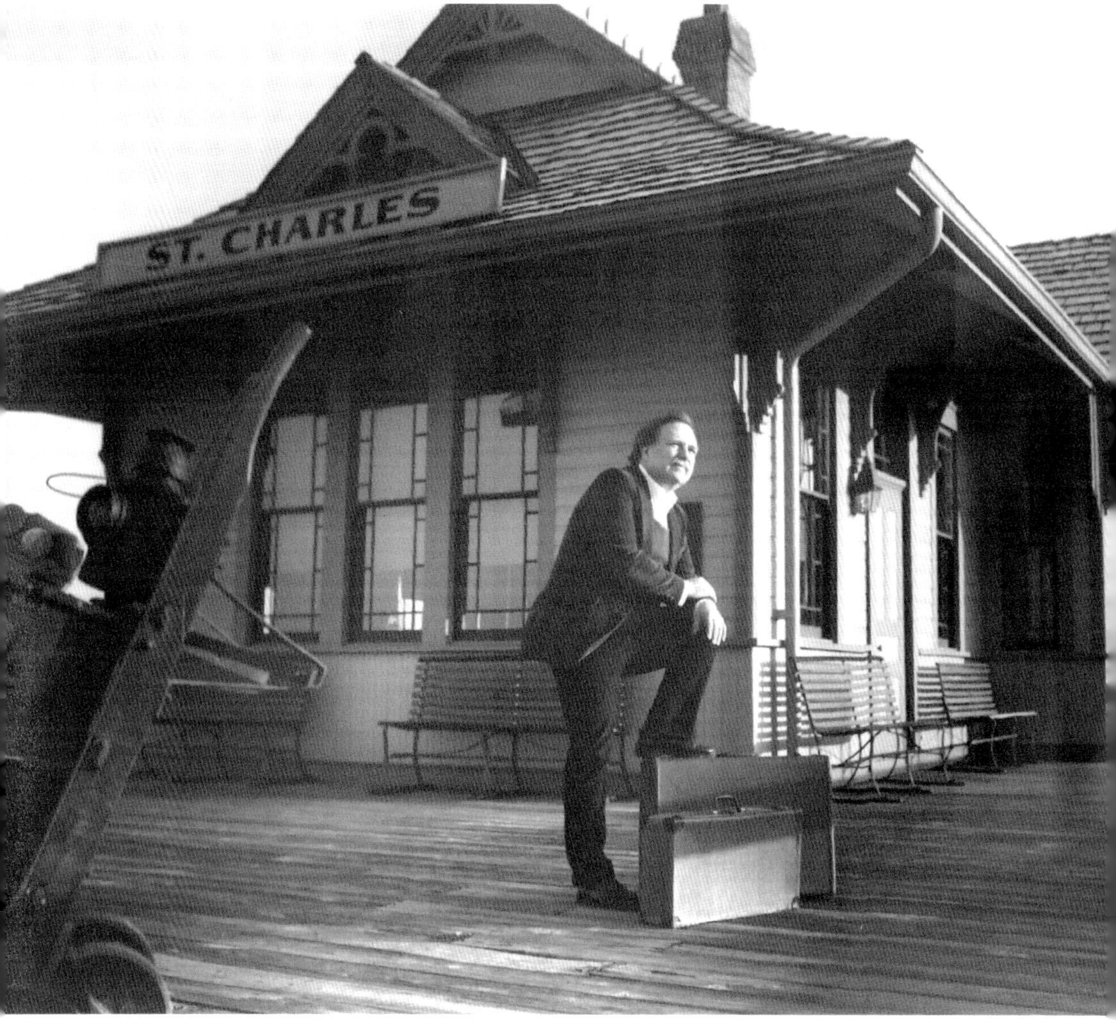

Archie Scott

A founding member of the South Main Preservation Society in 1972, Archie Scott served as president four times. Known by some as "Mr. Main Street," Scott purchased a home on Main Street in 1966 and spent the rest of his life promoting the restoration and preservation of the St. Charles Historic District. He served as chairman of the Special Business District and personally restored four buildings, leading a campaign to encourage other business owners and community leaders to do the same. Scott died on December 22, 2007, at the age of 65. He counted among his greatest accomplishments having saved the old mill, which is now Trailhead Brewery, and the Katy Depot, which now sits in Frontier Park. (Courtesy of St. Charles County Historical Society; photograph by Michael Schlueter.)

James H. Beardsley

During a time of great growth in St. Charles County, from 1982 to 1990, James Beardsley was the planning and zoning commissioner. He also sat on the advisory board of the Salvation Army and on the Tri-County Board of Directors for the United Way of St. Louis as chairman of the allocations committee and the members and agencies committee. He worked in real estate with Coldwell Banker and was a member of the National Association of Realtors and the Missouri Association of Realtors. He served as vice chairman of the community and legislative committee and was a member of the realtors political action committee of the St. Charles County Board of Realtors. Because of his expertise, the 11th Judicial Circuit Court often called on Beardsley to settle valuation disputes. (Courtesy of St. Charles County Historical Society; photograph by Michael Schlueter.)

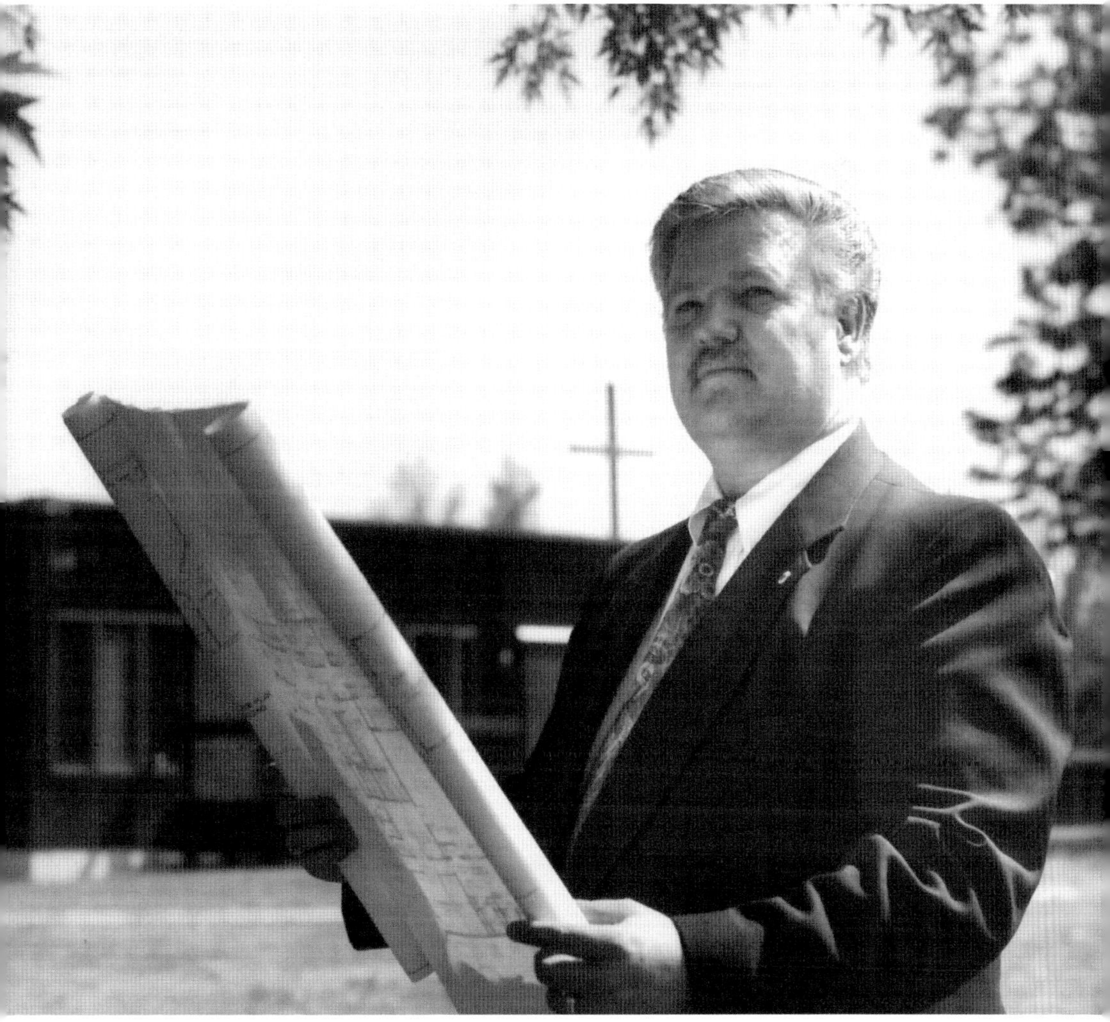

Dr. Robert J. Fleming

Robert Fleming opened his ophthalmology practice in St. Charles in 1955, after attending St. John's University and then serving three years in Europe under Gen. George Patton. He was awarded the Combat Infantry Badge and the Bronze Star. Dr. Fleming has served in many civic and professional organizations, including the St. Charles County Medical Society, the St. Charles Civic Ballet, the board of trustees of the City-County Library, and the board of directors of First State Bank. He also served as chief of staff at St. Joseph Hospital. In 1989, the St. Charles County Chamber of Commerce presented Dr. Fleming with a Lifetime Distinguished Service Award. (Courtesy of St. Charles County Historical Society; photograph by Michael Schlueter.)

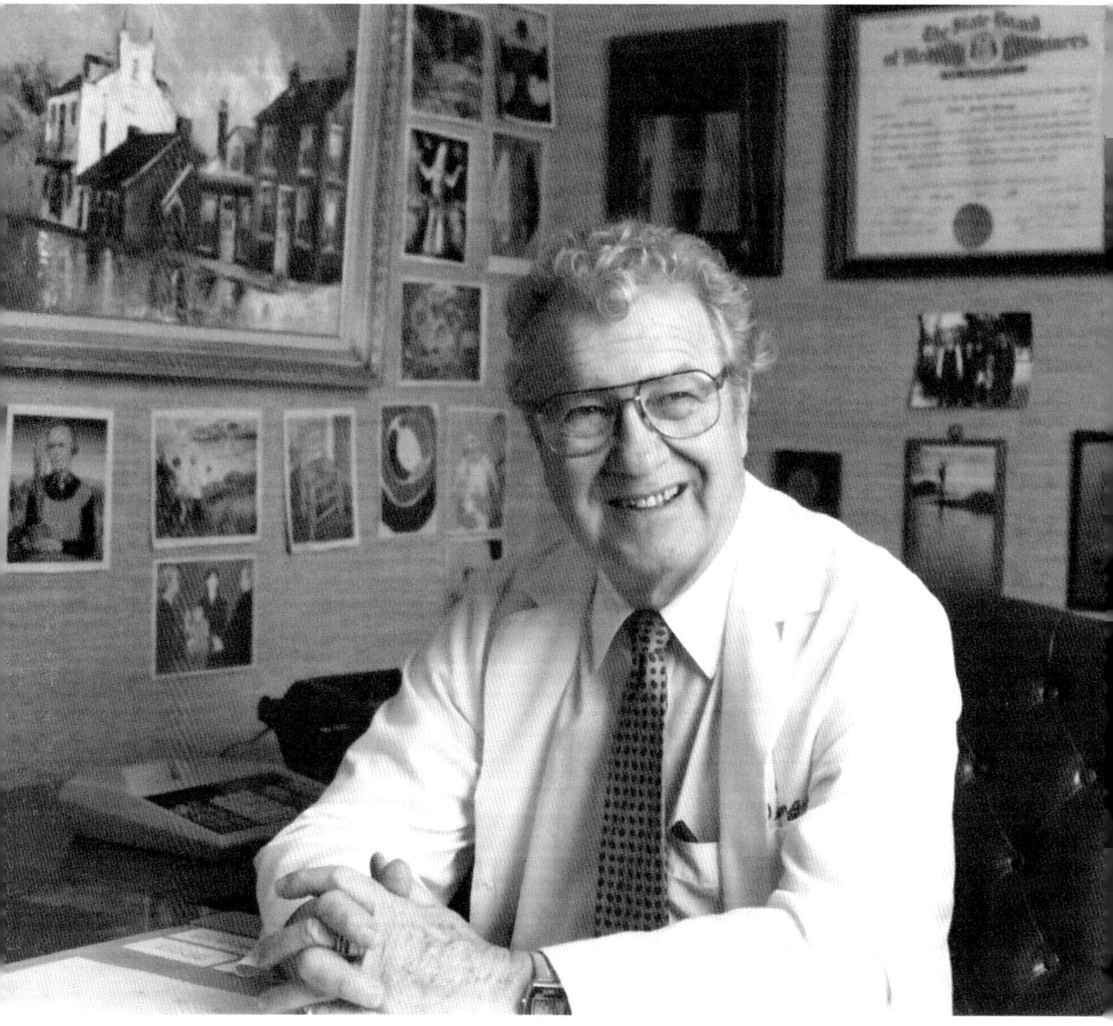

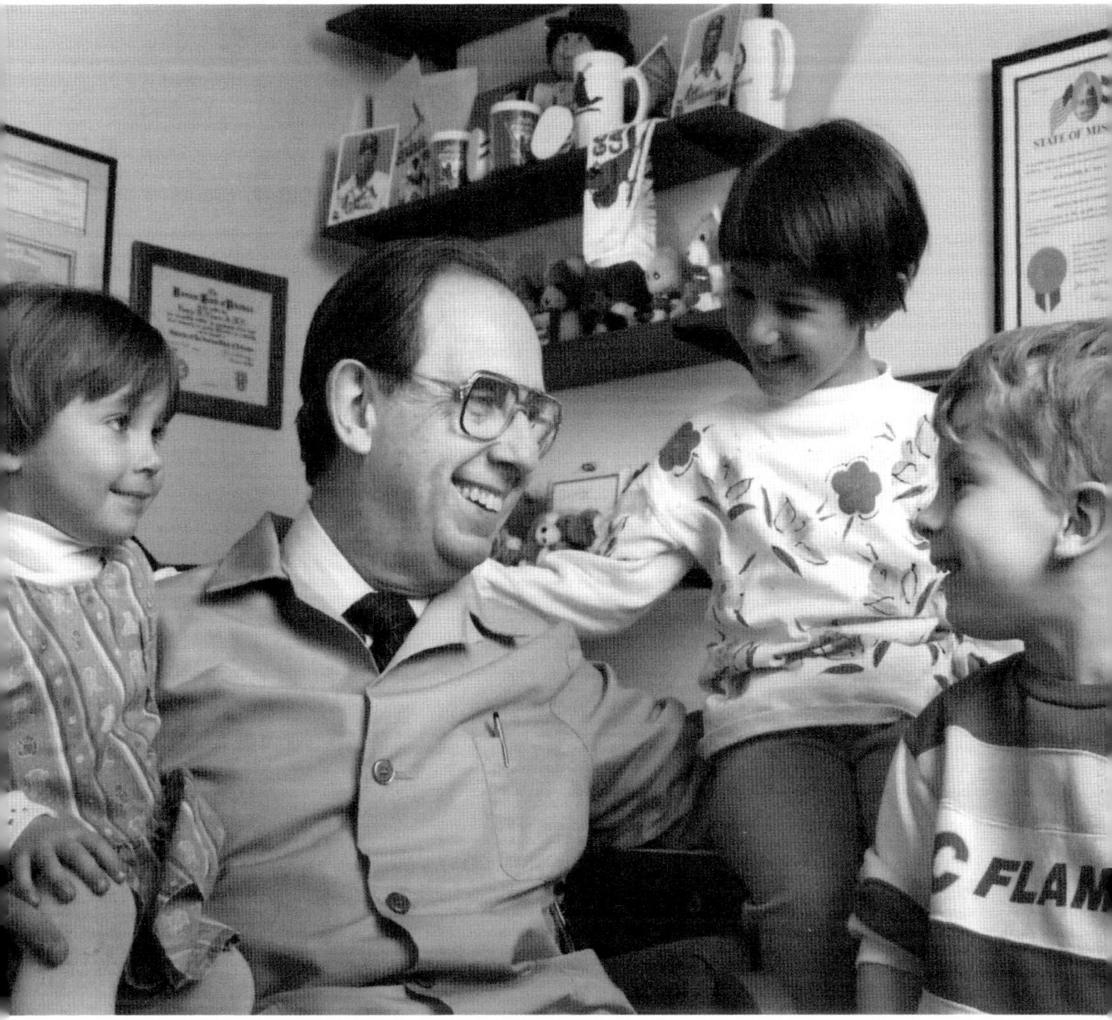

Dr. Henry W. Clever

Henry Clever began practicing pediatrics in St. Charles in 1963. He has served on the staffs of St. Joseph Hospital, St. Joseph Hospital West, and Barnes St. Peters Hospital. He has participated in many civic organizations, including the St. Louis Archdiocesan Board of Education, the School Advisory Board of Duchesne High School, and United Services. Dr. Clever has maintained membership in the Mental Health Commission of the Missouri Department of Mental Health, the American Academy of Pediatrics, the Medical Advisory Board for the March of Dimes, and dozens of other organizations and committees. The St. Charles County Chamber of Commerce gave Dr. Clever the 1990 Lifetime Distinguished Service Award and the 1998 Citizen of the Years award. (Courtesy of St. Charles County Historical Society; photograph by Michael Schlueter.)

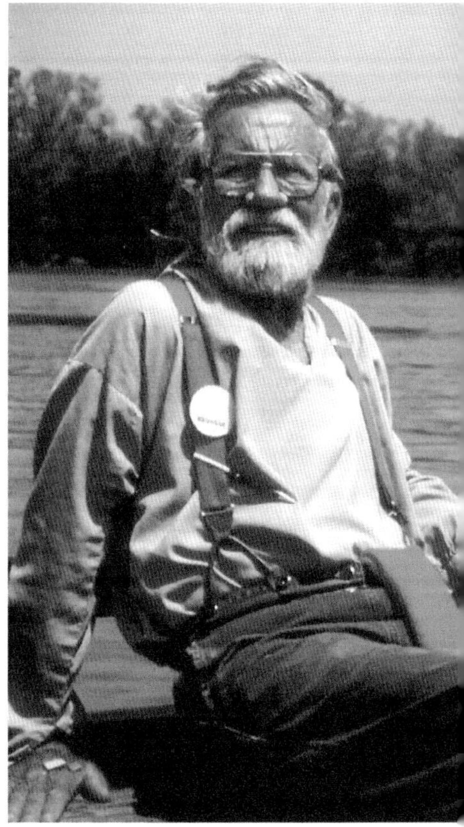

Glennon Bishop

Born and raised in St. Charles, Bishop, a World War II veteran, is widely known for building the Lewis and Clark keelboat replica, which took first place as a float in the national parade in Washington, DC, on July 4, 1992. Later, Glen and the Discovery Expedition crew built two pirogues and rebuilt the original keelboat after it was destroyed in a fire. Bishop is the recipient of the 1993 Discovery Award–Lewis and Clark Rendezvous, the 1996 Veterans of Foreign Wars Americanism Award, the 1995 St. Charles County Chamber of Commerce Lifetime Distinguished Service Award, and the 1998 Foundation of St. Charles Schools Distinguished Achievement Award. He has served as a leader in the Cub Scouts, Boy Scouts, and Sea Scouts; as city councilman (1966–1972); as chairman of the YMCA Organizing Committee (1967–1974); and as the St. Charles County Democratic Committee chairman (1968–1972). He also served on the riverfront planning committee and Landmarks Preservation Board for the City of St. Charles. A historic marker near the Lewis and Clark Boat House and Nature Center designates Bishop's Landing (below). (Right, courtesy of Jean Dryden and the Greater Saint Charles Convention & Visitors Bureau; below, photograph by author.)

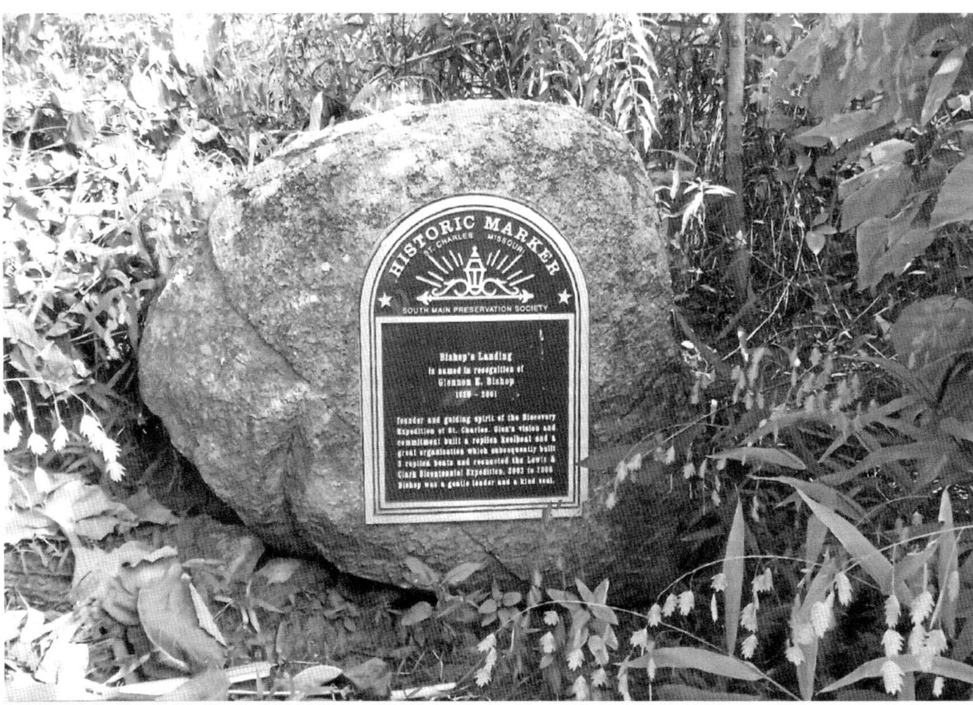

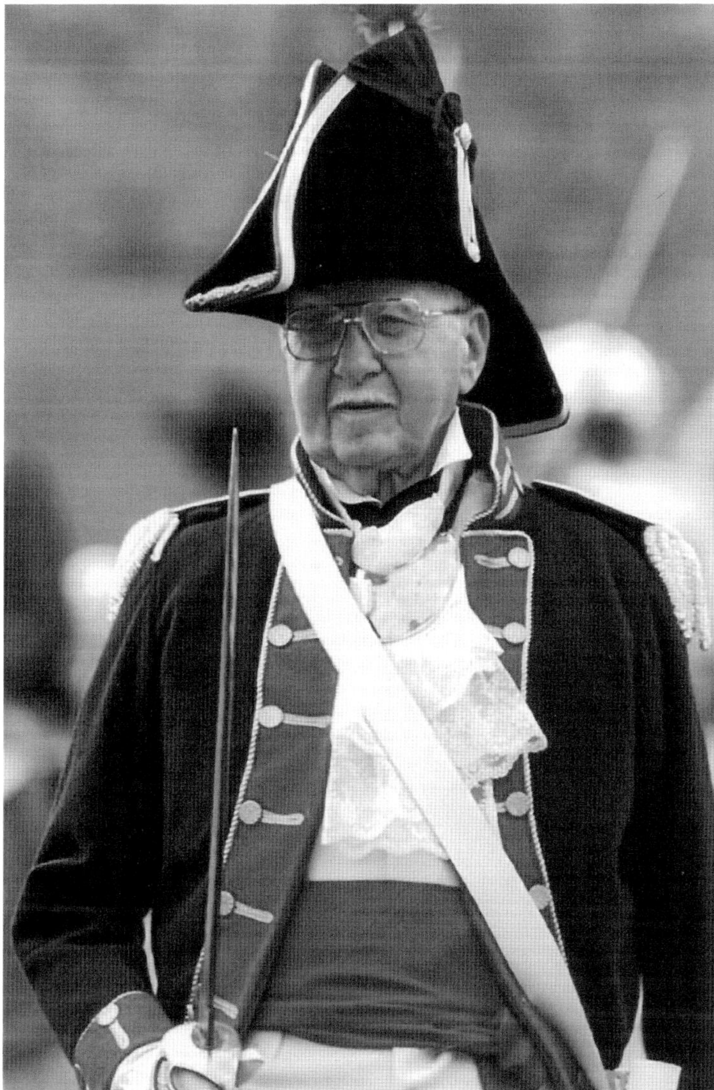

John Dengler

John Dengler owned and operated John Dengler Tobacconist, Inc., established by his father in 1917 in downtown St. Louis. It is believed to be the oldest continuous family-owned tobacco shop west of the Mississippi River. He moved his business to St. Charles in 1972 and became immersed in the preservation of buildings and traditions of the South Main Historic District. Dengler gave tours of South Main Street and served as president of the South Main Preservation Society in 1978 and 1979. He served on many professional organizations, committees, and boards. From 1987 to 1989, he was chairman of the Civil War Living History Days. He also founded the Lewis & Clark Fife and Drum Corps in 1992. Some of Dengler's recognitions include a William T. Kemper Foundation Community Service Award, the St. Charles County Chamber of Commerce Lifetime Distinguished Service Award, a Guardsman Award from the Departments of Army and Air Force for patriotic service, the Veterans of Foreign Wars 17th Annual Americanism Award, and the City of St. Charles second annual Discovery Award for "leadership in community progress." In addition, he was the first recipient of the Missouri Heritage Award. (Courtesy of Larry Muench at John Dengler Tobacconist.)

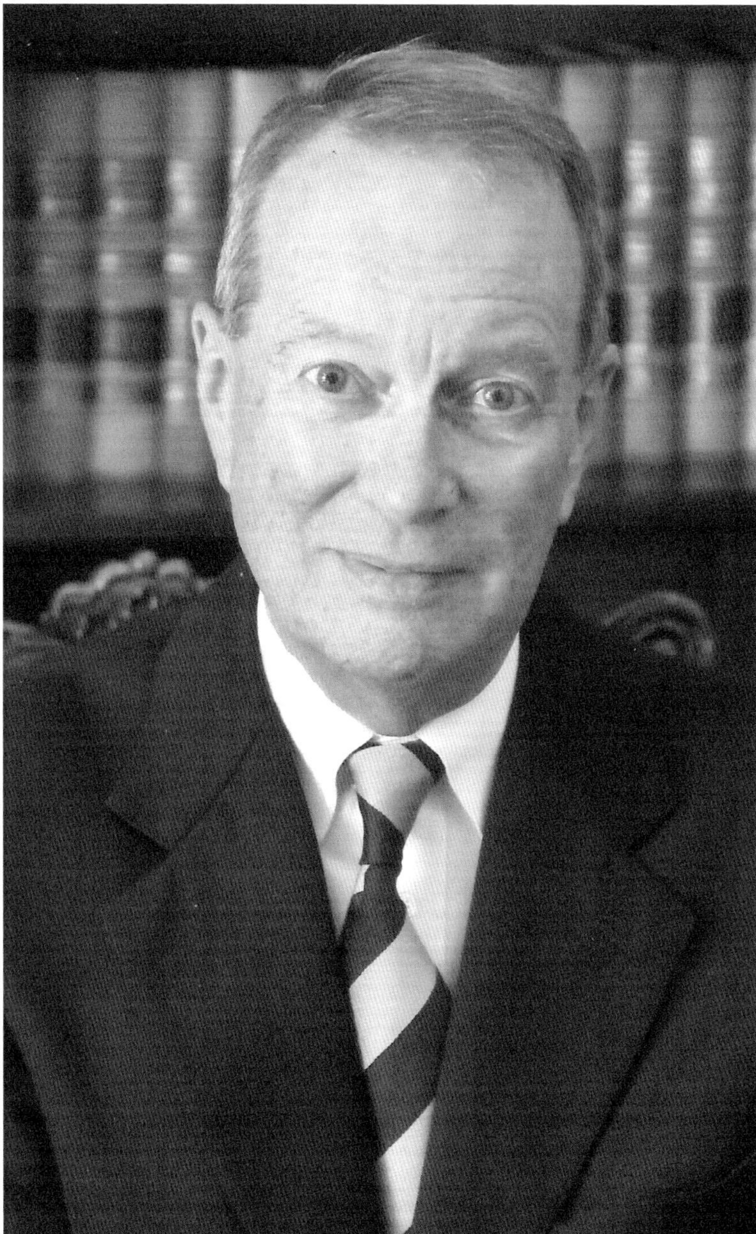

Keith Hazelwood

Keith Hazelwood is a partner at Hazelwood & Weber, LLC, in St. Charles. His practice deals with real estate matters, both transactions and actions before government agencies. He has for several years been selected by his peers as one of "The Best Lawyers in America." In 2014, he received the Best Lawyers' 2014 St. Louis Land Use and Zoning Law "Lawyer of the Year" award. Hazelwood's many civic activities have included serving on the St. Charles County Charter Commission, the board of the St. Louis Zoo, the Discovery Expedition of St. Charles, St. Louis 2004, FOCUS St. Louis, and St. Louis RCGA. The St. Charles County Chamber of Commerce awarded Hazelwood the 2004 Lifetime Distinguished Service Award and named him a 2008 Citizen of the Years. (Courtesy of Keith Hazelwood.)

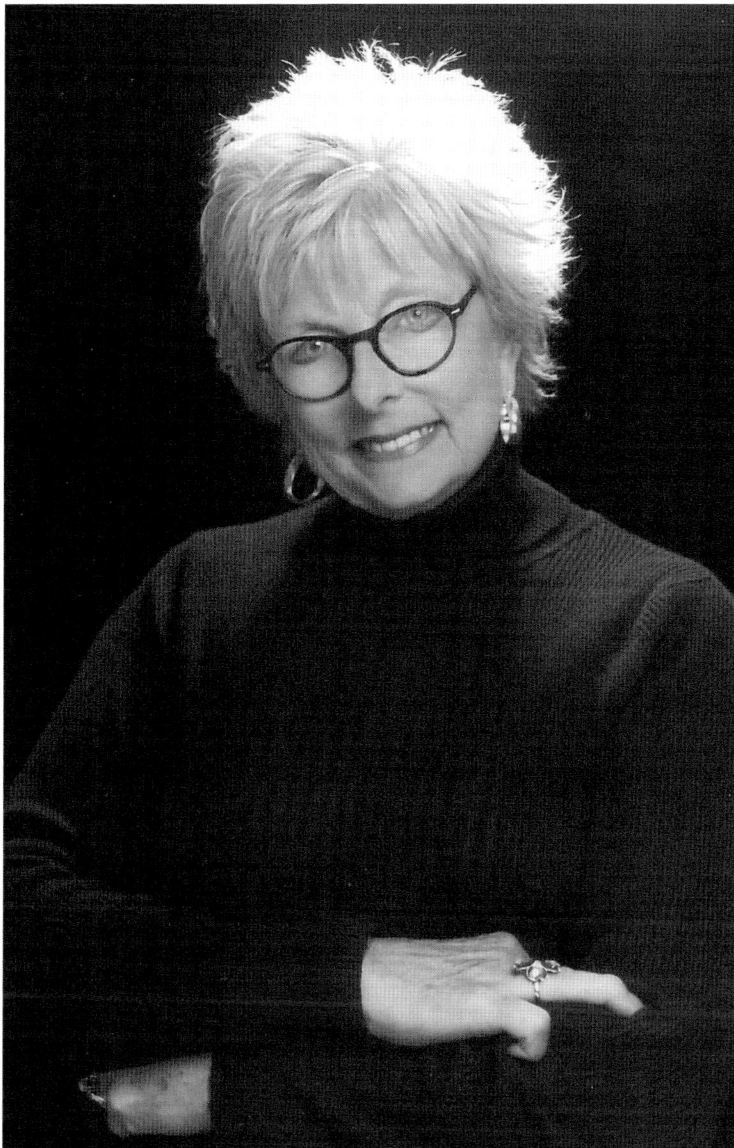

Ann Hazelwood

Ann Hazelwood first began making contributions to St. Charles as a preservationist, restoring a house on Main Street and serving as the president of South Main Preservation Society. In 1979, she opened Patches, Etc., operating three shops at one point. She is a certified quilt appraiser and served as the president of the National Quilt Museum. Her recognitions include Small Business Person of the Year, Retailer of the Year, and the St. Charles County Chamber of Commerce Lifetime Distinguished Service Award. She has served on the city and county's Economic Development Center (EDC) boards and the city's tourism commission. Hazelwood chaired the charter review commission under Mayor Robert Moeller and has served as president of the St. Charles County Chamber of Commerce. She and her husband, Keith Hazelwood, are the only married couple to have both served as chamber president. Ann's greatest passion has been writing, from Missouri travel books to a fiction series that features St. Charles. (Courtesy of Ann Hazelwood.)

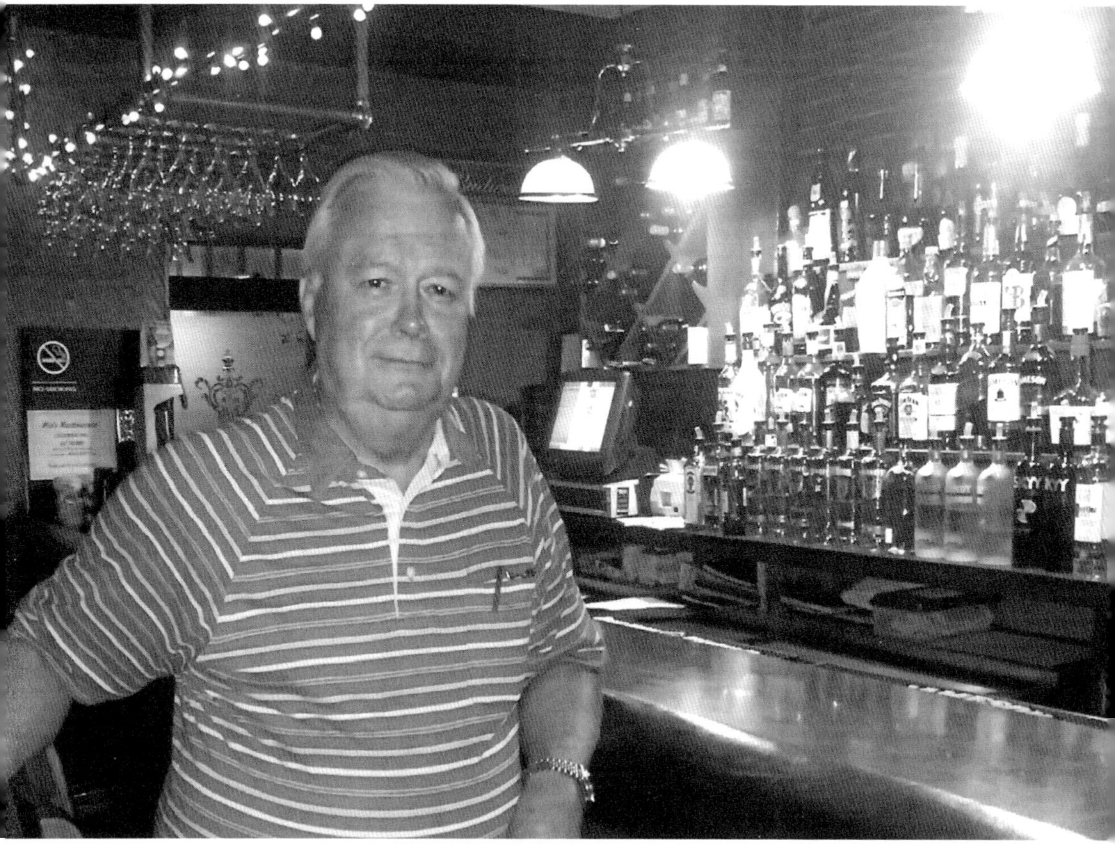

Ernie Dempsey

Ernie Dempsey arrived from Birmingham, Alabama, in November 1963 to work for McDonnell Douglas. He rented an apartment in St. Charles and began filling in as bartender at Pio's Restaurant. In 1970, Dempsey became Pio Pedrucci's partner, and in 1975, when Pedrucci retired, he became owner. Pio's is also where Dempsey first met his wife, Pedrucci's daughter Peggy. Dempsey said that when he first saw Peggy walk across the room at Pio's, he said, "I'm going to marry her." The couple was married for 47 years until Peggy's passing. Dempsey has served several years on the boards of the Boys and Girls Clubs and United Services and was chairman of the public works board for 17 years. Along with business partners, he has developed several properties, including the Columns Banquet Center, now owned by SSM. In 1994, Dempsey was the St. Charles County Chamber of Commerce Citizen of the Years. He served as a Missouri delegate to the Republican National Convention in New York City in 2004. (Photograph by author.)

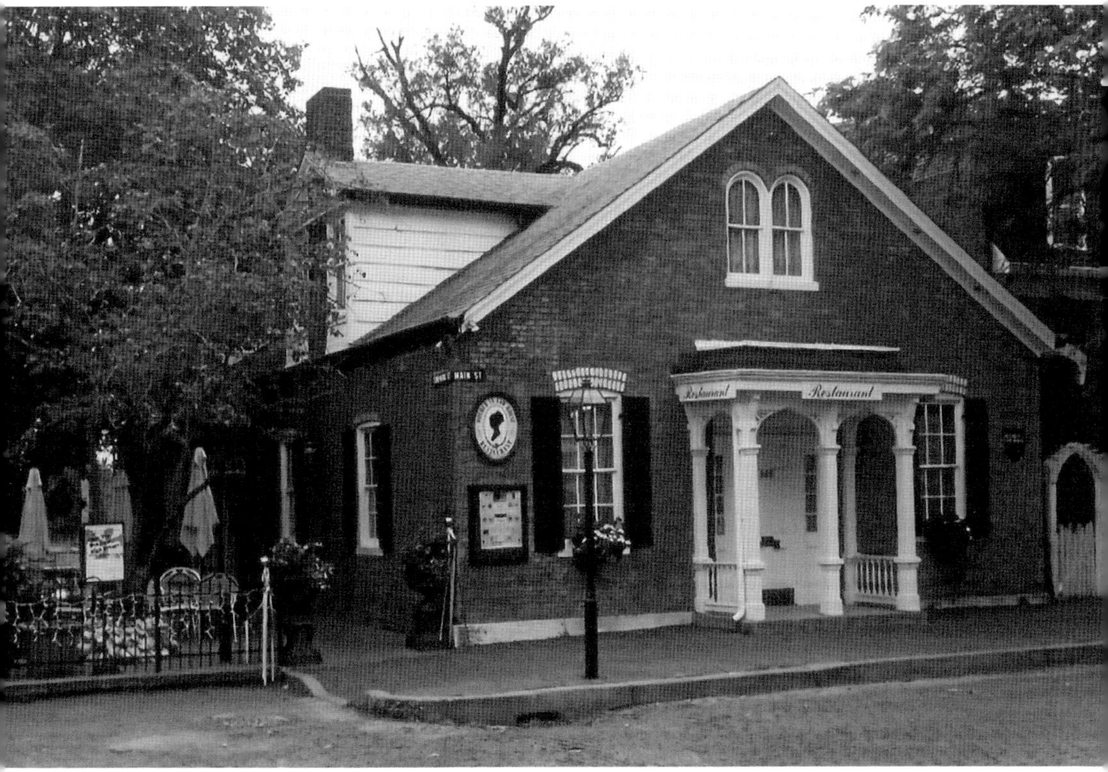

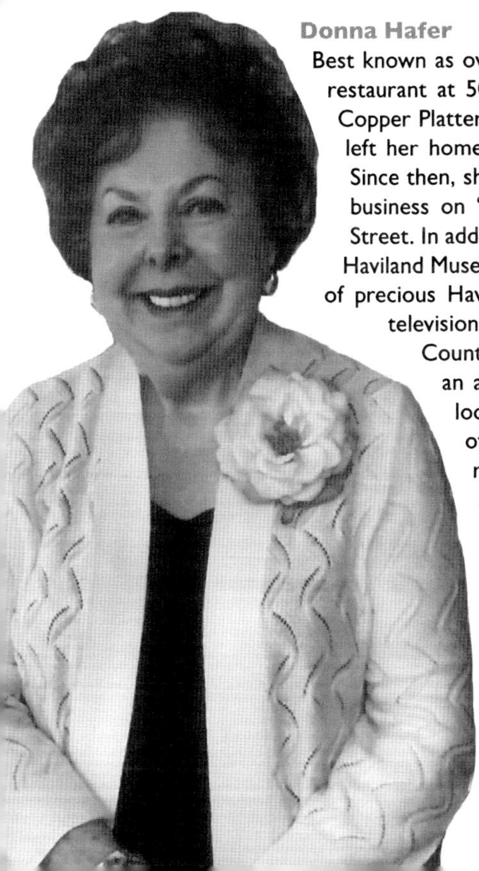

Donna Hafer

Best known as owner since 1981 of the popular Mother-in-Law House restaurant at 500 South Main Street, Donna Hafer also owned the Copper Platter restaurant on Main Street. As a young woman, Hafer left her home in Gillespie, Illinois, to attend Lindenwood College. Since then, she has done many things, including running an antiques business on "Stone Row" and restoring buildings on South Main Street. In addition to Mother-in-Law House (above), Hafer owns the Haviland Museum, 625 South Main Street, which displays many pieces of precious Haviland china. In 2008, Hafer appeared on the reality television show *Farmer Wants a Wife*, set in north St. Charles County. In one episode, Hafer taught women how to bake an apple pie. The Mother-In-Law House was also a date location on the show. A strong believer in the preservation of the historic district, Donna Hafer has received many recognitions, including a Lifetime Distinguished Service Award from the St. Charles County Chamber of Commerce in 1991. (Both photographs by author.)

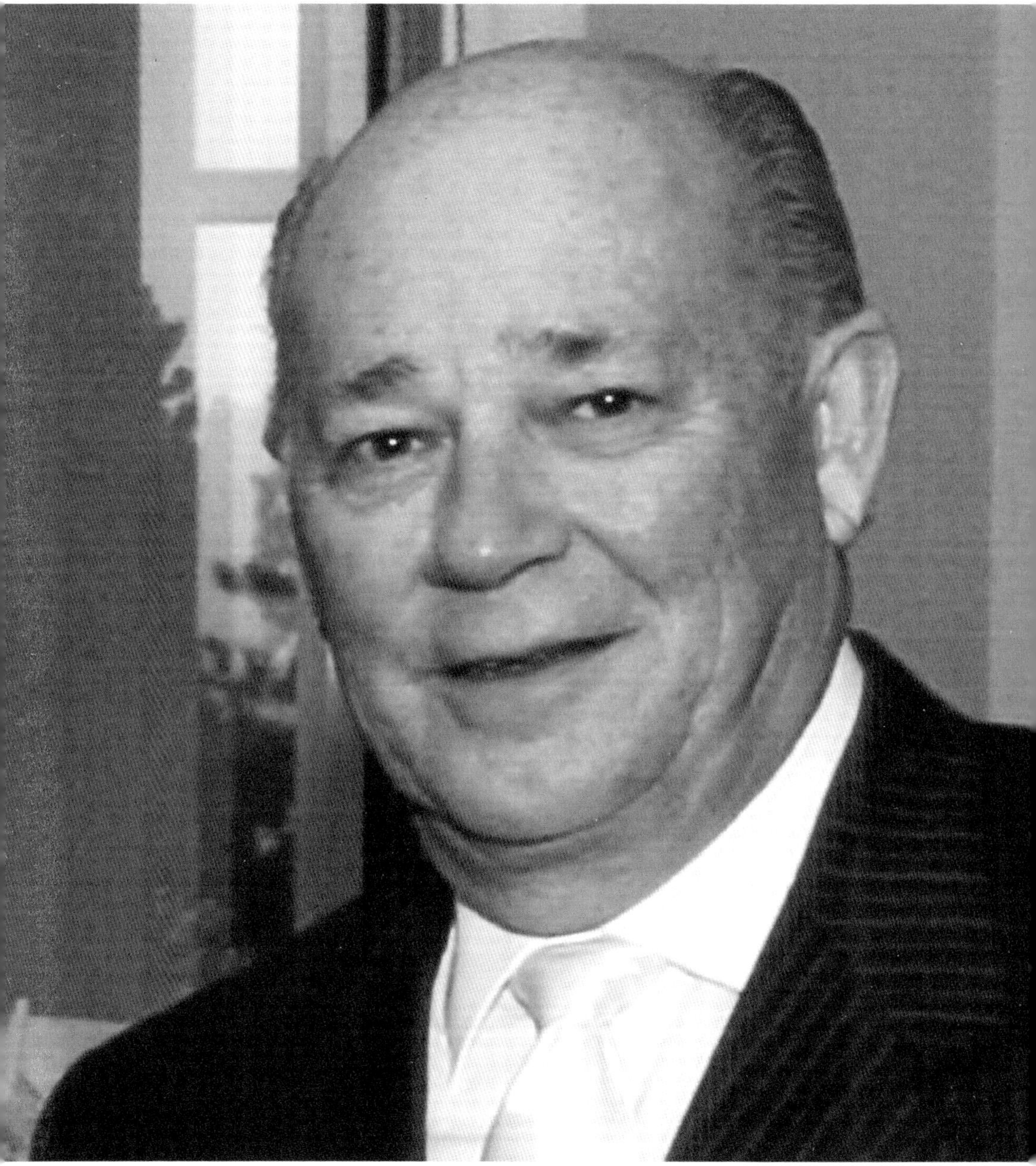

Jerry Scheidegger

Chairman of the board of Corporate Group, Inc., Jerry Scheidegger has served as a volunteer and board member for many community organizations, including St. Charles Goodfellows (president), the advisory board of Salvation Army, Bridgeway Behavioral Health, and William Woods University Parents Association. He has also served on the legal board and as chairman of the advisory board of Midwest BankCentre and the community board of Barnes-Jewish St. Peters Hospital and on the board at Lindenwood University. The J. Scheidegger Center for the Arts, Lindenwood's 138,000-square-foot fine-arts center, was named in recognition of his contributions to the institution. The St. Charles County Chamber of Commerce named Scheidegger Citizen of the Years in 2012. (Courtesy of Lindenwood University.)

CHAPTER FOUR

Government Leaders

In the more than 200 years since its settlement, St. Charles has had its share of dedicated government officials. The area's first commandant was Louis Blanchette, when the village was under Spanish rule, followed by Don Carlos Tayon and Don Santiago MacKay. When Missouri became a state, St. Charles was designated the temporary first state capital until the construction of the permanent capitol in Jefferson City was completed. This brought legends like Thomas Hart Benton and Alexander McNair to the area.

Edward Bates lived here, studied to become a lawyer, passed the bar, and later served as attorney general of the United States under Pres. Abraham Lincoln.

St. Charles has had its share of legendary mayors, too, such as Ludwell Powell, St. Charles's first elected mayor; Henry Vogt, a popular mayor and citizen; and Grace Nichols, the first woman to serve in that role in St. Charles. Of note also are Nathaniel Simonds, who came to St. Charles in 1801 from Vermont and served as state treasurer of Missouri from 1821 to 1829. Matthew Pitsch, a member of the Arkansas House of Representatives, has lived in several cities, including briefly in St. Charles.

Tom Dempsey also deserves mention. He spent several years in public office, serving in both the Missouri State House of Representatives and the Missouri State Senate. His service to the people of St. Charles is both noted and appreciated.

Alexander McNair

The first governor of Missouri when the state's first capitol was in St. Charles, McNair was born in Lancaster, Pennsylvania, on May 5, 1775. He attended the University of Pennsylvania, but he was forced to withdraw without completing his studies after the death of his father. McNair was commissioned first lieutenant in the Provisional Army in 1799 and moved to Missouri in 1803. His first foray into politics was as sheriff of St. Louis County and then US marshal of the Missouri Territory in 1814. During the War of 1812, McNair was the adjutant and inspector of the Missouri territorial forces. When Missouri gained statehood in 1821, McNair was elected the state's first governor, on August 28, 1820. While the capitol was being constructed in Jefferson City, at about the center of the state, several cities were considered for the honor of hosting the temporary capitol. St. Charles promised free meeting space if it was chosen. After being selected, the city was also the residence of Gov. Alexander McNair until 1824, when he completed his term and later accepted an appointment as the US agent to the Osage.

McNair died on March 18, 1826, and is buried in Calvary Cemetery in St. Louis. McNair Park in St. Charles is named for its famous resident, Missouri's first governor. (Courtesy of St. Charles County Historical Society.)

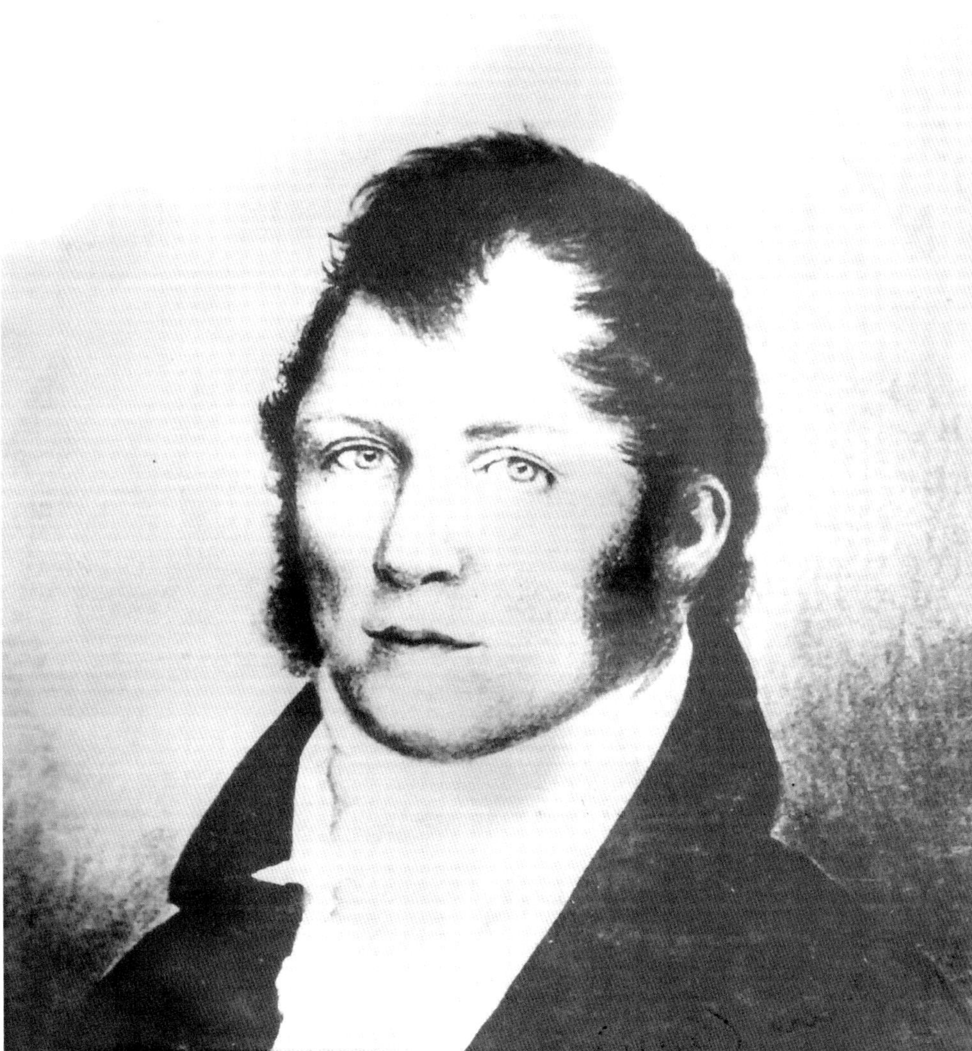

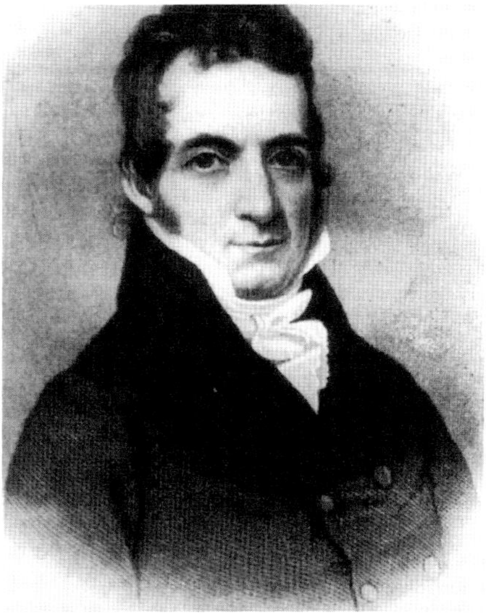

Rufus Easton

Born in Connecticut, Rufus Easton moved to St. Louis in 1803 to practice law. He was appointed judge of the Territory of Louisiana in 1805 by Thomas Jefferson, and he served as the first postmaster of St. Louis the same year. In 1821, when Missouri became a state, Easton was appointed attorney general. His daughter Mary Easton Sibley is known as the founder of Lindenwood College. Rufus Easton is buried at the cemetery on the Lindenwood campus. (Courtesy of St. Charles County Historical Society.)

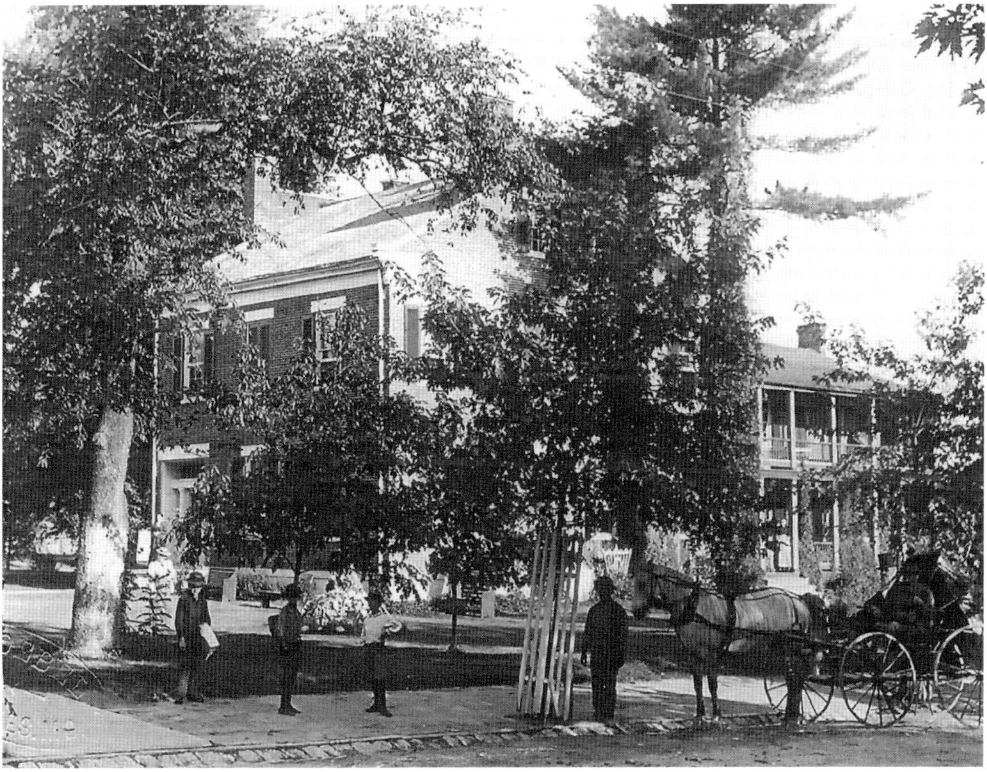

Ludwell Powell

In 1849, St. Charles was incorporated as a city, and on May 7 of that year, the first elections were held. Col. Ludwell E. Powell was elected mayor. A respected judge who had organized volunteers from St. Charles County during the Mexican War, Powell bought the land for the government that would become the site of Fort Kearney in Nebraska. Seen here is the home at Sixth and Jefferson Streets built for Colonel Powell when he was mayor. It later became the home of Dr. Charles Montgomery Johnson (see page 21). (Courtesy of St. Charles County Historical Society.)

Edward Bates

Edward Bates was the US attorney general under President Lincoln from 1861 to 1864. After serving in the War of 1812, Bates studied law with Rufus Easton and boarded with his family. He later became Easton's partner after passing the bar. In 1817, Bates and Easton organized the James Ferry, which ran from St. Charles to Alton, Illinois. (Courtesy of Library of Congress, LC-DIG-cwpb-05606.)

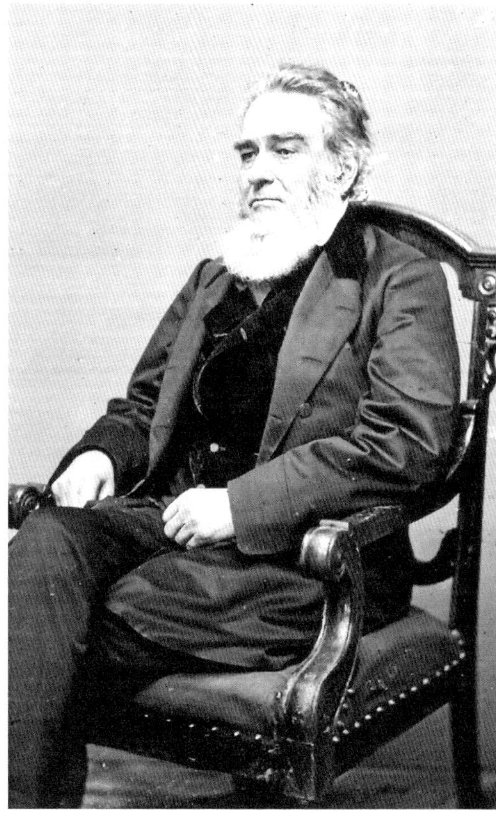

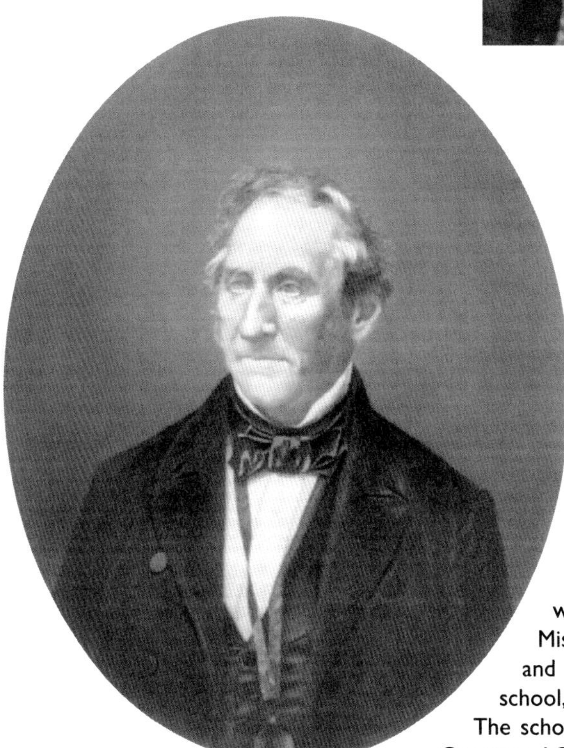

Thomas Hart Benton

Between 1821 and 1826, when St. Charles was Missouri's first capital, Benton was a Missouri senator. Benton School, built in 1896 and the St. Charles School District's oldest school, was named in Senator Benton's honor. The school closed in 2007. (Courtesy of Library of Congress, LC-USZ62-71877.)

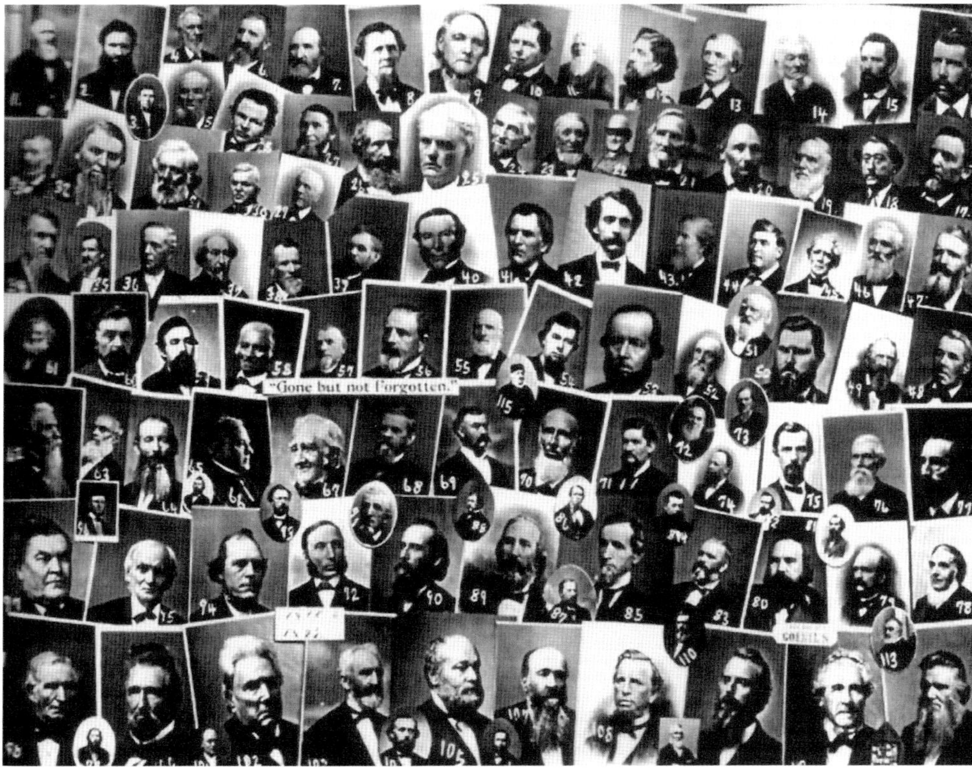

Arnold Krekel

A colonel in the Missouri State Militia, Arnold Krekel was the editor of the *Demokrat* newspaper and led the Radicals in St. Charles County during the Civil War. Pres. Abraham Lincoln appointed Krekel federal district judge in 1865. Colonel Krekel is pictured in this image, titled "Leading Business Men of St. Charles, Gone But Not Forgotten, 1860–1899." He is No. 103, in the bottom row, sixth from left. Edward Gut (see page 23) is No. 37, and Ezra Overall (see page 28) is No. 107. (Courtesy of St. Charles County Historical Society.)

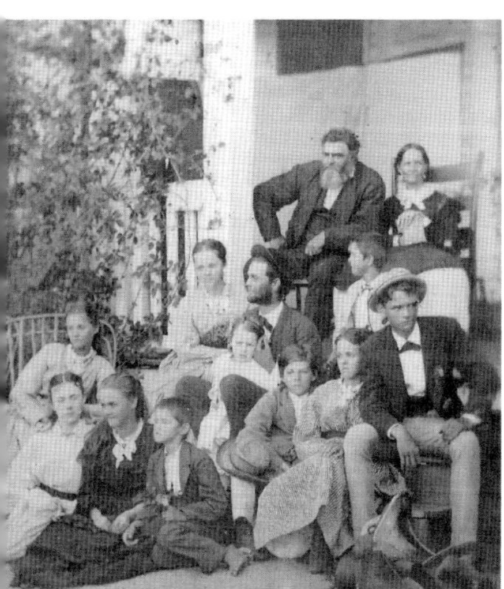

Barton Bates

The son of Edward Bates (see page 98), President Lincoln's attorney general, Barton Bates was a Union supporter during the Civil War, but he owned slaves. He was appointed and elected to the Missouri Supreme Court. Here, Colonel Bates (top row) poses with his family around 1872. (Courtesy of St. Charles County Historical Society.)

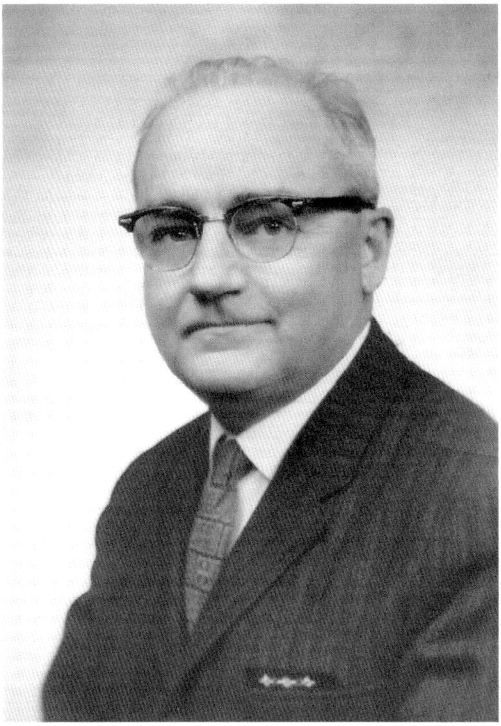

Henry Vogt

As mayor of St. Charles (1951–1958 and 1963–1970), Vogt oversaw projects related to hospital expansion, urban renewal, and historic preservation. Henry and his brother Bud founded the St. Charles Golf Course, which is now the site of a residential development and Vogt Brothers Park. Henry Vogt received the St. Charles County Chamber of Commerce Citizen of the Years award in 1967. Below, Vogt (center) is pictured at the St. Charles Police Department with Clifford Amrein (left), being sworn in, and former mayor Frank Brockgreitens. (Both, courtesy of St. Charles County Historical Society.)

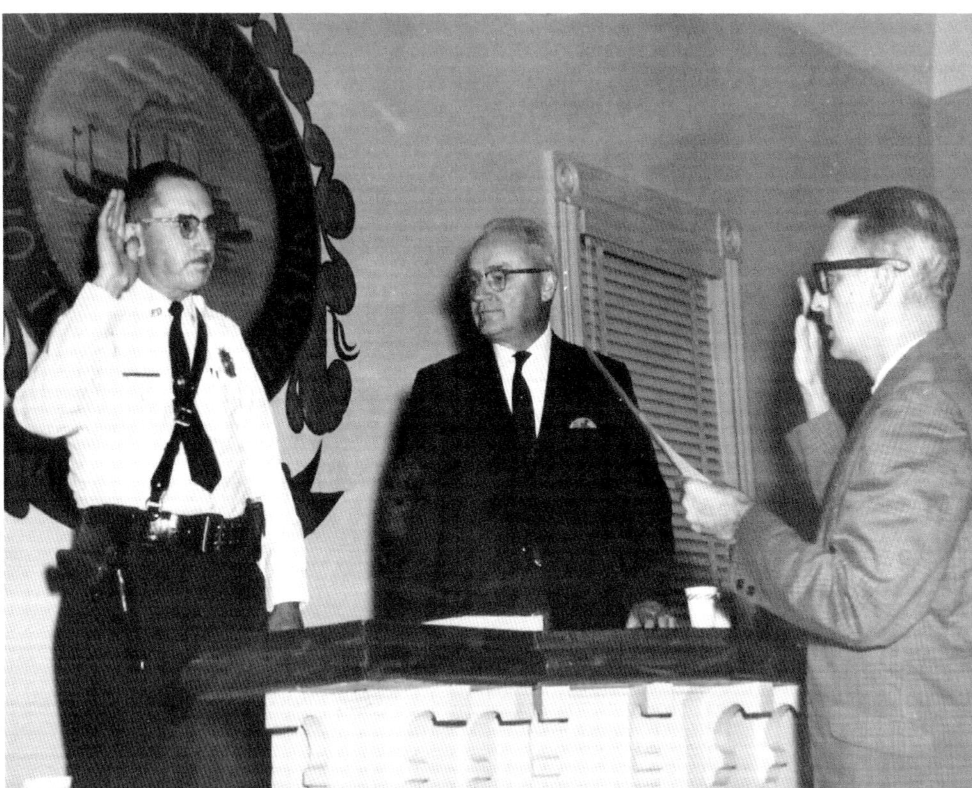

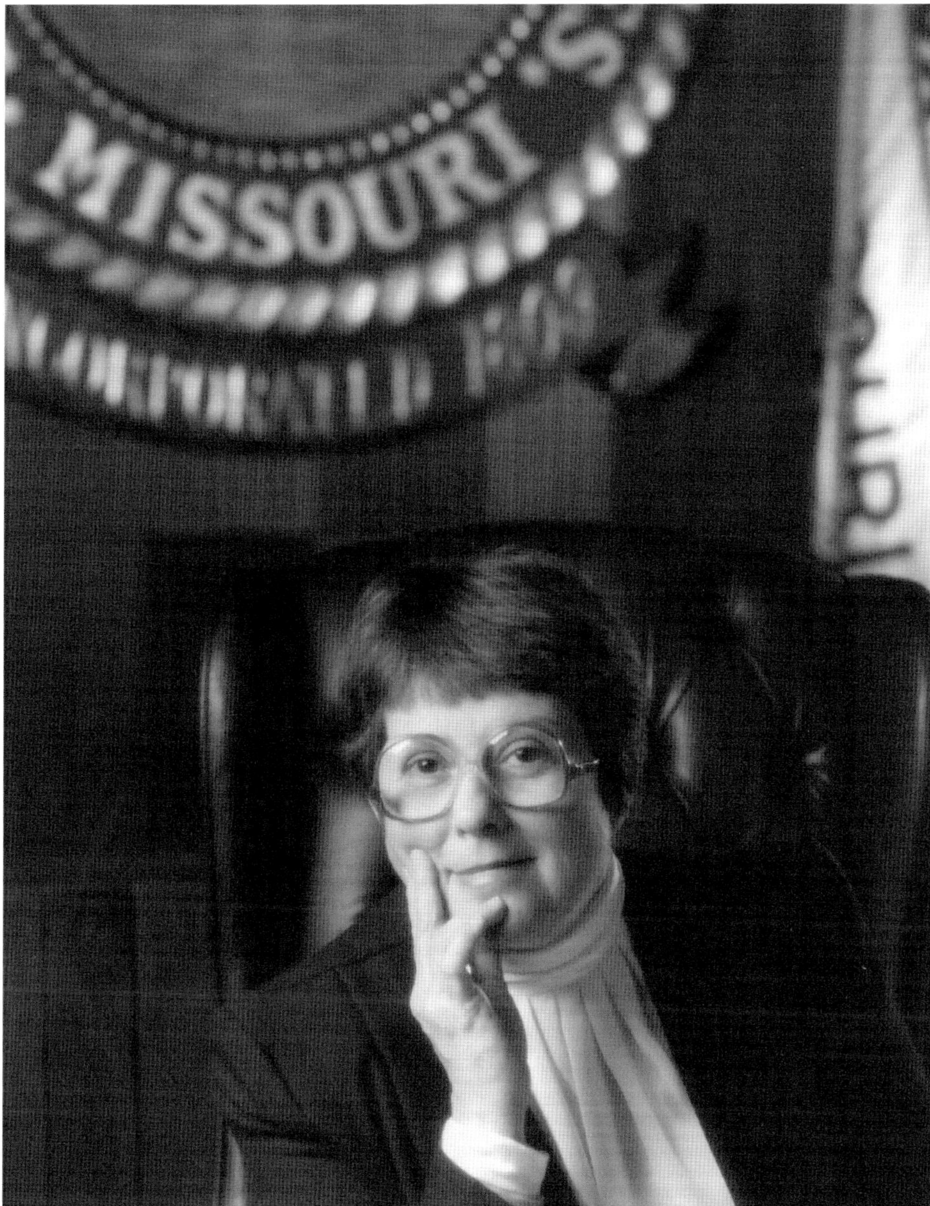

Grace Nichols

Grace Nichols owns the distinction of being the first female mayor of the city of St. Charles. She was elected in April 1987 and reelected in April 1991. Previously, she had practiced as a private attorney. She has served as chairperson of the public safety committee on the St. Charles City Council and as a member of the National League of Cities' community and economic development policy committee, the US Conference of Mayors' community development housing and economic development committee, the St. Charles County Bar Association, the Missouri Bar Association, the Illinois Bar Association, and many other organizations and committees. In 1998, the St. Charles County Chamber of Commerce awarded her the Lifetime Distinguished Service Award, and in 2007, she was named Citizen of the Years. (Courtesy of St. Charles County Historical Society; photograph by Michael Schlueter.)

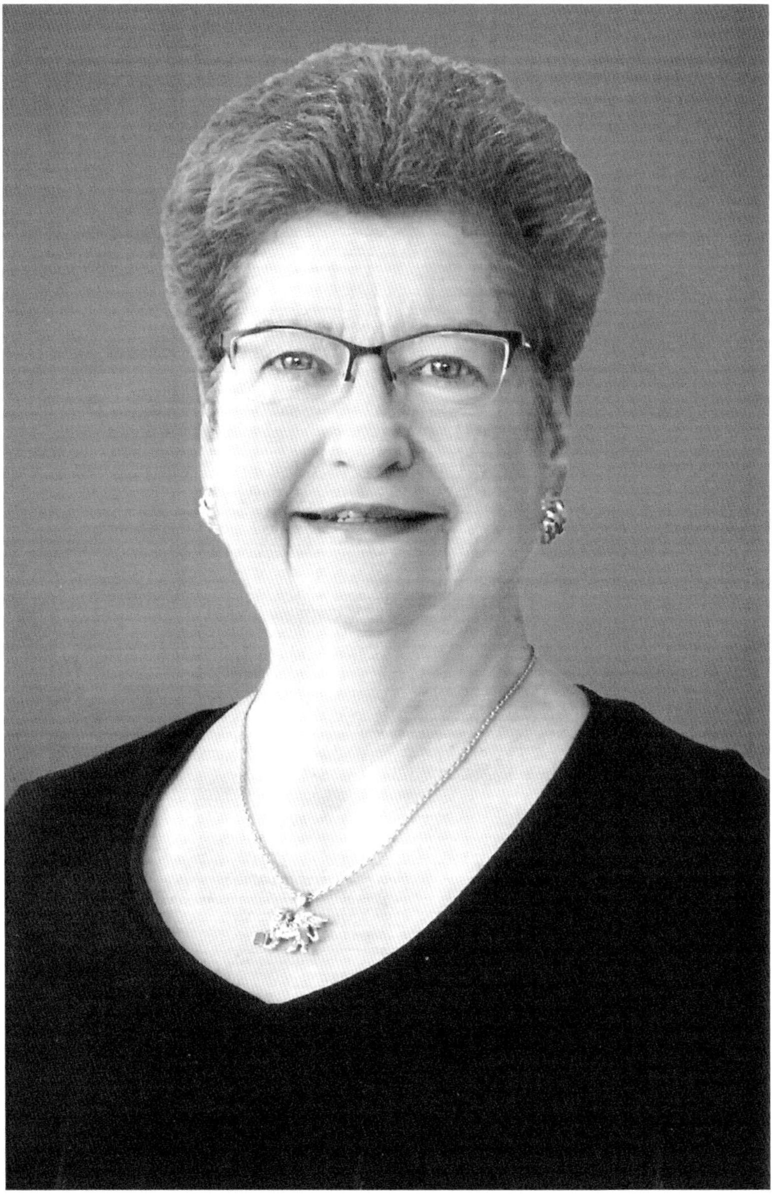

Lucy Rauch

Born and raised in St. Charles, Lucy Rauch was a member of the St. Charles County prosecuting attorney's office (1979–1982) and was elected to four-year terms as associate circuit judge in 1982, 1986, and 1990. She was appointed St. Charles County circuit judge in 1991 and elected to circuit judge in 1992 (by special election). She was reelected for six-year terms in 1994, 2000, and 2006, serving until her retirement in 2012. Rauch also served as presiding judge (1995–1998 and 2003–2004). Among the many committees and organizations she has served are the case processing time standards committee, the domestic relations committee, Salvation Army Advisory Board, Academy of the Sacred Heart Advisory Board, St. Charles County Bar Association, St. Charles Rotary Club, and Lindenwood University Board of Directors. Lucy Rauch was recognized by the St. Charles County Chamber of Commerce as a Citizen of the Years in 2014. (Courtesy of Lucy Rauch, photograph by Michael Schlueter.)

CHAPTER FIVE

Writers, Athletes, and Entertainers

A list of legendary and notable locals must, of course, include the musicians, athletes, entertainers, artists, and writers who make life so enjoyable. These are the people who give the public a respite from their everyday lives. They help broaden our perspectives and open our minds to new ideas. Of special note are Daniel Woodrell, award-winning novelist and author of *Winter's Bone*, and the many visual and performance artists who have displayed their work at Mosaics: Missouri Festival for the Arts and at the Foundry Art Center.

In the sports world, one St. Charles legendary local is football player Curtis Brown, who starred for St. Charles High School, went on to star at the University of Missouri, and then enjoyed a career in the National Football League. Another NFL player from St. Charles is Brandon Joyce. In addition to Mark Buehrle and Lou Brock, Major League Baseball is well represented with St. Charles athletes Tom Heintzelman, Dennis Tankersley, and Jacob Turner. Brett Gensler represents St. Charles in hockey. Connie Price-Smith is a legendary shot-putter, discus thrower, and four-time Olympian. Randy Orton is a legend in professional wrestling. St. Charles has also produced athletes who play in the National Basketball Association, such as Ryan Robertson and Josh Harrelson.

This chapter profiles the lives of many notable writers, athletes, musicians, and entertainers, from the world-famous Ambassadors of Harmony to the local band Serapis. These are the creative minds and talented people who brighten residents' days and make them proud to be from St. Charles.

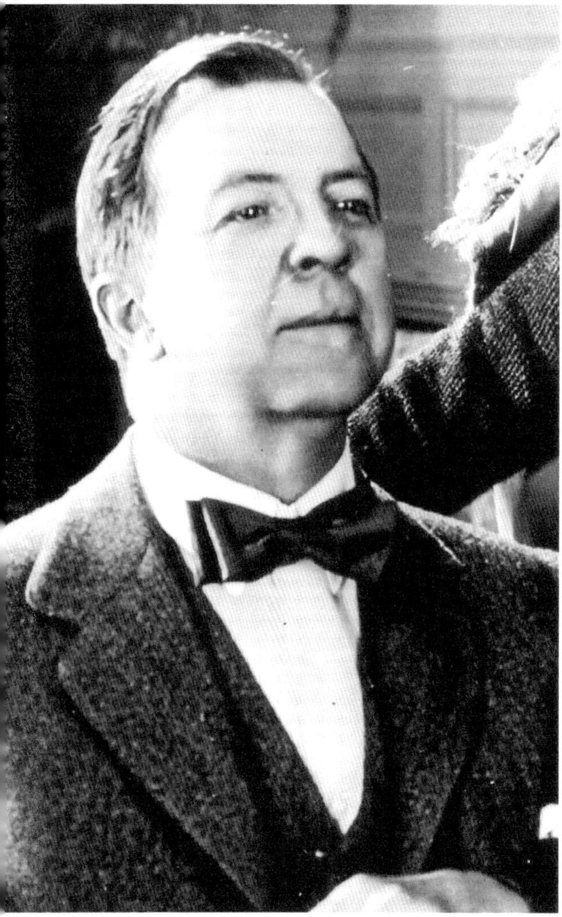

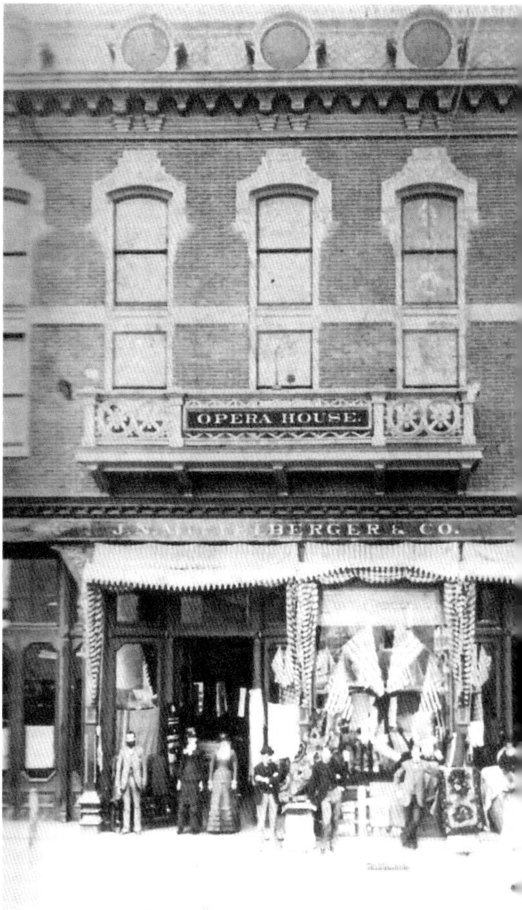

Rupert Hughes

Renowned author and playwright Rupert Hughes is believed to have written his first play in 1886 while attending St. Charles College. His brother Howard R. Hughes Sr., according to some records, was also a student at the school and starred in the play when it was performed at the St. Charles Opera House (right). Howard R. Hughes would later become best known as the father of tycoon Howard Hughes. (Both, courtesy of St. Charles County Historical Society.)

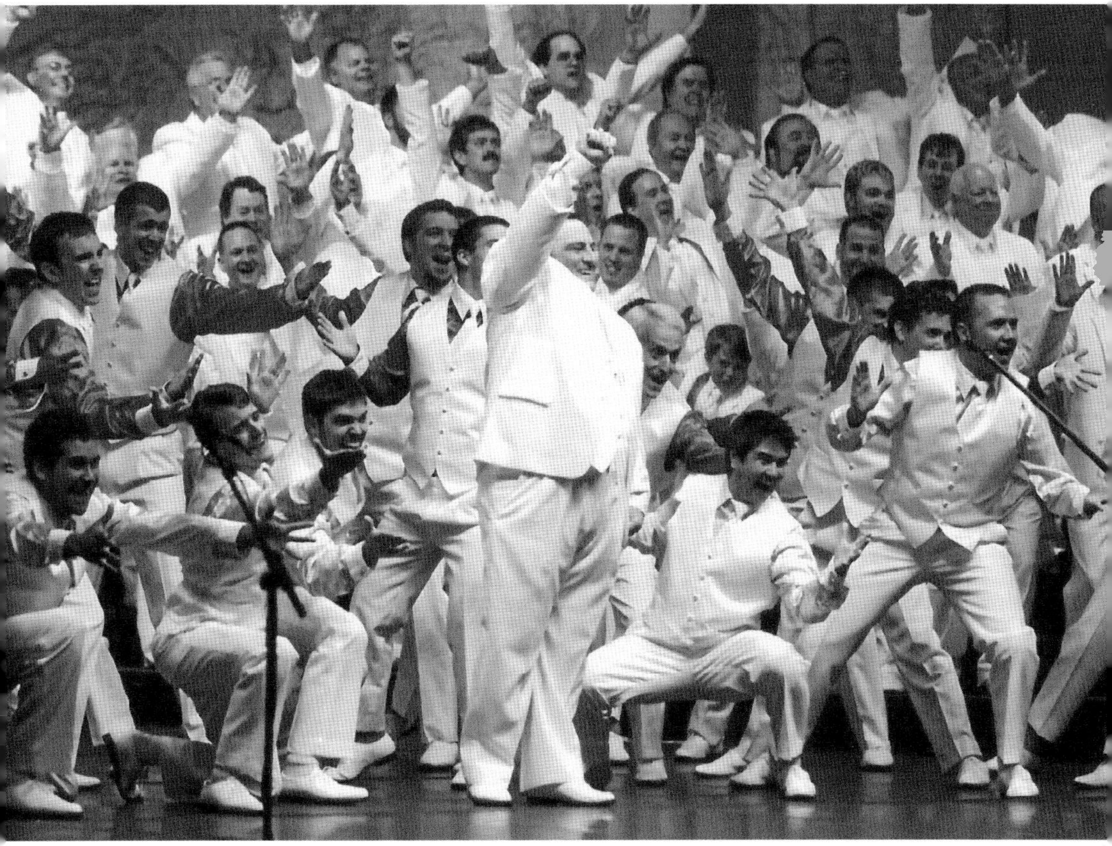

The Ambassadors of Harmony
The Daniel Boone Chorus was founded in 1963 in St. Charles. As it began winning competitions, the chorus renamed itself the Ambassadors of Harmony in 1991. Today, the men's a cappella chorus includes more than 160 voices and performs Broadway classics, barbershop, jazz, pop, and holiday favorites. Representing the St. Charles, Missouri, chapter of the Barbershop Harmony Society, the group has won three gold medals in the society's international contest and has performed across the United States and in England, Germany, Ireland, the Netherlands, and Sweden. (Courtesy of Barbershop Harmony Society, photograph by Lorin May.)

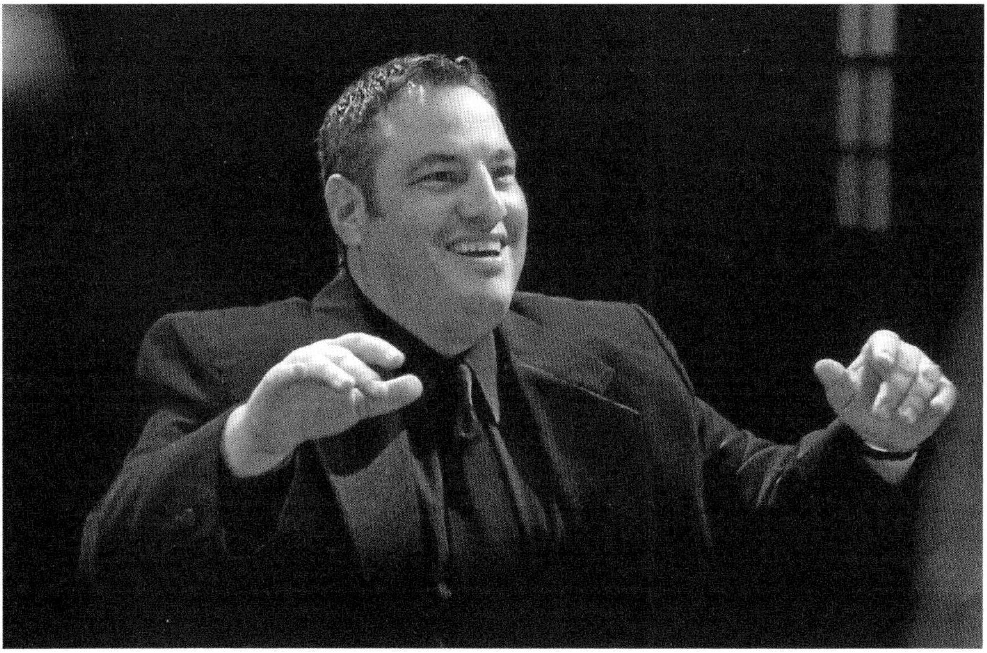

Jim Henry

Jim Henry, codirector of Ambassadors of Harmony, has led the chorus since 1990. He is the son of one of the early directors of the Daniel Boone Chorus, Bob Henry. A singer since childhood, Jim Henry is chair of the music department at the University of Missouri–St. Louis and holds a doctorate in music composition from Washington University. He also sings with Crossroads, the 2009 international champion quartet. The below photograph shows the Daniel Boone Chorus in 1964. The members are, from left to right, Lynn Broadfoot, Bob Mertins, John Forternberry, Bill Wallace, James Hamilton, John Flannagan, Bert Volker, Gordon Manion, Elmer Kemmery, Jerry Coen, Carl Daniels, Pat Murphy, and Doc Keough. (Above, courtesy of the Ambassadors of Harmony and University of Missouri–St. Louis Department of Music; below, courtesy of Ambassadors of Harmony.)

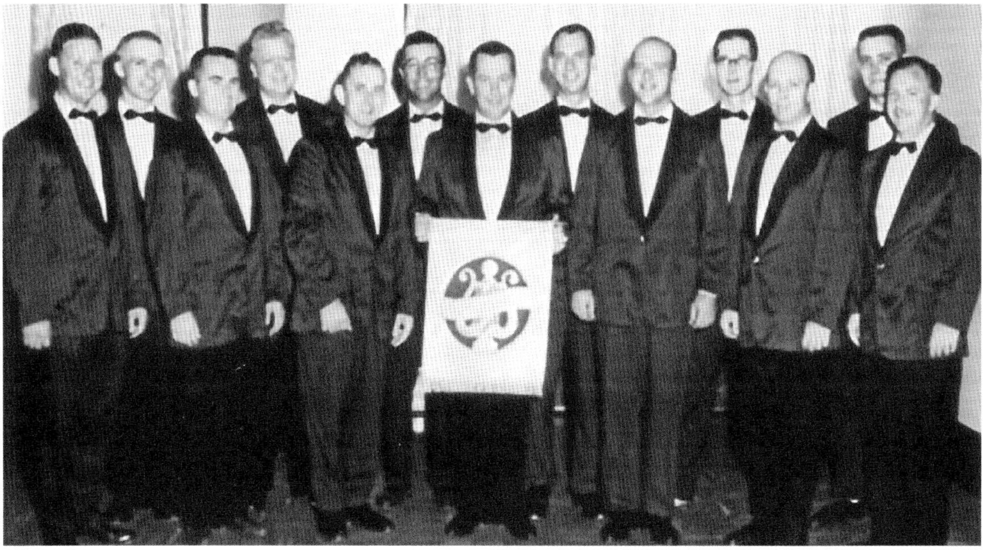

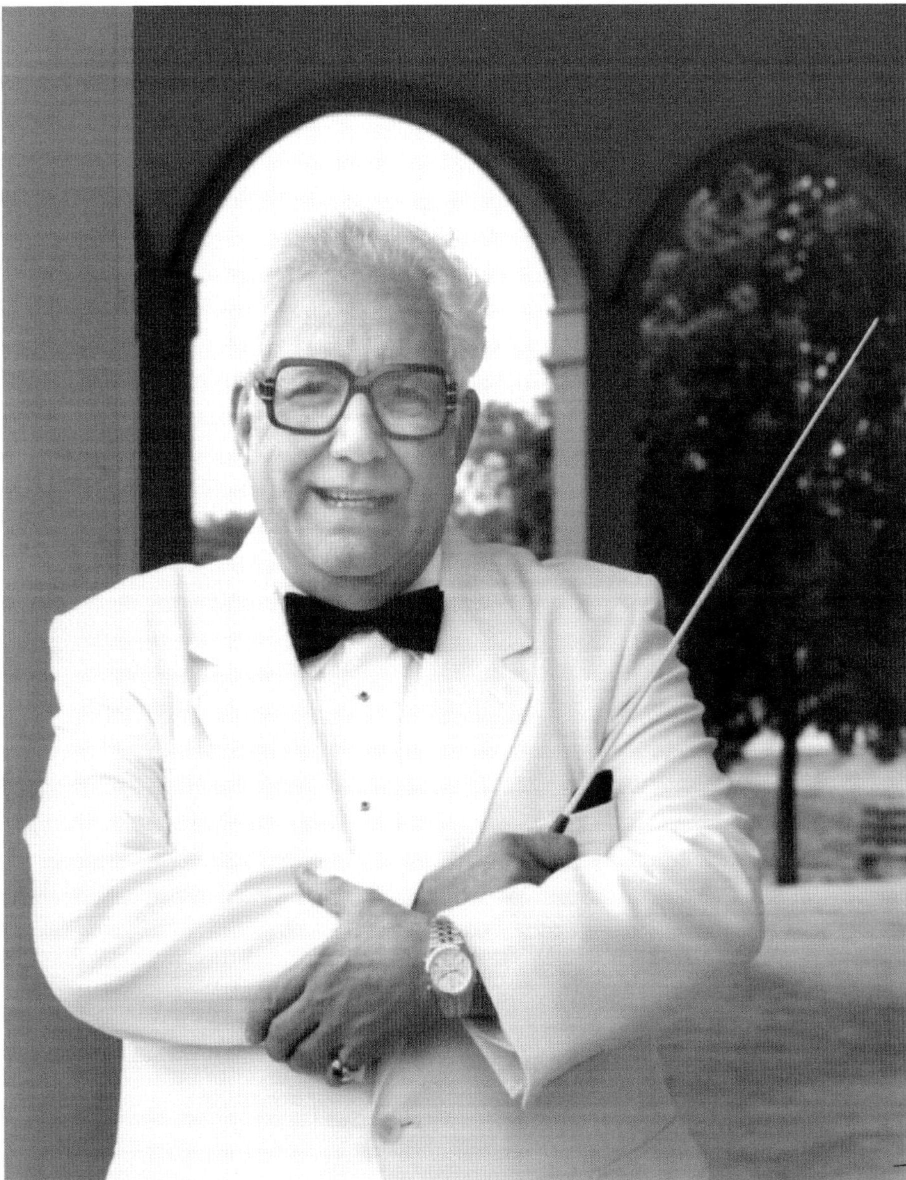

Marvin Hohman
Fondly remembered as "Mr. Music" by many St. Charlesans, Hohman studied music and earned a teaching certification through Harris Teachers' College in St. Louis. In the 1950s and 1960s, he conducted student bands in primary and secondary schools in St. Louis and St. Charles. In the 1960s and 1970s, he appeared throughout the St. Louis area with his Marvin Hohman Orchestra, a 16-piece big band, and as leader of smaller jazz combos, playing a wide range of social and dance music engagements. In the mid-1960s, Hohman moved to St. Charles, and from 1967 to 1999, he worked as a piano tuner/technician while operating a band instrument repair shop. For 20 years, he was conductor of the St. Charles Municipal Band. In 1992, the St. Charles County Chamber of Commerce awarded Marvin Hohman the Lifetime Distinguished Service Award. (Courtesy of St. Charles County Historical Society; photograph by Michael Schlueter.)

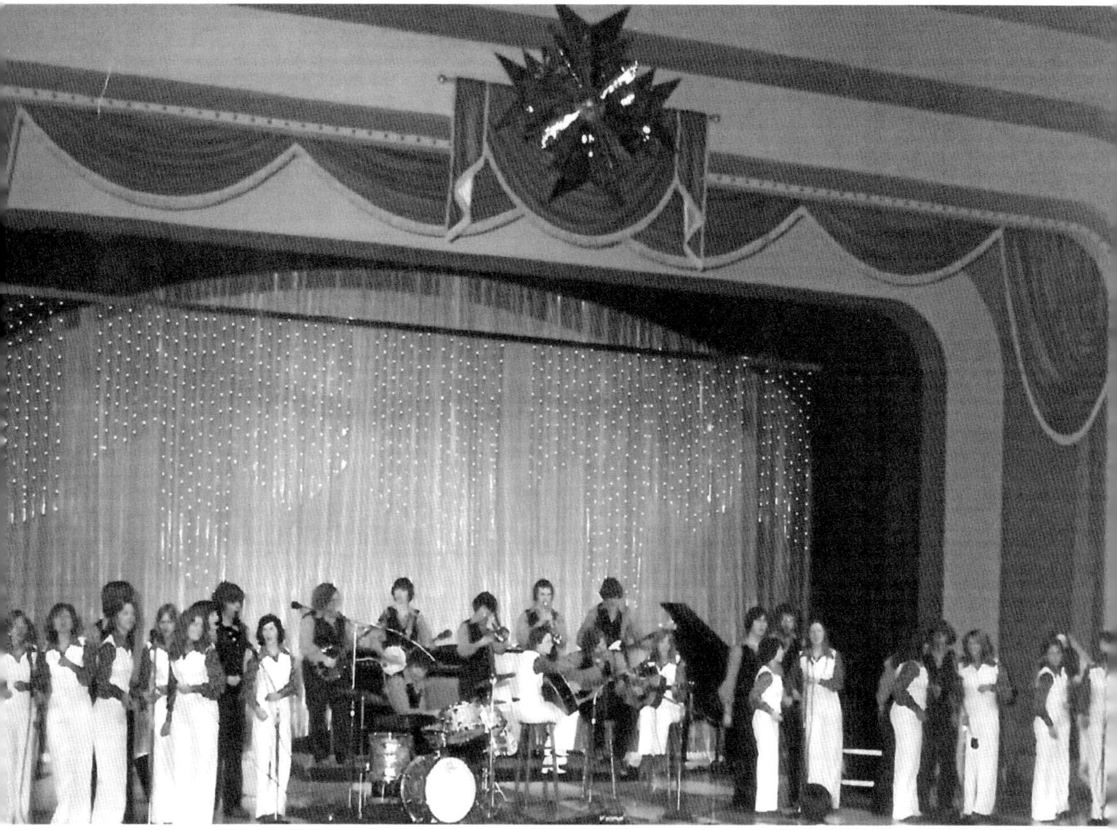

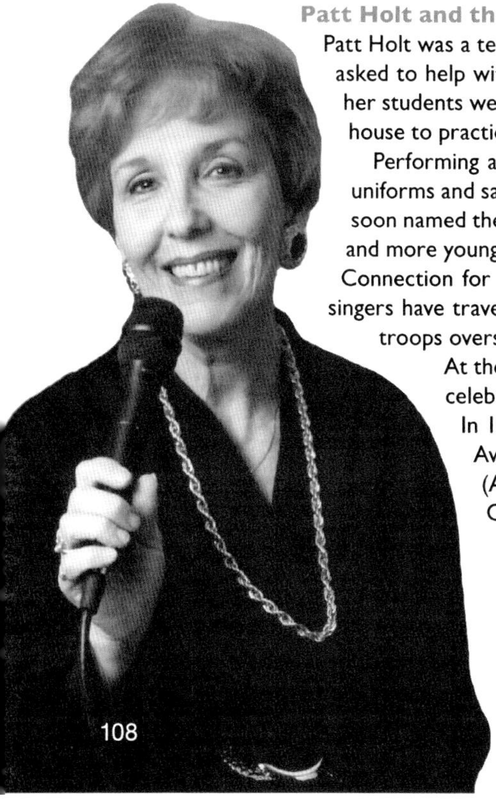

Patt Holt and the Patt Holt Singers

Patt Holt was a teacher at St. Charles Borromeo School in 1972 when she was asked to help with the music for a church service. But, when summer came, her students were not ready to quit singing, so she told them to come to her house to practice. The group became known as the Patt Holt Singers.

Performing at community fairs and fish fries, the teens wore hand-sewn uniforms and sang on the back of a flatbed truck. The chamber of commerce soon named the group "official ambassadors" for the city. As the group grew and more young adults became members, Holt developed other groups: The Connection for teens and Just Kids for younger singers. Today, Patt Holt's singers have traveled to Europe, Asia, and Africa and have performed for US troops overseas and for several American presidents.

At the group's 40th reunion in 2013, current and former members celebrated Holt as a teacher, mentor, and occasional matchmaker. In 1987, Patt Holt was awarded a Lifetime Distinguished Service Award from the St. Charles County Chamber of Commerce. (Above, courtesy of Todd Luerding; left, courtesy of St. Charles County Historical Society, photograph by Michael Schlueter.)

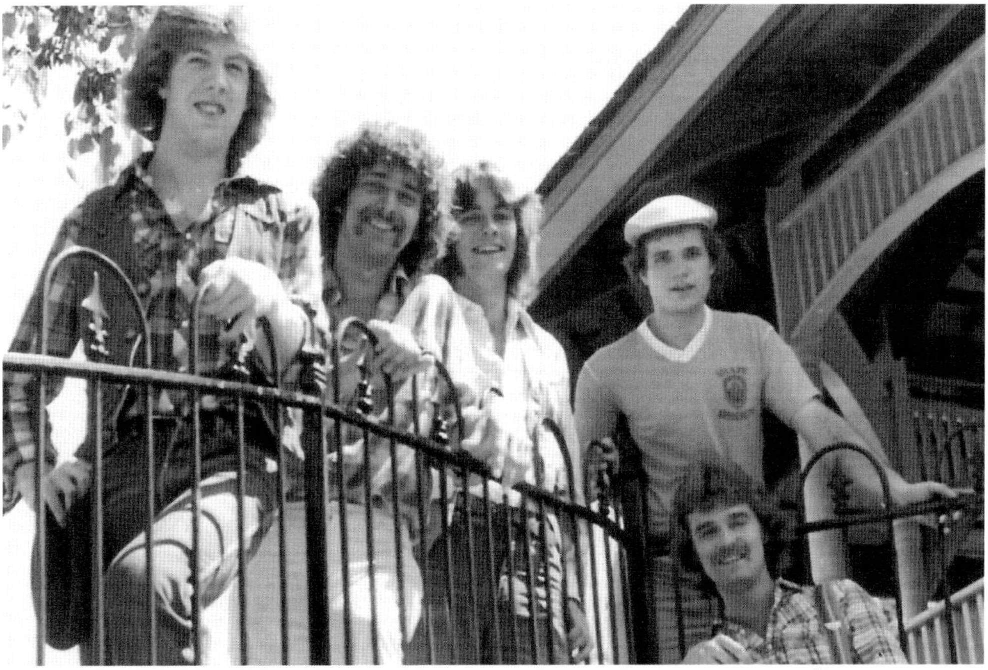

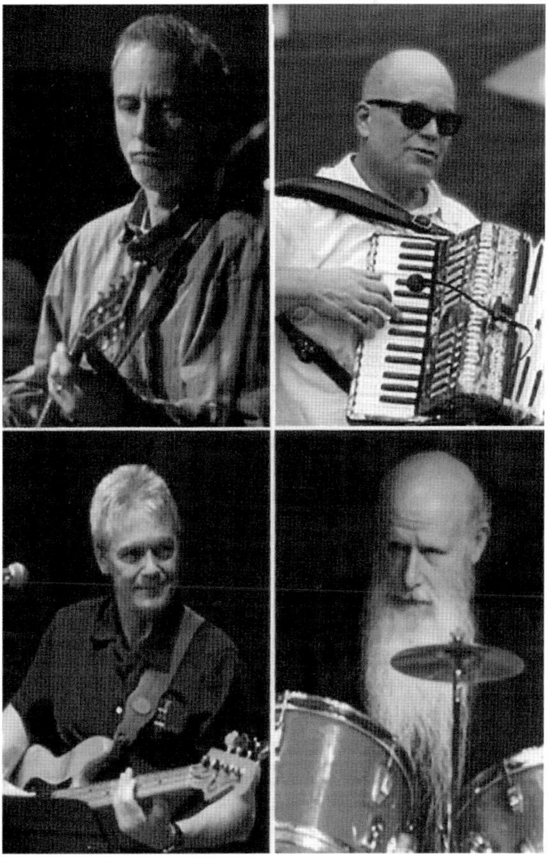

Serapis

One of St. Charles's longest-running and most popular local bands, Serapis has been together for more than 33 years. Todd Luerding, Gene Carroll, and Tony Chambers have known each other since their high school days in St. Charles. They formed Serapis in 1982, and Bob Gleason came aboard later. When not performing, Chambers is an award-winning photojournalist for KSDK in St. Louis. Luerding and Carroll work at St. Louis University, Luerding as a multimedia developer and Carroll as a technical director. Gleason owns Imagitrax. Some of the group's members are pictured above in a photograph from about 1981, when they called themselves Stone Mountain Band. They are, from left to right, Jonni Glaser (today a composer, arranger, and producer who has worked on Grammy-winning projects with major recording companies), Tony Chambers, Gene Carroll, Todd Luerding, and Steven Snyder. The photograph at right shows the band members today. They are, clockwise from upper left, Tony Chambers, Todd Luerding, Bob Gleason, and Gene Carroll. (Both, courtesy of Todd Luerding.)

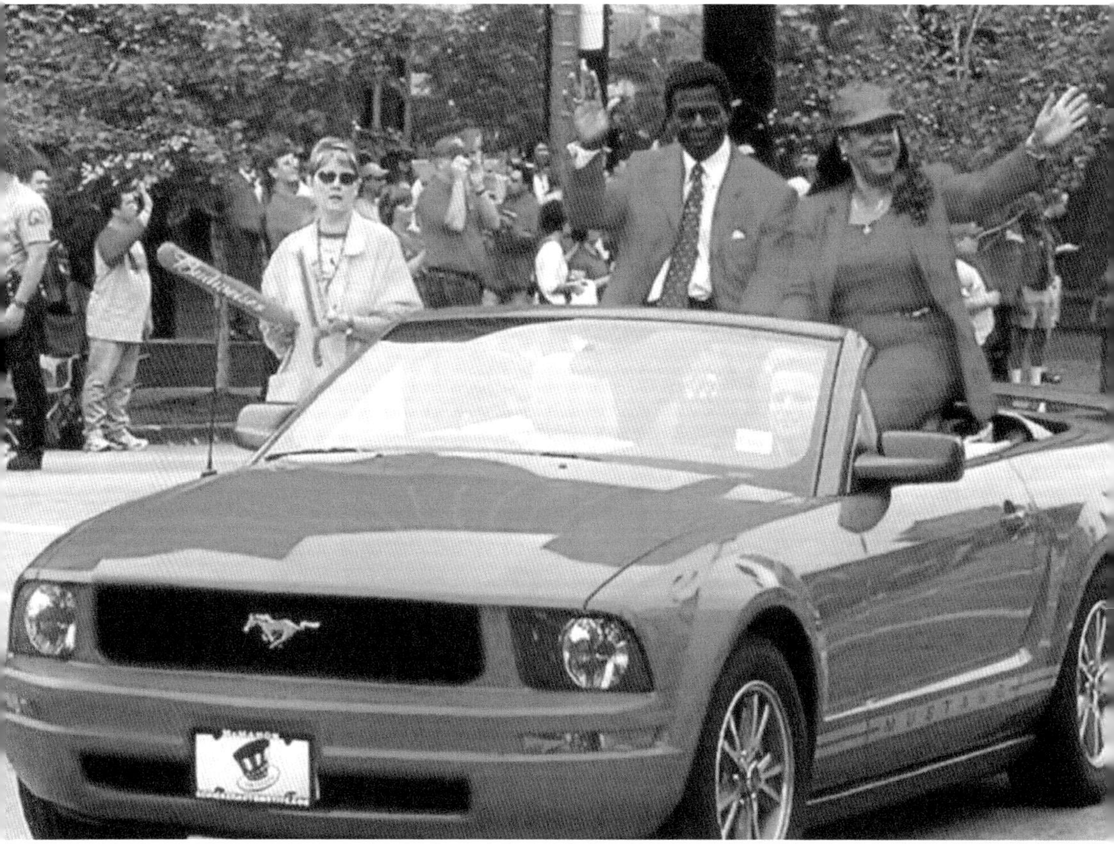

Lou Brock

Lou Brock is the only player in the history of Major League Baseball to have an award named for him while still an active player. A member of the National Baseball Hall of Fame, Brock, a former St. Louis Cardinal, was named one of MLB's Top 100 Players of the 20th Century. He and his wife live in St. Charles, and he is committed to many worthy causes. He is also a training instructor for the Cardinals. He is pictured here in October 2005. (Courtesy of Clayton Parker.)

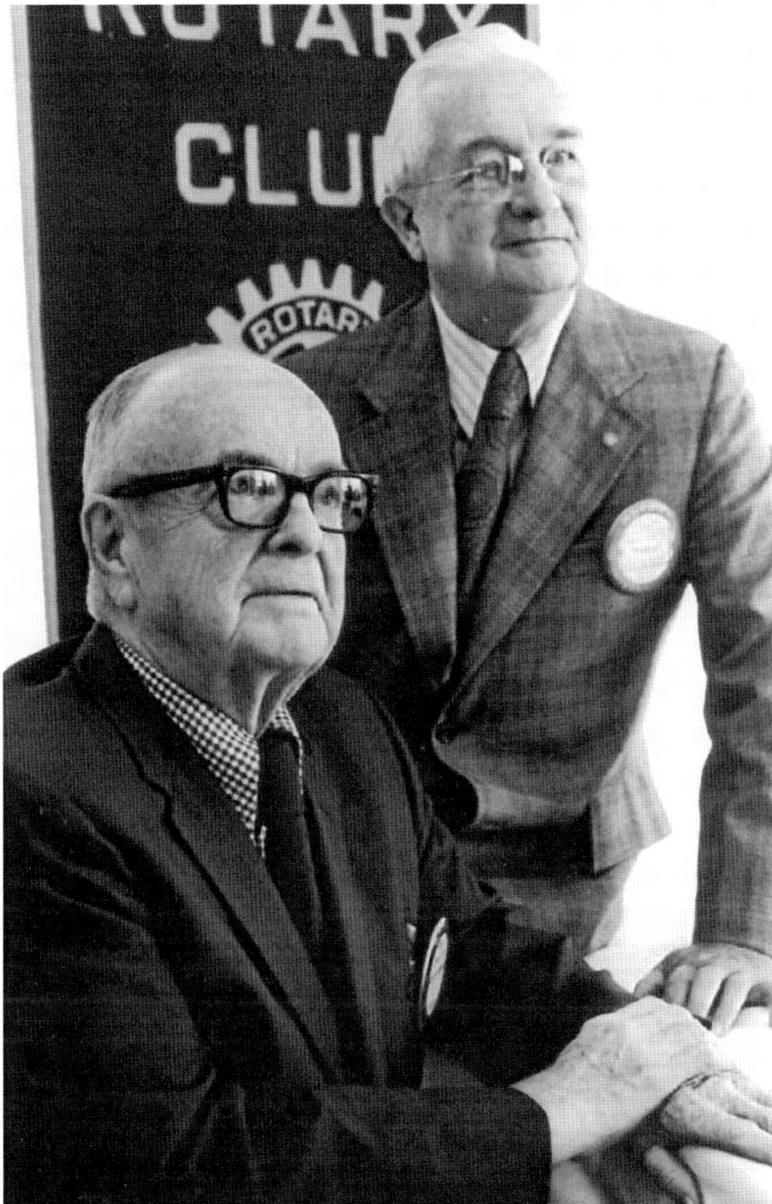

J. Ed Travis Jr.

Born and raised in Tarkio, Missouri, Ed Travis grew up playing football and starring for his high school team. He wanted to play for the University of Missouri but instead stayed at home and played for Tarkio College. His talent got him noticed, and he was slated to play for Mizzou starting in the 1917 season. World War I interrupted his dream for two years, but in 1919, "Brick" Travis played defense (earning his nickname) and starred for Mizzou. After his playing days, Travis moved to St. Charles and went into business. He was a charter member of the Rotary Club and participated in several committees and community endeavors, including the United Fund. He is a member of the Missouri Sports Hall of Fame as well as the College Football Hall of Fame. Travis was named Man of the Year by the St. Charles County Chamber of Commerce in 1958. (Courtesy of St. Charles County Historical Society.)

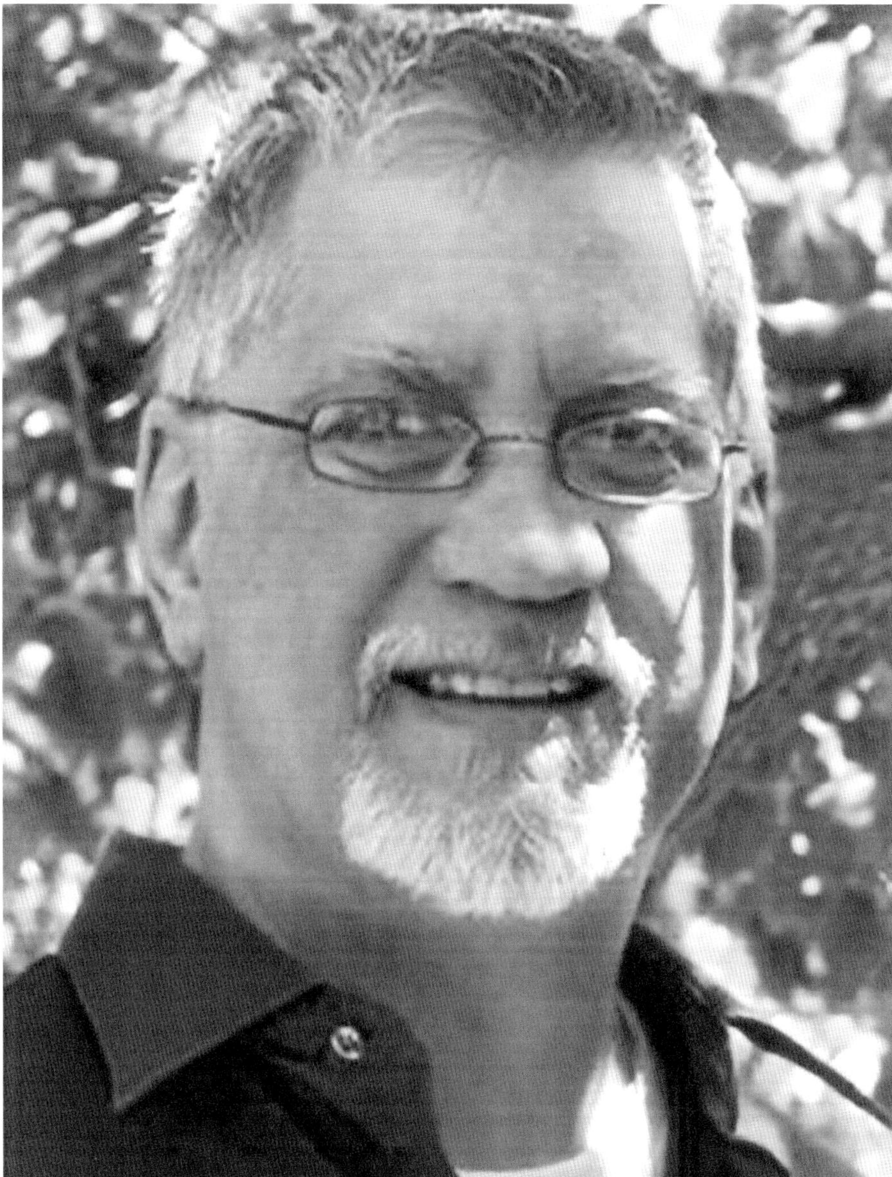

Mike Eisenbath

For 23 years, including 18 at the *St. Louis Post-Dispatch* covering Major League Baseball and the St. Louis Cardinals, Eisenbath was an award-winning sportswriter. Author of *Mark McGwire: The Power Hitter* and *The Cardinals Encyclopedia*, Eisenbath left sportswriting in 2002 to work for a large brokerage firm. His most recent book, *Hence My Eyes Are Turned Toward You: Confronting Depression with Faith and the Prayer of Jehoshaphat*, lays bare his personal struggle with clinical depression. His column "Man of the House" appears monthly in the *St. Louis Review*, and he writes for the web sites *Catholic Lane*, *Christian Review*, and *Catholic Stand*. With his wife, Donna, he presents "In Our Own Voice: Living with Mental Illness," a program sponsored by the National Alliance on Mental Illness. Eisenbath occasionally appears on the Catholic Relevant Radio Network. He has been praised by the editor at *Christian Review* and by others for having the courage to break the silence about living with depression. (Courtesy of Mike Eisenbath.)

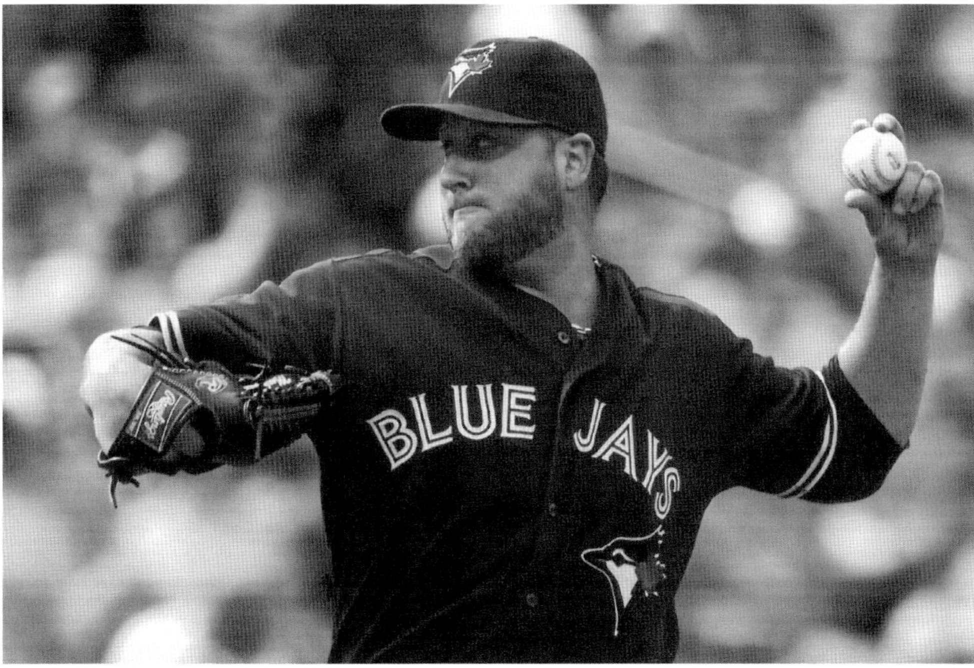

Mark Buehrle

Mark Buehrle grew up in St. Charles and attended Francis Howell North High School. He later attended Jefferson College in Hillsboro. Buehrle made his major-league debut as a pitcher with the Chicago White Sox and today pitches for the Toronto Blue Jays. In 2005, Buehrle pitched for the White Sox during their run to the World Series title. (Courtesy of Keith Allison at KeithAllisonPhoto.com.)

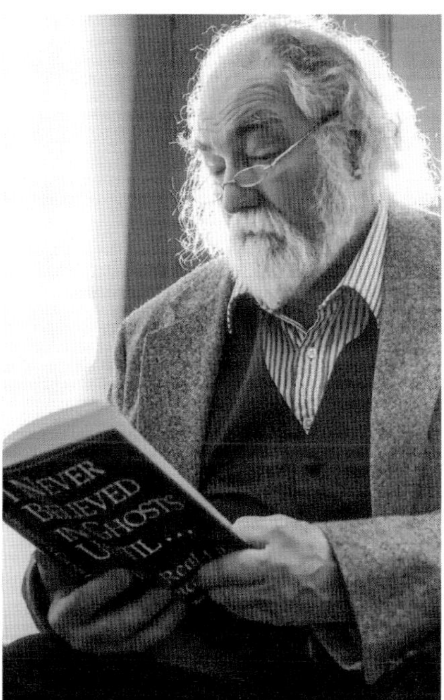

Dr. Michael Henry

Michael Henry is known in historic St. Charles as the man who leads ghost tours. A student of the paranormal for more than 30 years, Dr. Henry is the author of four non-ghost-related books, as well as *The Ghosts of St. Charles* (2010). A former educator, he has received several recognitions, including Teacher of the Year, Excellence in Education, and Excellence in Curriculum Development from the St. Charles School District. He is a former adjunct professor at Lindenwood University and has performed as a magician across the United States, the United Kingdom, and elsewhere. (Courtesy of Michael Henry.)

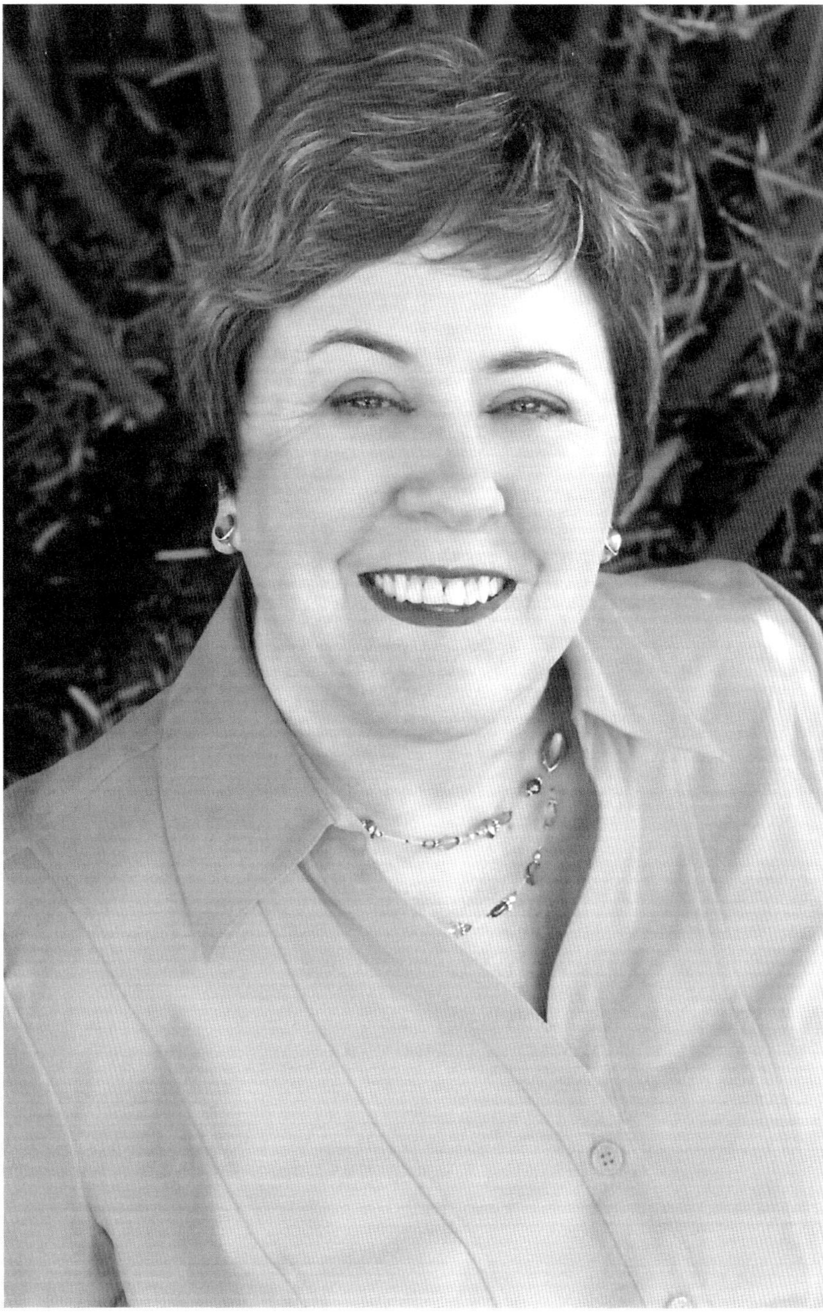

Bobbi Smith

Bobbi Smith has written more than 50 books and six novellas, several of which have made the best-seller lists of the *New York Times* and *USA Today* and at several retail outlets and booksellers. She is the winner of the Storyteller of the Year award from *Romantic Times* magazine, and over six million copies of her books are in print. The foreign rights to Smith's books have been sold in China, France, Germany, India, Israel, Italy, Russia, and Sweden. Using the pen name Julie Marshall, Smith has also written two faith-based contemporary novels. (Courtesy of Bobbi Smith.)

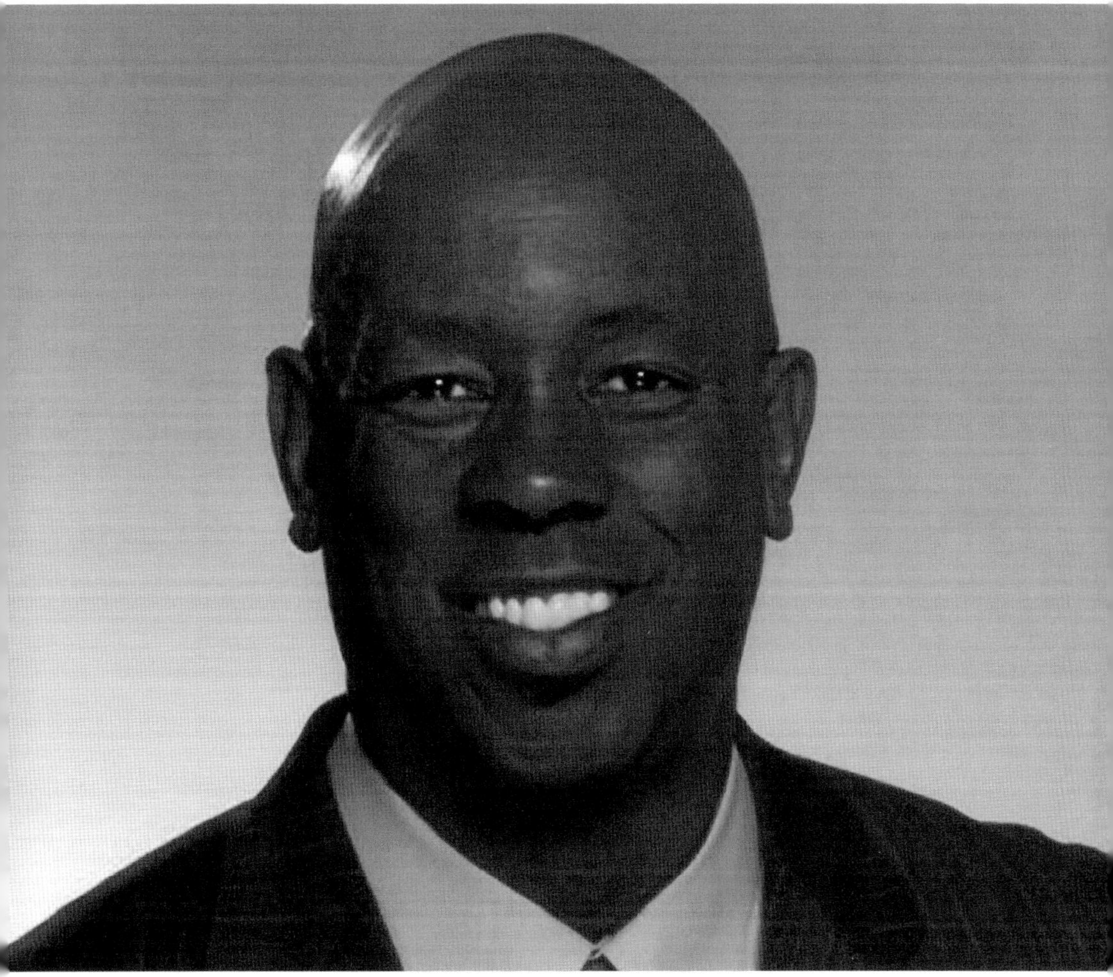

Art Holliday

Art Holliday grew up in St. Charles and attended St. Charles High School. A news reporter for KSDK in St. Louis, Holliday's work has been recognized with several awards, including three sportscasting Emmys (1985, 1988, and 1989). Holliday was inducted into the hall of fame of the Greater St. Louis Association of Black Journalists in 2001. He received the National Alliance on Mental Illness Media Award in 2002. In 2003, the University of Missouri–Columbia selected Holliday for its Faculty-Alumni Award. The fourth-floor residents of Mizzou's Excellence Hall named their floor Holliday House that same year. (Courtesy of Art Holliday; photograph by Doug Howell Photography.)

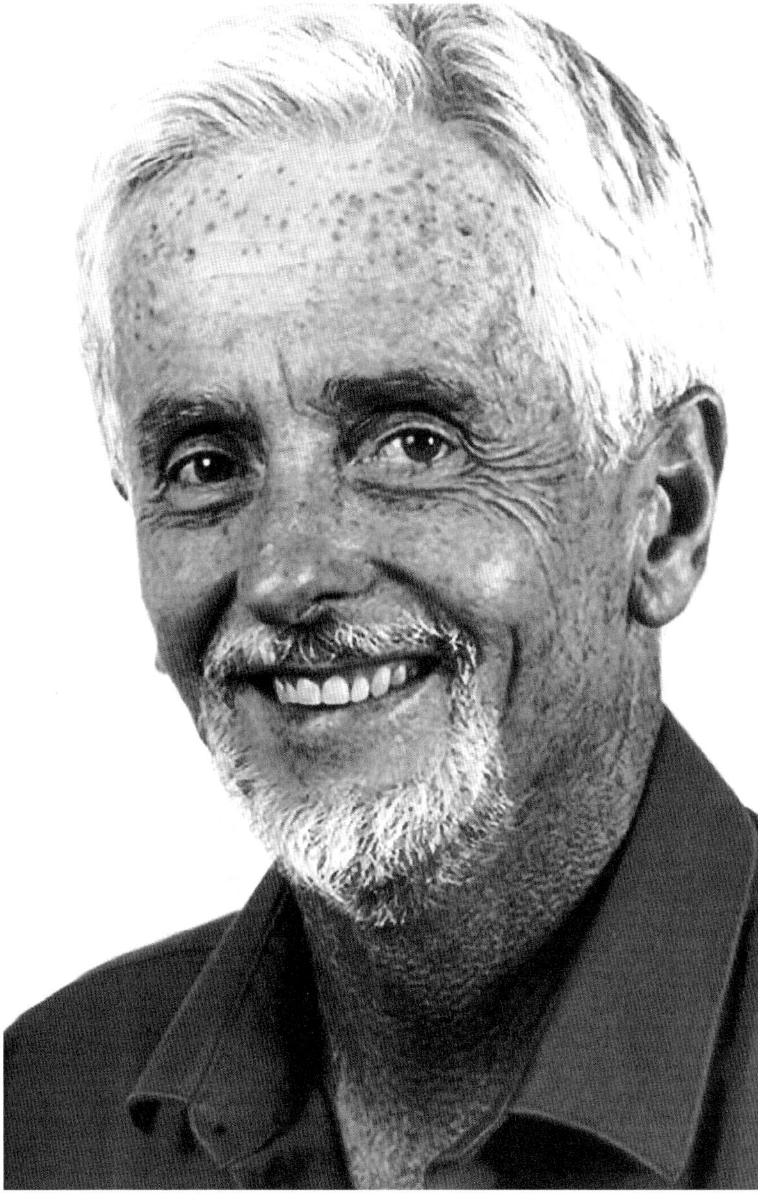

Steve Pokin

Many in St. Charles will remember Steve's "Pokin Around" column in the *Suburban Journals of St. Charles County*. Pokin left St. Charles about 2012 and is now a reporter at the *News-Leader* of Springfield, Missouri, where he continues to write the column. In 2007, while at the *Suburban Journals*, Steve wrote about the suicide of a 13-year-old girl in St. Charles County who killed herself as a result of cyberbullying. The story exploded nationally and internationally and was used as the storyline for a *Law and Order* episode. Based in large part on his reporting of that story, the Suburban Newspapers of America named Pokin the 2008 National Journalist of the Year. Pokin, who lived near Blanchette Park, said he misses running on the crushed stone of the Katy Trail, as well as the wonderful times he had sitting outside with friends at the restaurant Lewis & Clark's. (Courtesy of Steve Pokin; photograph by Nathan Papes/ *News-Leader*.)

CHAPTER SIX

Military and Law Enforcement

The sixth and final chapter of *Legendary Locals of St. Charles* is dedicated to all members of the armed forces who serve their country and to all members of law enforcement who serve their community.

In addition to a few legendary locals who served in the military and who were not mentioned in previous chapters, like Gen. Henry Hopkins Sibley and Col. George W. Tainter, included in this chapter are each of the law-enforcement officers who died while serving in the St. Charles community. John Blair, James Lamb, Fred Bergmann, Gary Stroud, and Grant Jansen worked for the City of St. Charles Police Department. The other three officers, John Dierker, Albert Musterman, and Richard Lee Henke, worked for the St. Charles County Sheriff's Department. We included the county department's officers for three reasons. First, the sheriff's office was located in the city of St. Charles at the time these officers served. Second, at least one of the officers (Musterman) lived in the city of St. Charles while serving. And third, all of these officers gave their lives in the service of their fellow citizens of St. Charles, city and county, and deserve mention.

May these officers, as well as members of the military who have lost their lives, always be remembered by the people of St. Charles, Missouri.

Gen. Henry Sibley

Henry Hopkins Sibley, born in Louisiana, came to live in St. Charles with his uncle George C. Sibley and aunt Mary Sibley, founders of Lindenwood College, after his father died when he was seven years old. He enrolled at West Point when he was 17, later fighting in the Mexican-American War and for the Confederate army in the Civil War. (Courtesy of St. Charles County Historical Society.)

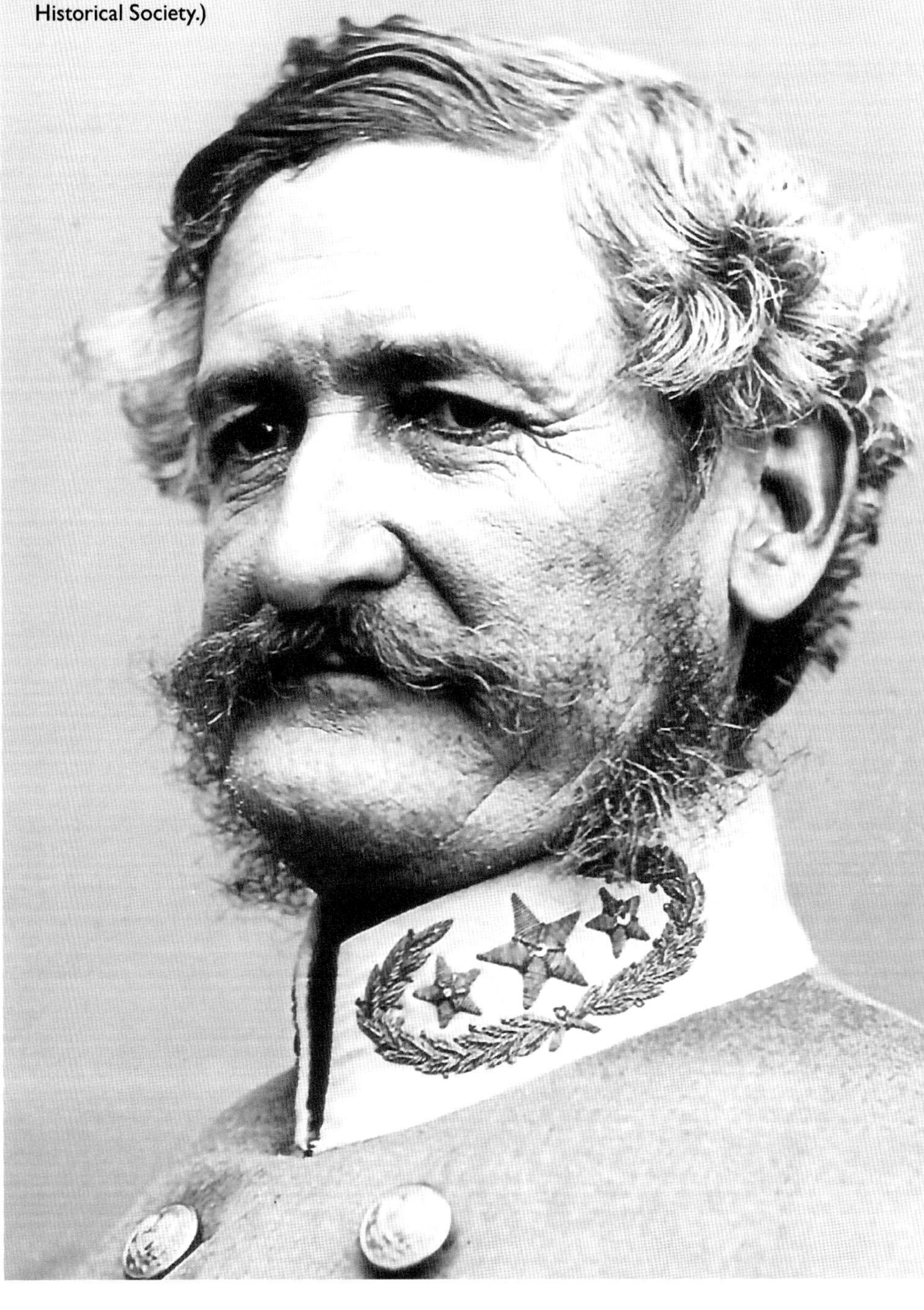

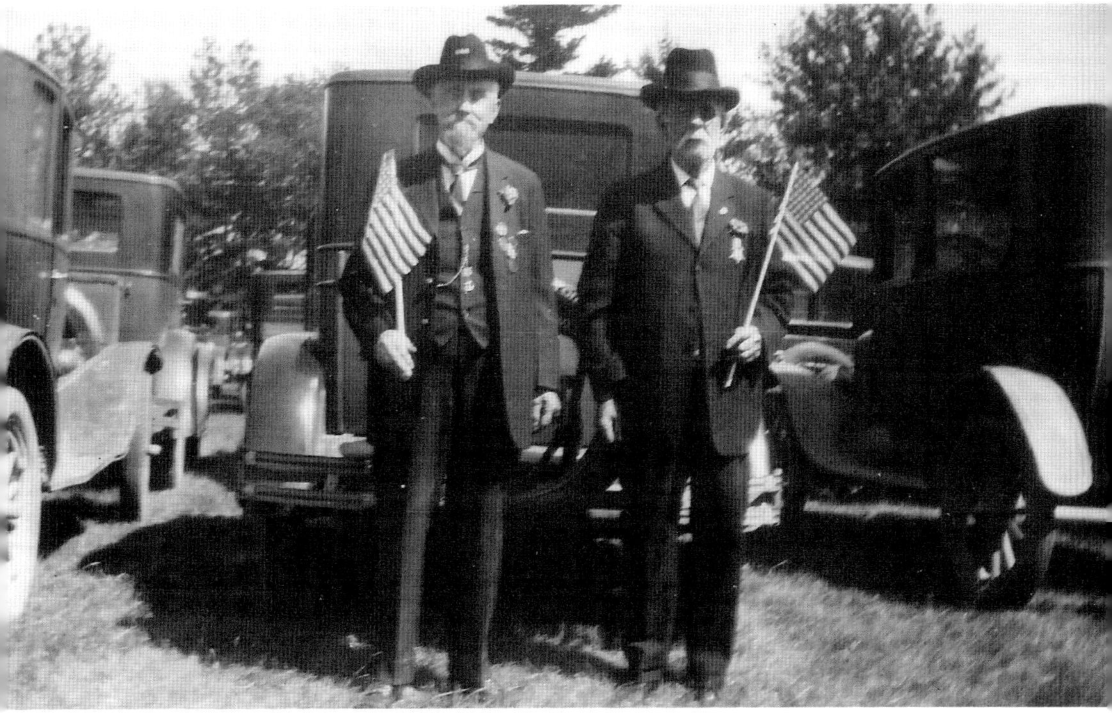

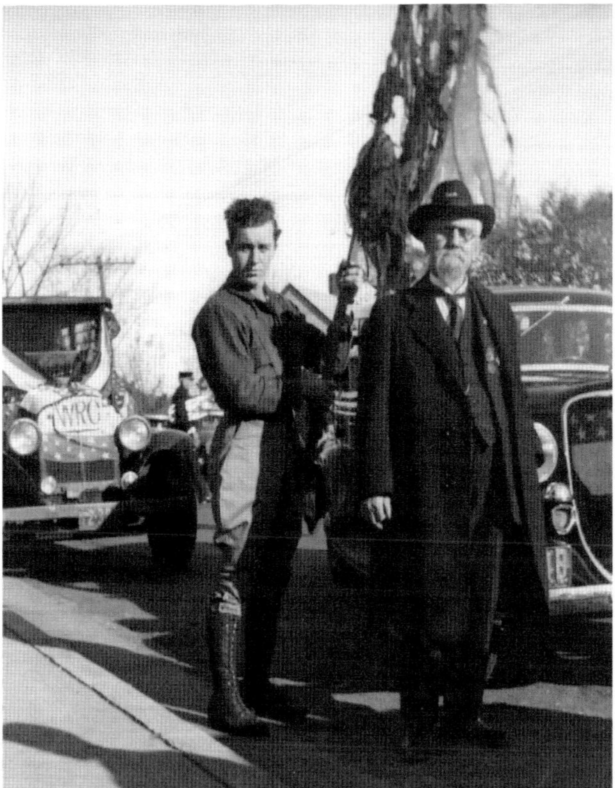

Col. George W. Tainter

Dr. Tainter was a dentist who had established his practice in Linn, Missouri. In 1861, he enlisted for service in the Civil War with the Army of the Potomac. After being wounded and discharged, he joined the Navy in 1862, achieving the rank of ensign and receiving a medal for distinguished service. In his later years, he enjoyed visiting his son's store in St. Charles, Tainter's Drug Store, and ordering pineapple malts. Dr. Tainter is pictured on the left with his grandson Gregory about 1926 or 1927 at the Armistice Day Parade. Above, Tainter (left) poses with an unknown friend. (Both, courtesy of St. Charles County Historical Society.)

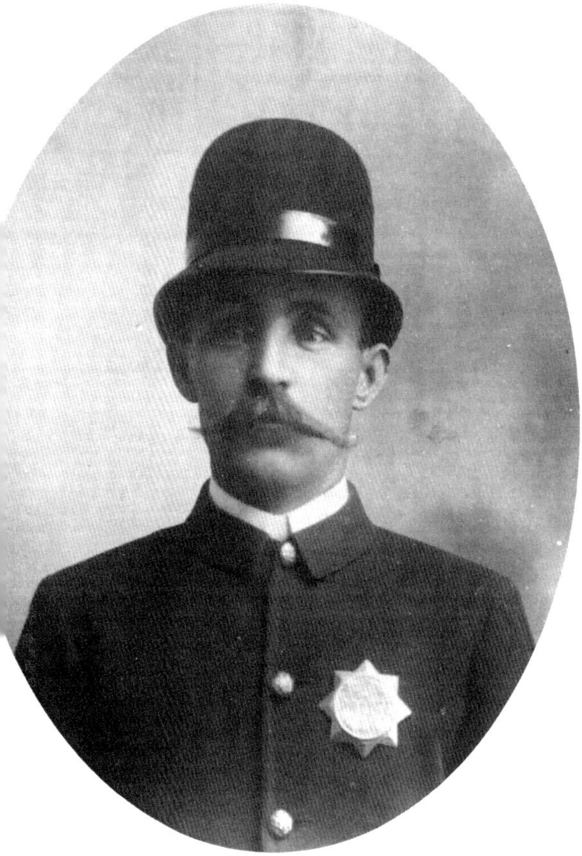

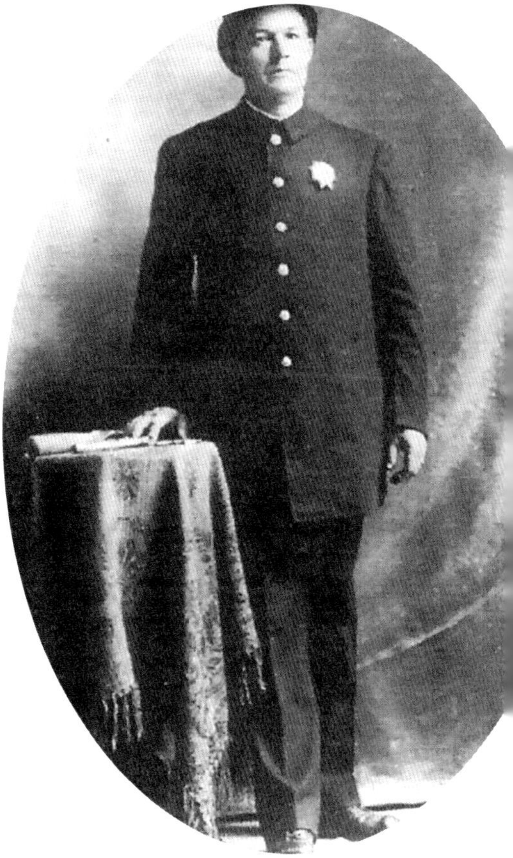

James David Lamb and John Blair

Patrolmen Lamb and Blair were shot and killed on December 6, 1913, while attempting to arrest three gamblers who had been told to leave town. Gunfire was exchanged, and Lamb (left) killed one of the suspects, Tom Allen. The other two suspects were captured by a posse a short time later about 10 miles east of St. Charles. Patrolman Lamb had been with the agency for 20 years. It is unknown how long Blair (right) was with the force. Andrew and Harry Black were charged with the murders and sentenced to death. (Courtesy of St. Charles County Historical Society.)

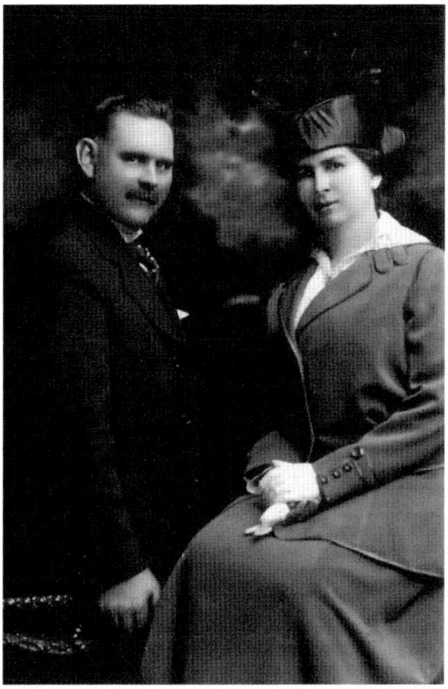

John H. Dierker

On April 5, 1916, Sheriff Dierker was shot and mortally wounded by a man he attempted to arrest for trying to shoot another man over a dispute about wages. Hours later, an angry mob trapped the suspect in a barn. When he appeared at the door and held up his hands, members of the mob fired at him. The suspect ran back into the barn and set it on fire, then appeared again at the door with his hands raised. This time, he was met by a hailstorm of bullets. At the time, Dierker had almost finished the second of two four-year terms as sheriff. He served from 1904 to 1908 and from 1912 until his death. Sheriff Dierker is pictured here with his wife around 1910. (Courtesy of St. Charles County Historical Society.)

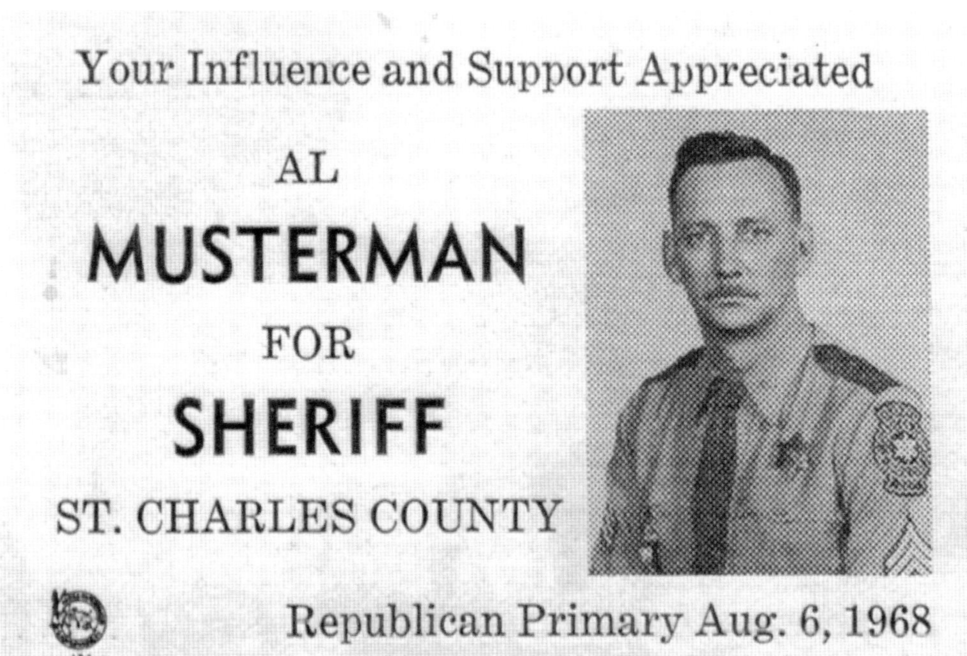

Albert H. Musterman

Lt. Albert Musterman was shot and killed on November 30, 1969, while making a traffic stop on Highway 61. The suspect had just murdered a witness who was scheduled to testify in a federal narcotics trial the next day. In connection with the death, two of the defendants in the trial were arrested and charged with murder. Musterman's killer was later caught and escaped several times, finally landing on the FBI's Ten Most Wanted list before being captured a final time. Lieutenant Musterman had served with the sheriff's office for nine years. (Courtesy of Will Hall and Gina Christine.)

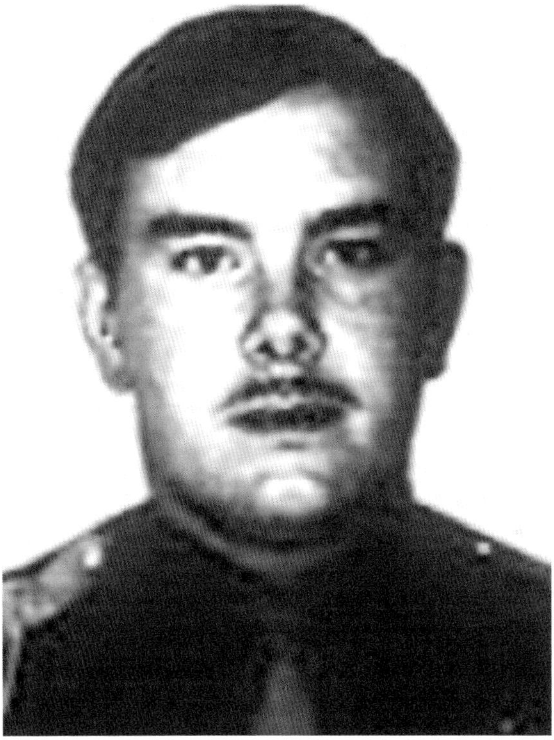

Richard Lee Henke
Deputy Henke was struck and killed by a drunk driver on February 4, 1971, while manning a roadblock. Checkpoints had been set up after a house in Weldon Spring was burglarized earlier in the day. The suspect's vehicle was stopped one mile west of the hit-and-run scene at another roadblock. Richard Henke had been a deputy sheriff for 18 months. (Courtesy of National Law Enforcement Officers Memorial Fund, Washington, DC.)

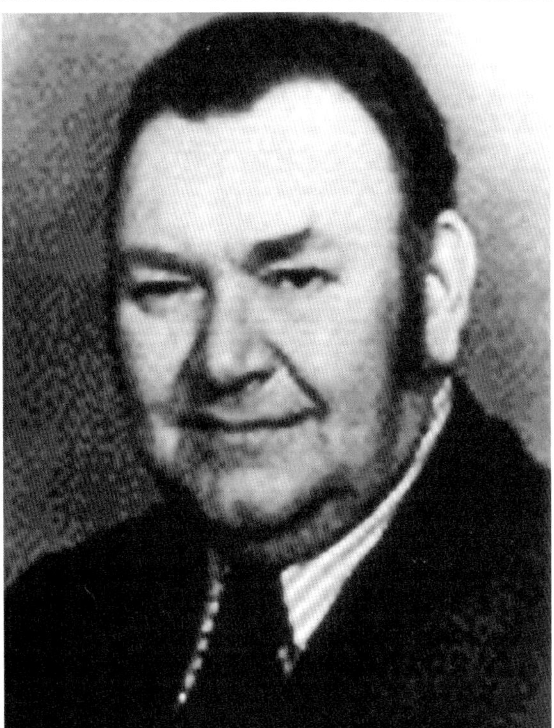

Fred Bernard Bergmann
Reserve officer Bergmann was shot and killed on September 12, 1976, when he and another officer responded to a burglary-in-progress at a local business. Officer Bergmann came through a rear door to investigate and was shot and killed as he entered the business. The suspect was apprehended a short time later. (Courtesy of National Law Enforcement Officers Memorial Fund, Washington, DC.)

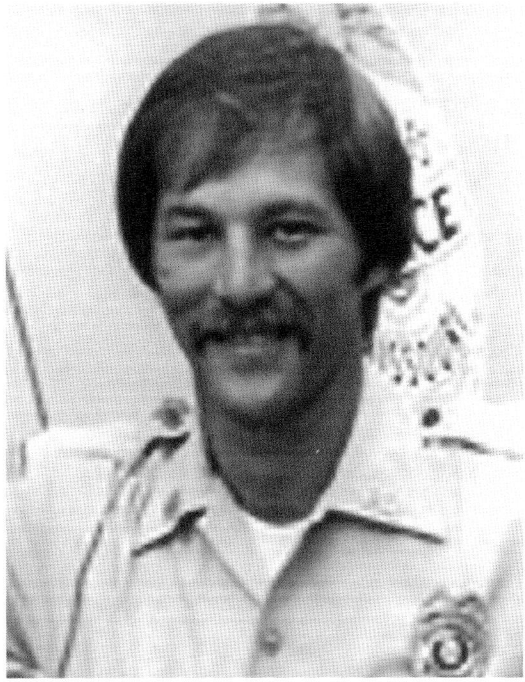

Gary R. Stroud
Officer Stroud was shot and killed on October 24, 1977, while investigating a report of a man walking around with a shotgun. The suspect fired through the windshield of Stroud's patrol car. The suspect was captured minutes later after he crashed his car into a utility pole. He was convicted of capital murder and sentenced to life. Officer Stroud had served with the St. Charles Police Department for 18 months. (Courtesy of National Law Enforcement Officers Memorial Fund, Washington, DC.)

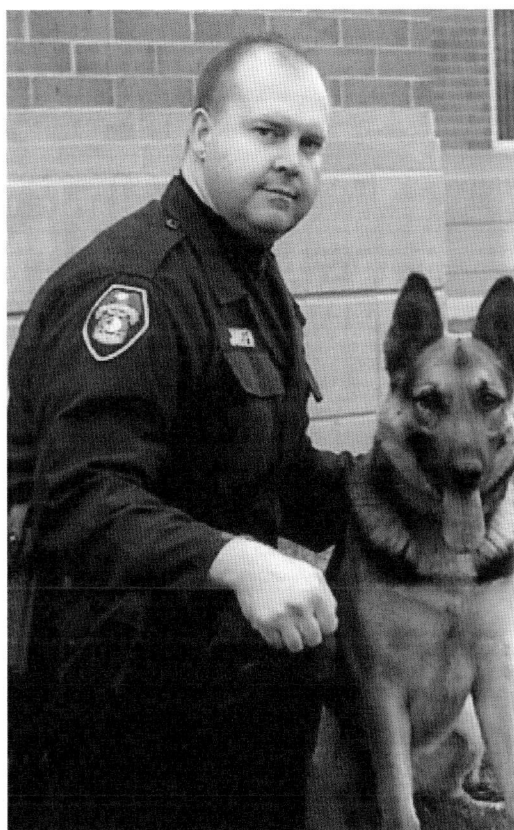

Grant Anthony Jansen
A member of the St. Charles Police Department, Officer Grant Jansen was killed on September 10, 2008, in a single-vehicle crash on Spencer Road when his car left the roadway. His K-9 partner was not injured. Officer Jansen had served for 20 years. (Courtesy of National Law Enforcement Officers Memorial Fund, Washington, DC.)

ABOUT THE ST. CHARLES COUNTY HISTORICAL SOCIETY

The St. Charles County Historical Society was founded in 1956, incorporated in 1958, and is dedicated to the preservation of documents and artifacts related to St. Charles County history. The society preserves primary and secondary source materials relating to the county, publishes a monthly newsletter and a quarterly publication called *St. Charles County Heritage*, and sponsors various activities to promote the preservation and study of history.

The historical society is located at 101 South Main Street in St. Charles in a house built over 185 years ago. The building was originally known as the Market and Fish House and contained booths for produce, a scale to weigh wagonloads of goods, outside oil lamps, and a public bulletin board. The town band often played on the market steps to entertain people who sat on nearby benches while waiting for the mail coach to arrive at the post office.

The building lost its roof in the tornado of 1876, and it was later replaced. In 1886, the building became the St. Charles City Hall. A new city hall was built in 1973, and the building at 101 South Main Street was placed on the National Register of Historic Places on November 14, 1980. It became the home for the St. Charles County Historical Society in July 1982.

BIBLIOGRAPHY

A History of St. Charles, Missouri During the First Two Hundred Years of American Independence. St. Charles, MO: City of St. Charles and the St. Charles American Revolution Bicentennial Planning Commission, 1976.

The Boone Society. "Missouri Boone Sites." www.boonesociety.org

Breslow, Lori. *Small Town*. St. Charles, MO: The John J. Buse Historical Museum, 1977.

Brown, Jo Ann. *St. Charles Borromeo, 200 Years of Faith*. St. Charles, MO: The Patrice Press, 1991.

Bryan, William S., and Robert Rose. *St. Charles County Missouri: Biographical Sketches from Pioneer Families of Missouri*. St. Charles, MO: St. Charles County Genealogical Society, 1993.

Buse, John J. *In His Own Hand: A Historical Scrapbook of St. Charles County, Missouri*. St. Charles, MO: John L. Buse, 1998.

Ehlmann, Steve. *Crossroads: A History of St. Charles County, Missouri*. Bicentennial ed. St. Charles, MO: Lindenwood University Press, 2011.

Flynn, Cleta. *Through a Woman's Eyes*. St. Charles, MO: St. Charles County Historical Society, 2014.

Franciscan Sisters of Mary Archives, SSM Healthcare.

Greater St. Charles County Chamber of Commerce. "Citizen of the Years." www.gstccc.com

Historic Main Street: St. Charles, Missouri. Volume 1, Nos. 1–3. St. Charles, MO: Heritage Manor Publishing, Inc., 2005, 2006.

Olson, Edna McElhiney. *Historical Saint Charles, Missouri*. St. Charles, MO: 1967.

One Hundred Years of Medicine and Surgery in Missouri. St. Louis: *St. Louis Star*, 1900.

Popp, William. *The Life and Works of Rudolph Goebel*. St. Charles, MO: St. Charles County Historical Society, 2010.

Schultz, Robert G., ed. *Heritage Treasures: An Anthology of Articles from 20 Years of the St. Charles County Heritage*. St. Charles, MO: St. Charles County Historical Society, 2006.

St. Charles County Historical Society Archives. www.scchs.org

Willard, Francis Elizabeth, and Mary Ashton Rice Livermore. *American Women: Fifteen Hundred Biographies*. Rev. ed. New York: Mast, Crowell, & Kirkpatrick, 1897.

INDEX

INDEX